Translation

CSLI
Lecture Notes
No. 221

Translation
Linguistic and Philosophical Perspectives

Martin Kay

 **CSLI**
PUBLICATIONS Center for the Study of
Language and Information
Stanford, California

Copyright © 2017
CSLI Publications
Center for the Study of Language and Information
Leland Stanford Junior University
Printed in the United States
21 20 19 18 17   1 2 3 4 5

Library of Congress Cataloging-in-Publication Data

Names: Kay, Martin, author.

Title: Translation : Linguistic and Philosophical Perspectives / Martin Kay.

Description: Stanford, California : Center for the Study of Language and Information, 2017. | Series: CSLI Lecture Notes no. 221 | Includes bibliographical references and index.

Identifiers: LCCN 2017006017 | ISBN 9781575868455 (hardcover : acid-free paper) | ISBN 1575868458 (hardcover : acid-free paper) | ISBN 9781575868714 (softcover : acid-free paper) | ISBN 1575868717 (softcover : acid-free paper) | ISBN 9781684000272 (electronic) | ISBN 1684000270 (electronic)

Subjects: LCSH: Translating and interpreting. | BISAC: LANGUAGE ARTS & DISCIPLINES / Translating & Interpreting.

Classification: LCC P306 .K39 2017 | DDC 418/.02–dc23

LC record available at https://lccn.loc.gov/2017006017

CIP

∞ The acid-free paper used in this book meets the minimum requirements of the American National Standard for Information Sciences—Permanence of Paper for Printed Library Materials, ANSI Z39.48-1984.

CSLI was founded in 1983 by researchers from Stanford University, SRI International, and Xerox PARC to further the research and development of integrated theories of language, information, and computation. CSLI headquarters and CSLI Publications are located on the campus of Stanford University.

Visit our web site at
http://cslipublications.stanford.edu/
for comments on this and other titles, as well as for changes
and corrections by the author and publisher.

Contents

1

Introduction

"Translation", like many English words, can be used to refer to an artifact, or to the process that gives rise to the artifact. A person undertakes the *translation* of a text, thus creating an artifact that we call a *translation*. There is little doubt in the minds of most people about what a translation is and, therefore, at least grossly, what the activity that gives rise to one involves. On closer inspection, we shall see that much of what it involves is far from obvious.

According to Wikipedia

> Translation is the interpreting of the meaning of a text and the subsequent production of an equivalent text ...that communicates the same message in another language.[1]

The trouble with this, of course, is that it relies on words like "interpreting", "meaning", "equivalent", and "message" that are so bound up with the notion of translation as to leave us with a definition that is dangerously close to circular. In later chapters, we will attempt to tease the notion apart into components that are, to the extent possible, distinct from it and from one another. We do not expect to be entirely successful in this endeavor, but we do hope to shed some light in places that generally remain wrapped in darkness. For the remainder of the current chapter, however, we propose to ignore all definitions of translation, appealing only to the intuitions that we rely on for everyday discourse.

There is a small number of situations in which we routinely encounter translations though, in most of them, we may neither know nor care that that is what they are. We read translations of reports

---

1. Wikipedia contributors. 2008. "example." In *Wikipedia, The Free Encyclopedia.* 13 May 2008 11:51 UTC. https://en.wikipedia.org/w/index.php?title=Translation&oldid=212089293

1

from the foreign press and the speeches by dignitaries and politicians, originally written or spoken in languages we do not know. We take note of the fact that they are translations only on the rare occasions when we are told that a word we had not known before was borrowed from another language or when we learn that the translation contains some word or phrase that only approximates the meaning of the original. In the 1980s, the Russian words *perestroika* (перестройка) and *glasnost* (гласность), referring to two of the reforms introduced by Mikhail Gorbachev, were adopted as part of the English language. The words mean approximately *restructuring* and *openness* respectively.

On March 6, 2009 Secretary of State Hillary Clinton presented the Russian foreign minister Sergei Lavrov with the gift-wrapped red button bearing the inscription *peregruzka* (перегузка) which she had been told was the Russian for *reset*. The message she had hoped to convey was that America wished to place its relations with Russia on a new footing. The effect was, if anything, the opposite of this because the Russian word *peregruzka*, at least according to Mr. Lavrov, in fact turns out to mean *overcharged* or *overloaded*. The word they actually wanted was *perezagruzka* (перезагрузка). Naturally the incident attracted the attention of the press, and the public was allowed a glimpse of problems that can arise in communication between two people who speak different languages.

Much was made of John F. Kennedy's use of the words "Ich bin ein Berliner" on June 26, 1963 in a speech before the Berlin wall. Someone noted that word *Berliner* can be used in some parts of Germany, though generally not in Berlin, to refer to a jelly doughnut. Some went on to claim that a German, wishing to say "I am a Berliner" would in fact say "Ich bin Berliner", omitting the word *ein*. Even this is not true. What the president said was, in fact, just what most Berliners would have said in these circumstances. However, there are many Germans for whom *Berliner* can indeed mean *jelly doughnut* so that the phrase was at least a potential cause for merriment in some places. If the situation were somehow transposed to Frankfurt, and the speech had been given entirely in English, the English-language press would have quoted *I am a Frankfurter*, which would have caused more laughter at home than in Germany. For the most part, news reports do not turn on linguistic subtleties, real or imagined, and we remain generally unaware of the fact that we are reading a translation. When we read a story, factual or fictional, ancient or modern, the question of whether or not the words are the original ones or a translation very rarely arises. This is, of course, exactly the situation that a translator generally strives to achieve.

1.1 Pedagogical and Word-for-Word Translation

Many first encounter translation in school in the course of learning a foreign language. It is only in the school setting that we see translation as it is actually being done. Indeed, we have the experience of doing it ourselves because language learners are frequently called upon to translate into, and out of, the language they are learning, though this practice used to be more common than it is today. Unfortunately, this *pedagogical* translation gives a very distorted view of what translation is like in other settings. Learning a foreign language and learning to translate between it and one's native language are quite different enterprises. Pedagogical translation is used as a simple way of conveying the meanings of foreign words and phrases and, perhaps more importantly, of satisfying the teacher that the student has learnt the particular words and constructions the lesson was intended to instill.

Notice that a rather halting translation might in fact serve this latter purpose better than a smooth and idiomatic one. The French teacher who asks for a translation of "I do not think you should continue your studies" will probably not be satisfied with "A mon avis, il ne vaut pas la peine de poursuivre tes études." (literally: "In my opinion, it is not worth it to continue you studies").[2] What the teacher wants is "Je ne crois pas que tu doives poursuivre tes études", because this requires a subjunctive form ("doives") of an irregular verb ("devoir", (SHOULD)), which was very probably the point of the lesson.

Pedagogical translation has little to do with translation as it is actually practiced by professionals. However, it has a considerable amount to do with common perceptions of translation and, in particular, with the way it is viewed by workers in the field of machine translation. The proportion of the people in that field with any experience of the kind of translation that is actually done to fill the practical needs of the world is almost vanishingly small. Consequently, the approaches taken to it, though they differ in many ways, are almost invariably modeled on classroom exercises of the kind to which students are routinely subjected during the early stages of learning a foreign language. The student is expected to have memorized a set of words and phrases in the language, paired with English counterparts. When memory fails, the student has recourse to the lists in the relevant chapter of the text, or the vocabulary listing at the end of the book, or a small bilingual dictionary. Some words and phrases have more than one counterpart

---

2. Example from LinguisTech. 2017. *Translation Services*. Accessed April 6, 2017. http://LinguisTech.ca/.

in the other language so that the student must know what to look for in the surrounding context in order to choose the right one.

Certain pairs of counterparts have received so much attention that they have become familiar to people that have almost no other knowledge of the language in question. A student who takes up a new language will expect it to have two words corresponding to the English verb *know* because French has *savoir* and *connaître*, German *wissen* and *kennen*, Italian *sappere* and *connoscere*, and so forth. The distinction between *ser* and *estar* in Spanish is equally celebrated, doubtless because these verbs translate *to be*, the commonest verb in English. A student who is translating "know" into French, or "be" into Spanish must by all means use one of the approved pair and not some other expression that might, in fact, be possible in the given situation.

The words the student chooses must be rearranged to reflect differences between English and the foreign language. Thus, in Romance languages, adjectives must often be moved to a position following the noun they modify and pronouns arranged in carefully specified order before the verb and German verbs must be placed in the second or the final place in the sentence, depending on criteria that the student must master. If the right counterparts are chosen and the rules properly applied, the result will meet the teacher's needs and, to that extent, will be a translation.

What I am calling "pedagogical translation" is the closest we generally get to what is commonly referred to as *word-for-word* translation. We have all learnt at one time or another that there is generally something wrong with word-for-word translation, but it is like what we have been taught to do in school and it is perhaps not entirely clear what an alternative would be like.

If we look at all closely at any kind of translation, including that done in the school room, we soon see that it can never be really word for word. We learn in class that the French for *realize*, in its commonest interpretation, is *se rendre compte* and that you need the two words *ne* and *pas* to translate the English word *not*. The teacher wants to know that we have mastered these things and calls on us to translate *I did not realize it.* Good students that we are, we work out the details, and come up with *Je ne m'en suis pas rendu compte*, thus showing our mastery of several more or less subtle things. The *ne* and the *pas* must be separated, with just the right things between them. Because *se rendre compte* has this *se* in it, we have learnt to recognize it as a so-called *reflexive* verb, and we must therefore use the auxiliary verb *suis* instead of the default *ai*, and so forth. The teacher needs to be assured that we have mastered all these things. But the basis of it all is that *did not* is a fixed phrase that is paired with *ne...pas* in the vocabulary listing, and *se rendre compte* with *realize* They are not single words, but they are short phrases that can be collected in vocabulary lists and memorized for the exam. In other words, they function very like single words.

It goes without saying that the English word *realize* has other meanings, as when we talk of realizing a profit or a dream. It is also the case that French does have a verb *réaliser*, which can sometimes be used to translate the *realise*. But *se rendre compte* maybe the commonest equivalent and it is probably the one that the teacher can make most of.

In the following chapter, we will explore a model of translation that is quite similar to the one we have characterized here as pedagogical translation because it will turn out to be instructive to see how far it can be pushed and where it breaks down. We will find that it can be pushed quite far but that, when it breaks down, it may leave us in a desperate situation. We will discover that the ordinary journeyman translator has problems suddenly thrust upon him for which this model provides no guidance.

1.2 Adaptation

Most non-pedagogical translation is done by professional translators. When amateur translation is used for serious purposes, it is usually because the person who does the translation, or the person employing their services, or both, have misjudged what is required to do the job adequately. Consequently, both run the risk of considerable embarrassment. The one place where translators who might reasonably be thought of as amateurs routinely do work of high quality is in certain kinds of *literary* translation. When a publisher commissions a translation, it is usually from a professional, who is, however, often paid very little for the work. But literary translations are sometimes labors of love produced by writers with literary pretensions of their own and who think of translations as being, at least in some measure, original creations.

In his preface to the "Translation of Ovid's Epistles" (1680), a work that has been influential among people that theorize about translation, John Dryden distinguished "metaphrase", or turning an author word-for-word, and line-by-line, from one language into another, from "paraphrase", or translation with latitude, where the author is kept in view by the translator, so as never to be lost, but his words are not so strictly followed as his sense. And he distinguished both of these from "imitation", now often referred to as *adaptation*, which is really a new work, inspired by one in another language. In literary circles, however, this last has been commoner than those we would be more willing to call translation today. In recent times, its most prominent exponent was doubtless Ezra Pound who produced stunning poetic works which purported to be translations from many languages, including ancient Egyptian, Latin, Greek, Anglo-Saxon, Provençal and Chinese. While the literary value of these works is widely acknowledged, their value as translations is a matter of considerable controversy.

Pound did not know Chinese. His so-called *translations* from this language are based on notes made by Ernest Francisco Fenollosa, an American historian of Japanese art at Tokyo Imperial University, who also did not know Chinese. Fenollosa's notes were copious and meticulous, providing lists of supposedly corresponding pairs of words and occasional supposed translations of complete lines. Eric Hayot writes "That Pound's translations are successful has been taken by any number of critics as a literary miracle, by others as literary fraud" (2004).

To a large extent, a literary translator, or adapter, has more or less tacitly defined the nature of the enterprise he engages in and his readers' satisfaction is the measure of his success. Edward Fitzgerald's translation of the Persian *Rubaiyat of Omar Khayyam*, first published in 1859, immediately became part of the English literary canon, a position it retained for at least a hundred years. As a translation, however, it sometimes departs so far from the original that some of its quatrains cannot be confidently traced to any particular one in the Persian text. Fitzgerald felt justified in taking the approach he did to his original, because it was part the culture he was born into which did not routinely distinguish adaptation from translation and encouraged a total disdain for people they judged inferior, like Persians.

1.3 Globalization and Localization

One of the approaches to machine translation is known as *interlingual* translation. The basic idea is to translate a document into an artificial intermediate language, known as an *interlingua* in a first stage, and then, in a second stage, to translate that into the target language. The interlingua is an artificial language designed to abstract away from the tiresome idiosyncrasies of natural languages, treating all meanings in a uniform manner. The idea goes back to the seventeenth-century philosophers Descartes and Leibniz. The term *universal characteristic* (*characteristica universalis*) was coined by Leibniz to refer to his notion of a universal language using numbers in which to express more accurately than is possible in ordinary languages mathematical and scientific ideas.

We shall have more to say about interlinguas in due course. In particular, we shall find many reasons to doubt that they can constitute a viable strategy. There has, however, come to be a process that is very reminiscent of it that is standard practice in the preparation of products that are intended to be sold on broad global markets. This process has two aspects, referred to as *globalization* and *localization* respectively.

To understand the distinction between globalization and localization, and how it relates to translation, we should consider together, the product itself and all the ancillary material—documentation, packaging, advertising, etc—that goes with it. The globalization phase consists in removing from this package as much as possible of what ties it to a particular country, part of the world, or language. If one version of the product will require electric current at 240 volts and 60 cycles, while another requires 120 volts and 50 cycles, then this difference is restricted to as small a part of the total product as possible, say the power-supply unit. To take care of this difference, different power supplies may be needed in different versions of the product, but no other difference will be required. An even better solution would be to design a single power supply that would work on either kind of current so that, for this purpose, at least, the products would not have to be distinguished at all. If the laws in different countries require different insulation or shielding materials, then places are identified and the differences minimized. Here, as in other places, it may be possible to eliminate the differences by simply adopting the more demanding standard. Only where the cost of this would be prohibitive need the distinctions be maintained.

As we said, these processes are carried out, not only on the product itself, but on all the material that goes along with it. In particular, all the places need to be located where linguistic differences would play a role. These include documentation, words on buttons, knobs and dials, inscriptions on boxes and packages, and so forth. Some of these things will require a major translation effort. Others can be made simpler and less error prone by words that have similar functions in different languages, by a symbol, or the word in a designated member of the set of languages, so that these can be replaced automatically later. The idea of this globalization enterprise is to minimize and simplify the localization step in which the differences among the various versions of the product that cannot be avoided are actually realized.

The purpose of globalization is to minimize the amount of localization work that will be required. This is the work that has to be done separately for each of the languages, cultures, and legal jurisdictions in which the product will be sold. If it has been found possible to use a power supply that can adapt itself to different voltages and frequencies, then this is a piece of localization that will not have to be done at all. If graphic symbols have been found to replace words on some buttons and switches, this will also reduce the localization required.

A crucial part of the localization process is generally not seen by the consumer of the product at all. It involves providing for the service and maintenance of the product. For this purpose, each individual replaceable part of the product must be stored in various warehouses, where it must be carefully distinguished from other parts from which it differs, however slightly. To this end, each part is given a number in a master *parts list* in the manufacturer's home language. This list is then translated into the languages of the other places where the product will be sold, making sure that different parts have different names, however small the differences among them may be.

In principle, the arduous and costly exercise of naming all the parts does not have to be done because the number is all the would be required to order a particular one from the warehouse. This does not work in practice, because maintenance people and, more particularly, members of the general public, need to refer to these things so that a more mnemonic way of naming them is required. Setting up this kind of system, for any but the most trivial of products, can be very demanding and can involve unexpected pitfalls.

Suppose, for example, that two parts of the product are held together by one or more pins that pass through holes in these parts. The pins are split for part of their length so that the sides can be bent in opposite directions, thus preventing them falling out. It is a device that makes sense only when the parts do not need to be held together particularly tightly or with accurate alignment. In the United States, a pin that is designed to be used in this way in known as a *cotter pin*. In Great Britain, a cotter pin is more like a wedge that is driven into a whole. It is slightly smaller than the hole at one end and slightly larger at the other so that it can be driven only part way through and, if it is driven hard, it holds the pieces together quite firmly. It would be most misleading to use this word for the same item in the two regions of the world.

Many examples of this kind can be found in British and American English, and there are, of course, far more in more distantly related languages. The term *wrench* refers to a mechanic's tool in both dialects.

In Britain, however, it refers only to a tool that grips the object to which it is applied. So a plumber uses a wrench to hold a piece of pipe while screwing something onto it. Another tool, called a *spanner* is used to hold a nut, the head of a bolt, or any other object that has been provided with flat surfaces, or faces, for just this purpose. In the United States, both of these tools are referred to as *wrenches* and the distinction between them is made in some other way when necessary. One may, for example, refer to a *crescent wrench*, which is the simplest kind of spanner.

1.4 Translation and Interpretation

Foreign wars bring nightly accounts of the adventures and misadventures of correspondents and the people they refer to as their "translators". In the terminology that professional translators use, such people would be described as "interpreters" rather than "translators" because they work with spoken rather than written language. Typically, an interpreter listens to a speaker, and then conveys what has been said in another language, also by speaking. A translator works from a written document, and delivers a written document in another language. Both translators and interpreters would be quick to point out that the enterprises are different in any number of ways.

There are, of course, borderline situations, such as when documents are passed out, say at a seminar attended by speakers of more than one language. If someone goes over these documents, saying what they mean in other languages, the words they speak are said to constitute a *sight translation*. The result of transcribing a recording of professional interpretation would rarely look like what a professional translator would produce working from a transcript of the original because an interpreter works under entirely more stringent constraints than the translator.

This book is about translation. What it has to say about interpretation will be confined almost entirely to this section. This is not to say that translation and interpretation do not have a great deal in common. Clearly, both can be done only by someone who has a good command, not only of the two languages, but also of the subject matter being treated. Simplifying greatly, one could say that interpretation is translation that is done under great time pressure. However, the interpreter is frequently forced to adopt compromises that would be unacceptable in a translation. This is a matter about which this book will have a considerable amount to say, because one of the main problems that it will address is that of what makes translation difficult, and whatever this is presumably also makes interpretation difficult. In addition to the difficulties that arise in both enterprises, the interpreter must often cope with input that is ill-formed in various ways; where sentences are started but never finished, and where there are asides, interruptions, and the like.

The situations in which interpretation is carried out are very diverse. We therefore routinely talk about different kinds of interpretation. The most important distinction is between *simultaneous* and *consecutive* interpretation. In the former, the interpreter is generally speaking at the same time as the original speaker. While lay people have good reason to regard this as a heroic undertaking, there are also particular difficulties in consecutive interpreting, where the interpreter speaks after the main speaker. Most notable is simply that of remembering everything that has been said so that the interpretation will not leave out anything significant. An important consideration is therefore clearly how frequently the original speaker pauses so that the interpreter can catch up. The speed of the original delivery can clearly have a crucial effect on the quality of simultaneous interpretation and on the stress placed on the person doing it. The consecutive interpreter will sometimes interrupt when the original speaker goes on too long, and the simultaneous interpreter sometimes has a button he can press that causes a light to come on on the speaker's podium as a request to slow down.

The simultaneous interpreter generally sits in a soundproof booth and hears the speaker through headphones which prevent the original speaker's voice from being picked up by the interpreter's microphone. They also reduce the extent to which the interpreter hears his or her own voice. There is a separate booth for each language for which interpretation is being provided and there are generally two interpreters assigned to each booth. They take turns, each interpreting for twenty to thirty minutes, which is about as long as interpreters can work at a stretch. Some simultaneous interpreters can work without this equipment, such as in a seminar or in a luncheon meeting, but this is quite rare.

Consecutive interpretation generally occupies less time than the original. In conferences and similar situations, it is often expected to take about a third of the time. The reasons for this are not carefully articulated, but some of them are fairly obvious. In the typical case, the speaker is formulating thoughts on the fly. There is therefore quite a lot of reformulation, abandoning of sentences that do not work out for some reason or other, and material that it inserted only to give the speaker time to think. To try to render all of this in the interpretation would be not only unnecessary, but also very difficult. What is effectively a summary can therefore actually be more effective than a rendering that follows the original more closely. The simultaneous interpreter clearly has much more limited scope for this kind of reformulation.

A distinction is made between short and long consecutive interpretation on the basis of the frequency with which the original speaker pauses to allow for interpretation to take place. In the short variety, the speaker pauses every few sentences, whereas in the long variety, the interpreter may have to wait until the end of an entire speech. Because of the memory load imposed by the long variety, interpreters often take notes. These function in a different way from the notes that we take of lectures and the like in ordinary life. Shorthand might seem to be ideal for this purpose, but it falls down for two reasons. First, because these notes are required to aid recall over a relatively short time span, they can omit a considerable amount of detail. They must require as little of the interpreter's attention as possible, so that this can be focused on the speaker. Second, the notes ideally serve to recall the content of what was said without reproducing the actual words that were used. They therefore typically take a graphic rather than a linguistic form. The system that an interpreter uses is very personal and generally will not be understandable by another interpreter.[3]

Several interpretation specialties are widely recognized. There are, for example, interpreters that specialize in *legal* or *courtroom* work. This clearly requires special knowledge of legal terminology and a sensitivity to distinctions which, while of minor importance in everyday life, may be crucial in a legal setting. Furthermore, the interpreter is generally held to particularly stringent standards when interpreting certain participants in a trial, notably the defendant.

Some interpreters specialize in *community* and *escort* interpretation. The former can occur in a variety of settings—in hospitals and doctor's offices, when parents meet teachers, at meetings with parole officers, and so on. Escort interpretation is what takes place when, say, a reporter takes an interpreter along, or official visitors to a foreign country are provided with an interpreter who accompanies them on their visit.

Sign language interpretation also constitutes a special variety. While it can obviously be done in both directions, it is most commonly encountered simultaneously in meetings involving some deaf participants. It does not involve soundproof booths or special electronic equipment. The interpreter simply stands in a place that is in clear view of the audience and interprets what is said.

---

3. A detailed discussion of note-taking by consecutive interpreters can be found in Rozan 2004.

1.5 Translation in the World

Translation, loosely construed, is presumably about as old as language. Narrowly construed, it operates only on written text and delivers written text as output, and would therefore only be as old as writing. One of the best known early examples is the Septuagint, translation of the Hebrew Bible into Koine Greek commissioned by Ptolemy II Philadelphus, the Greek king of Egypt, in the third century, and completed in the first century BC. The translation was made in Alexandria and was widely used by Hellenistic Jews, many of whom were no longer conversant with Hebrew. The name "Septuagint" comes from the fact that some seventy (or seventy-two) translators were involved in the translation and one story has it that there were six translators from each tribe, and that each group of six worked in a separate room. In spite of this, the groups all produced identical translations. If this story were true, it would be remarkable indeed because even very straightforward texts can give rise to quite divergent, though arguably equally good, translations.

The Bible is generally held to be the most translated text in the world, resulting in many versions in many languages and giving rise to much strife and controversy. St. Jerome's translation of the Greek New Testament into Latin at the end of the fourth century AD, and known as the Vulgate, became the version authorized by the Catholic church. Martin Luther's 1521 translation of the Greek Bible into German played an important role in bringing about the German reformation. The English King James Bible published in 1611 was important for similar reasons in England. A total of forty-seven different translators worked in six committees to produce it.

Much of ancient Greek philosophy and science was preserved through the European dark ages by the Arabs in Mesopotamia, which is approximately modern Iraq. In AD 762, the caliph al-Mansur, who was much influenced by Persian culture, moved the capital of the Islamic Empire from Damascus to the newly founded city of Baghdad. He established there a palace library, sometimes referred to as the *House of Wisdom* which also became a major center for translation into Arabic or Persian, and also Greek scientific and philosophical works. In the Middle Ages, many of these found their way back to Europe through southern Spain, notably Córdoba, where they were translated into Latin and, later, Spanish.

The importance of translation in the modern world would be hard to overstate. Estimating the number of translators in the world, or in any part of it is difficult because a large number of translators work part-time, often in their own homes. A report form the United States Bureau Of Labor Statistics (2015) put the average salary of a full-time translator at around \$45,000, and increase of about 50% in ten years. The report puts their average pay at \$21.84 per hour and expects the number of people involved in the work to increase by 46% between 2012 and 2022.

According to a report from IbisWorld (Diment 2016), a market research organization in industrial and business forecasting, translation services are expected to keep on growing and reach \$37 billion in 2018. The largest company involved in such services is U.S. military contractor Mission Essential Personnel. Their revenues increased by some \$100 million in 2014. The second largest, Lionbridge, grew by more than \$20 million. As of 2012, Common Sense Advisory expected the language services market to grow at an annual rate of 12.17%, reaching \$33.523 billion by the end of the year.

As a result of globalization and localization, corporations must routinely have correspondence, contracts, user manuals, advertising material—documents of almost every imaginable kind—translated back and forth among several different languages. The Boeing Dreamliner uses materials coming from over thirty countries in some of which there are multiple suppliers. Interactions with each of them must be in accordance with carefully drawn up agreements that are understood by both parties. More than 50% of the sales made by the Caterpillar Corporation are outside the United States. The equipment they sell is complicated and therefore requires large amounts of documentation. That documentation is intended to be read for the most part by people who cannot be expected to know English. In any case, many countries require that the documentation accompanying imported equipment be in their official language.

Increased need for translation comes not only from the expansion of international trade and finance and the need to provide product literature in many languages. It comes also from the greatly increased sophistication and complexity of the products themselves as a result of which a great deal more documentation is typically required. Along with this go greater requirements for company executives and technicians to travel to foreign countries which, together with expansions in the tourist industry, leads to an altogether greater demand for multilingual literature related to travel.

The European Union's translation service, the Directorate-General for Translation, produced 1.76 million pages of output in 2012. A page is 1,500 typed characters, so that makes 2.64 billion characters. The types of documents involved, in order of priority, are

1. Proposed laws, policy papers ("communications") and Commission consultation documents.
2. Consultation documents to or from national parliaments and correspondence with national authorities, companies and individuals.
3. Websites and press releases.

The cost of this amounts to €330 million a year, or about €0.60 (roughly $0.80) for every EU citizen. From 2004 to 2007, the number of official EU languages doubled from eleven to twenty-three, but Commission translation costs increased by only 20%. According to certain very rough estimates, the cost of all language services in all EU institutions amounts to less than 1% of the annual general budget of the European Union. Divided by the population of the European Union, this comes to around €2 per person per year.

The European Union now has twenty-four official languages for the twenty-seven member countries. The languages and the countries in which they are used are as follows:

1.	Bulgarian	Bulgaria
2.	Croatian	Croatia
3.	Czech	Czech Republic
4.	Danish	Denmark
5.	Dutch	Netherlands and Belgium
6.	English	Ireland, Malta and United Kingdom
7.	Estonian	Estonia
8.	Finnish	Finland
9.	French	Belgium, France and Luxembourg
10.	German	Austria, Belgium, Germany and Luxembourg
11.	Greek	Cyprus and Greece
12.	Hungarian	Hungary
13.	Irish	Ireland
14.	Italian	Italy
15.	Latvian	Latvia
16.	Lithuanian	Lithuania
17.	Maltese	Malta
18.	Polish	Poland
19.	Portuguese	Portugal
20.	Romanian	Romania
21.	Slovak	Slovakia
22.	Slovene	Slovenia

23.	Spanish	Spain
24.	Swedish	Finland and Sweden

Some countries have more than one national language and some languages belong to more than one country.

The European Union has a permanent staff of some 1,750 translators, sometimes referred to as "linguists", and six hundred support staff. The laws of the European Union must be promulgated in all of the official languages and, furthermore, each version is deemed to be *authentic*. What this means is that no version has precedence over any other, so that legal cases can be argued on the basis of any of the texts or, indeed, on any subset of them. If the lawyer for a Pole who is suing an Italian sees a way of construing the Finnish version of the relevant rule or statute in a way that seems to favor his position, he can base his case on that version. It is therefore of the uttermost importance that, to the extent possible, these translations should allow just those interpretations allowed by the original. Each of them is, after all, not simply a translation of the law, but the law itself.

True authenticity is an ideal which, in many cases, cannot be achieved. From time to time, it is discovered that the translation of a law in one of the languages contains an error. Perhaps it is an error that would normally be considered of little consequence. Nevertheless, a case may come up, perhaps some time after the promulgation of the law, that makes the error suddenly crucial. The original policy was to correct the mistake, making the change retroactive back to the original promulgation. As more and more mistakes came to light, it became clear that this was unworkable. The only alternative, and the one which is now in force, is to admit that the law was ambiguous up to the time of the change. Clearly, this leaves open the possibility of some sharp legal practice.

The majority of the documents generated by the European bureaucracy are formulated in English, and most of the remainder in French or German. A large number of them must then be translated into twenty-six other languages. A nontrivial number of documents, however, must be translated from each of the twenty-seven into the remaining twenty-six languages, so that the capability must be available for translating between any of the 506 pairs of languages.

When a new country joins the European Union, and causes the number of official languages to increase, the entire body of legislations, treaties and the like must be translated into this new language. At present, this amounts to some ninety thousand pages of text. The responsibility for this, which lies with the country concerned, can be daunting—it amounts to more than two pages for each of the approximately forty thousand people on the island of Malta. In 2006, the European Union estimated that it had spent around €800 million on translation.

At the end of 1992, the European Union adopted rules requiring all technical manuals for equipment and hardware sold in member countries be written in the user's native language. But even without such a requirement, the globalization of industry and commerce makes it increasingly important to have such material in several languages. This is a major part of the process of localization which, in addition to the translation of documentation, requires such things as insuring that equipment meets health and safety requirements in the target countries, electrical insulation is in accord with local standards, and so forth.

1.6 Translation as an Art or a Craft

Most translators regard themselves as artisans. They learn their craft in professional schools. In the United States, there are many universities that offer Master of Arts and doctoral degrees in translation, but these degrees are often oriented towards research in the field, and do not always reflect competence in the craft. In other countries, schools of translation and interpretation issue certificates guaranteeing a minimum level of competence and constitute the principal gateway to the field. Some legal procedures in the United States require a "Certificate of Accuracy" to accompany a translation. This consists of a statement, signed by the translator and notarized by a Notary Public, declaring that the translation is complete and accurate to the best of the translator's knowledge. They therefore say more about the translator's good will than his competence.

Certified translations of personal documents such as birth certificates, marriage certificates, university and high school diplomas are called for in a variety of settings and there are translators that specialize in providing them. More demanding are longer and less standardized documents such as contracts and treaties, not to speak of legal statutes themselves.

We have already spoken of the special difficulties attending the translation of laws and statutes in the European Union. The translator of these types of document must clearly understand the legal terminology used in the documents and of subtle but often crucial distinctions that can result from replacing one term by another which, in ordinary usage, would seem hardly different at all. But there is more to it than that. Legal documents clearly often contain parts where it is crucial to strive for meticulous accuracy. What this requires in practice is maintaining the vagueness or ambiguity of a passage where the writer wishes to avoid making unnecessary commitments. Not surprisingly, work of this kind is frequently revised, edited, and revised again by several different translators.

Another difficulty with legal translation arises when not only two languages, but also two legal systems are involved. Presumably, we may not expect to find a ready translation for terms like "alimony", "value added tax" and "double jeopardy" in few parts of the world where the legal system was not fairly closely related to our own. The approach that a translator takes to problems like these depends on the function that the translation will be expected to fill. The most difficult situation is the one in which the translation is expected to be authentic which, as we have said, is often the case in the European Union or in bilingual countries. Recall that an authentic translation is one which, for legal purposes, can be used interchangeably with the original. Common law prevails generally in Canada with the exception of Quebec, which uses civil law on the French model. But there are many situations in which Canadian federal law requires authentic translations. This can obviously lead to extreme conflicts.

The severity of the requirements placed on the journeyman translator can approach those placed on the literary translator. The most obvious such situations arise in public relations. Advertising does not aspire to the beauty of a Shakespearean sonnet, but the linguistic subtleties involved can be great and the perils of failure are extreme. There are humorists that specialize in real and imaginary mistranslation of advertising slogans like "Nothing sucks like Electrolux", and the Spanish version of "Avoid embarrassment: use Parker pens" which could be read approximately as "It won't leak in your pocket and make you pregnant". Humor aside, the difficulty of maintaining the impact of an advertisement while maintaining an appropriate level of sensitivity to the target culture can clearly be challenging. Often, entirely different advertisements are required rather than simply translating any single original. The marketing of wine in Europe is a case in point. In much of Northern Europe, wine is a drink for special occasions whereas, in the south, it is an everyday drink. So a different approach to its marketing is presumably appropriate. A widely known example of an infelicitous choice of words in international marketing was the original choice of "Ke-kou-ke-la" as the name for Coca-Cola in China on the grounds of phonetic similarity. It was later discovered that this can be taken to mean "bite the wax tadpole" or "female horse stuffed with wax" in some dialects. It was replaced by "ko-kou-ko-le" which translates as "happiness in the mouth". It is reported that a sign on American-made medical containers which read: "Take off top and push in bottom," was not well received in Britain for supposedly linguistic reasons.

Charging by the word is not generally practicable in interpretation, where rates are quoted by the hour and generally lie in the range from $50 to $100. The lowest rates are for community interpretation and situations where little technical knowledge is required. Rates in the mid-range are charged for courtroom proceedings, medical settings, and many business situations. Simultaneous and telephone interpreting is charged at the higher rates, as is interpretation requiring considerable technical knowledge.

1.7 This Book

Most of the writing that is done about translation falls into one of two categories. The first is instructional material intended for use in the training of translators. The typical member of this category presents in each chapter a passage representing a different subject or style of writing, together with notes on difficulties that might arise when translating it into another language. The second consists of war stories from a translator hero recently returned from battling the untranslatable.

This book fits neither of these models. Our main concern will be with the activities of the ordinary journeyman translator in the course of his ordinary nine-to-five job. Some of the questions we shall ask will be apparently so simple as to hardly seem worth asking at all, such as what properties a pair of texts have to have that cause us to acknowledge that one is a translation of the other. Otherwise put: what is a translation anyway? Translators must clearly know more than one language. A person who learned two languages together from their earliest childhood, so that they have two native languages, is a *bilingual*. So is a bilingual necessarily the best, or even a good, translator? If not, then what is it that a good translator knows that a bilingual may not? Is translation always possible, or do some otherwise unremarkable texts have properties that make them untranslatable into at least some other languages? Are some languages easier or more difficult to translate into or out of?

We do not expect to answer all these questions, but we do expect to come away from the experience with a clearer understanding of what translation is and how it is done.

A remark needs to be made on one aspect of the language used in this book. From time to time, we will write things like the following: *When a translator is confronted with a situation of this kind, he must decide....*

This usage constitutes a contravention of widely accepted norms concerning sexist language. Using *he* in this generic way may seem to be excluding or marginalizing women. But something equivalent to this usage clearly needs to be found and considerable ingenuity has been devoted to the search.

One solution consists in inventing orthographic hybrids like *(s)he* and *he/she*. The trouble with these, apart from the fact that they are ugly, is that, while they can be written and read, they cannot be spoken and one should surely not write what cannot be discussed because it cannot be read aloud.

As a generic pronoun, *he* is a relative newcomer to the English language. It was first recognized in an Act of Parliament in 1850,[4] which said *words importing the masculine gender shall be deemed and taken to include females* (Barker and Moorcroft 2002). Previously, this function had been generally filled by the pronoun *they*, which continues to fill it in some usages today. But *they* has come to be deprecated by some pundits on the grounds that it seems to ascribe plurality to clearly singular entities. But it has the altogether more serious defect that, in many situations, it simply does not work. The sentence *When a translator is confronted with a situation of this kind, they must decide among these alternative* just does not mean what is intended. Still worse would be *When a translator is confronted with a situation of this kind, they must decide whether the rules applies to themselves.*

Using *he or she* in place of the generic *he* can also give rise to sentences that are so complicated as essentially to lose their meaning. Consider *When a translator is confronted with a situation of this kind, he or she must decide whether he or she should take the rule as applying to himself or herself.* As the sentence gets longer, the problem can easily get worse and worse.

Another solution to this problem which is increasing in popularity, is to use both *he* and *she*, shifting between them more or less randomly. So, we will sometimes get *When a translator is confronted with a situation of this kind, she must decide....* The trouble with this is that some readers, including the present writer, reacts quite differently to the sentence depending on which version of the generic pronoun it contains. We read the one containing *he* smoothly and, all else being equal, assimilate the intended meaning. Encountering the one with *she*, on the other hand, is like following a television drama that is suddenly interrupted by a commercial. Yes, yes. We should not belittle women,

---

4. Interpretation Act of 1850 (13 & 14 Vict. c. 21) also known as "An Act for shortening the Language used in Acts of Parliament" or Lord Brougham's Act.

members of particular races, or the adherents of other religions, and we should be kind to children and animals. Now, what were you saying?

We will frequently use generic *he* in this book, while strongly disapproving any acts, linguistic or other, that tend to disparage anyone. We use it because, for us at least, it is the only alternative that works.

2

A Model of Translation

Everybody knows what a translation is. A translation is a text produced with the aim of conveying the same meaning as a text in another language. The translation process results in an artifact that we also refer to as a *translation*. Based on no more than this idea, two people who know the same two languages will generally agree on whether one text is a translation of another. They may be uncertain which text is the original, and which the translation, but they will agree on whether their meanings are sufficiently similar for one to be a translation of the other.

A pair of bilinguals that took this characterization of translation seriously could presumably disagree on whether one of a pair of texts was a translation of the other only if they disagreed on whether they meant the same thing. So, if we want to gain a better understanding of translation, we need to tease apart the properties that a pair of texts must have that might lead us to say that they have the same meaning. Here things start to fall apart.

Meaning is a notoriously slippery notion. Many gifted and determined people have devoted substantial parts of their lives to it and left many of the problems it raises largely unresolved. If we seek a better understanding of translation, we must expect to find ourselves frequently retracing their steps and possibly also our own. The best we can hope for may be that we will not have to follow these worthy people down every blind alley that they have explored.

2.1 The Order of Events

We might expect the question of whether one text is a translation of another to be easiest to solve if they contained instructions for the fulfillment of some task. We could then give the original text to a speaker of the source language, and the purported translation to a speaker of

the target language, and observe what they did as they tried to follow the instructions. If they exhibited essentially the same behavior,
we would presumably have substantial evidence that they were reading
translations. To be specific, let us consider a set of directions about
how to reach the Charles de Gaule airport from a particular apartment
in the center of Paris. Here is one of the texts:

Text A
Go up the hill from the apartment to Place Monge. Take the Metro
from there to the Gare du Nord. From the Gare du Nord, take the
RER, line B, to the airport.

We can simplify this preliminary investigation by letting the purported translation also to be in English. Here is a candidate:

Text B
You can get to the airport on the RER, line B from the Gare du Nord.
You can reach the Gare du Nord by taking the Metro from Place
Monge. The Place Monge is just up the hill from the apartment.

If each of these was given to a different native speaker of English who
did not know the way from the apartment to the airport, and if the
routes they describe do indeed lead to the airport, then we may suppose
that that is where they would both end up. We need also to assume
that our two subjects share some important background information so
that they would, for example, know what to make of the terms *metro*
and *RER line B*.

The reader of text B might have a little more difficulty in understanding the instructions because the order in which they describe the
events is the reverse of the one in which they are actually expected to
occur. Text A describes them in their "natural" order. This difference
might also be sufficient to disqualify either text as a translation of the
other. If we imagine text B to be a translation of text A, then we must
assume that the translator had some compelling reason to rearrange the
events so that they appear in a less natural order than they do in the
original, and maybe no such compelling reason comes readily to mind.
Suppose, however that this passage occurred not in a text intended to
be taken as a set of instructions, but as a counter to the argument that
there is just no way of getting from the apartment to the airport using
public transport. Under these circumstances, it makes much more sense
to work back from the goal. We know you can get to the airport from
the Gare du Nord. So lets see if you can get to the Gare du Nord. Well,
yes, that can be done on the RER line B, and that is just up the hill
from the apartment.

If the argument is more persuasive when presented in this order, then we might suppose that the translator chose it for this reason. But we might still be reluctant to allow the translator the license required for such a radical reordering. If we take text A to be the translation, then it might be easier to believe that the translator considered a more natural order would improve the intelligibility of the result sufficiently to justify the move. But we might still be concerned whether, in so doing, he was assuming too much license. If the texts were longer, and the process they describe consisted of more finely articulated steps, our concerns about their wholesale reordering would presumably increase.

Let us therefore take it that a translation of nontrivial length should consist of a sequence of shorter translations. If one segment immediately follows another in text A, then its translation should follow the translation of the other in text B. We must probably remain flexible on just what should be allowed to count as a segment, but something of approximately the size of a sentence seems like a reasonable place to start. We know that one sentence is sometimes translated by two or three and that two or three are sometimes translated as one. Within a sentence, it is generally impossible to maintain strict parallelism between words or phrases. One reason for this is that, on this level, the order falls largely under the control of the grammars of the languages rather than any ordering implicit in what they refer to. In English, an adjective normally precedes that noun it modifies, whereas in Romance languages like French or Spanish, this order is often reversed. The verb in a German subordinate clause must come at the end. There are three theoretically possible ways of ordering the major constituents of the commonest kind of sentence, Subject, Verb, and Object. By far the greatest number of languages generally put the subject at the beginning. A third important class, including Classical Arabic, puts the verb at the beginning. In other languages, different considerations, such as information structure, are more important in determining the way the constituents of a sentence are ordered. English and German regularly use *fronting* to mark the new element in a sentence, as in *Broccoli, I cannot stand* or *Das würde ich nicht sagen* (THAT I WOULD NOT SAY).

If the source text, or some part of it, does not describe a temporal sequence of events, the argument that the translations of the sentences should be in the same order as the originals may be less compelling but, nevertheless, substantial departures from this order would presumably require some justification. It may not be clear why the author chose this order, or even whether he had any strong reason for choosing it, but it is his text, after all, and the translator should not make gratuitous changes to it.

2.2 Grain Size

Our first observation about the nature of translation, namely that big translations are made up of smaller ones, is less than profound. The same will be true of the second. Consider the following pairs of text as translations of one another:

Text C

Go out of the front door and turn left. You will pass three turnings on the right, the third being only for pedestrians. Turn right at the next possibility following this one and continue straight ahead, until you come have the possibility of turning half left along a wide boulevard at the end of which you will see an impressive building with a lot of gold leaf on the roof. That is the building you are looking for.

Text D

Go west along the river and cross by the Pont du Carrouselle. Go through the Louvre and up the Avenue de l'Opéra. The opera house is at the end of that street.

This example, like the earlier one, consists of directions for reaching a destination, in this case, the Paris opera house, from a particular location on the left bank of the Seine. This time, the order of events is the same and the key items referred to in the two texts—notably bridges and streets—are the same. But the way in which they are referred to is completely different. If you turn left after going out of the front door, you will be going towards the west. In this particular context, *turn left* and *Go west* give rise to exactly the same behavior on the part of a person who follows the instructions. To this extent, they therefore mean the same thing. Passing three bridges and turning right at the fourth means that one turns right at the *Pont du Carrouselle*, whether one realizes it or not. But having recourse to this very special knowledge is clearly not required to achieve an adequate translation. To do so is therefore gratuitous and detracts from the quality of the result.

It does not require a detailed analysis to put the quality of this supposed translation severely in doubt. It is sufficient to observe that the two texts differ greatly in length so that, if the longer text is the translation, then it probably contains more information than the original, most of which probably did not need to be there. If the shorter text is the translation, then information from the original has probably been omitted. Recall, however, that the criterion we adopted for adequacy in the translation of a set of instructions is that both texts should elicit the same behavior on the part of people that follow them and this criterion could be met in the present case.

As we have seen, a pair of texts could elicit the same overt behavior, even though the information in each of them was not strictly the same. A good translation is presumably one that adds and subtracts as little as possible and maintains the ordering of the various items of information as much as possible. There are two main reasons why this is generally possible only to a limited extent, both of which we will explore more thoroughly in later chapters. The first has to do with the lexicons of the two languages, and the other with their grammars.

Often, there is no item in the lexicon of one language that can be used to refer to just the same set of objects in the world that can be referred to by a given word in another language. The French word *cousin* can usually be translated into English as *cousin*, though the French word can only be used to refer to a male cousin. Going in the other direction can be more problematic because the English text may not make it clear whether the person in question is male or female. This example is on the border between lexicon and grammar. For a more thoroughly grammatical example, consider the translation of reported speech in German which requires the subjunctive if the writer does not wish to stand behind the content of the reported speech, but which can be in the indicative if it is patently true or if it enjoys the reporter's support.

Perhaps what is at fault here is our criterion. There is a *prima facie* case against it because it is limited to texts whose only purpose is to give instructions. On the other hand, this may be less of a restriction than it seems to be at first sight because there is a sense in which just about any text can be construed as a set of instructions. In the general case, they are instructions to the reader to construct a sequence of mental states, each built by modifying the preceding one in the sequence. It is often tempting to think of a mental state as corresponding to a mental picture, even though it will generally be a poorly specified one. The reader of text C is invited to construct an initial picture with three turnings. The last is important because it is there that he is called upon to do something specific. The reader of text D must also construct a mental picture with a turning corresponding to the third one referred to in text C, but it is referred to in a way that does not require a picture to be constructed of the other two turnings. The reader of text D must have a stored image of what the *Pont du Carrouselle* is if he is to able to recognize it. This requirement is not made of the first reader. What is important is not that the readers should have the same mental images when they are in corresponding mental states but that the particular parts of the images needed to move on to the next one should should have certain important properties in common.

Observable behavior that a text may elicit from a receiver in the real world can apparently not be taken as revealing anything consistent about the meaning of the text. If a text consists of instructions to its receiver, then they are instructions that are carried out in a private mental world. At a given point in the text, the writer hopes to have established a certain mental state in the reader that he hopes to modify in some fairly specific way with the next word, or phrase, or sentence, that he writes.

We can, of course, not observe mental states and the ways in which one of them can be modified to become another. Indeed, the very notion of a mental state is very imprecise, leading to the suspicion that our search for a more precise notion of what translation is may lead only to a vicious circle.

2.3   The Word Level

We now take a different perspective and examine an excerpt from a pair of sentences in English and French, one of which is known to have arisen as a result of translating the other. We will take it that the French version is the original, though little will turn on this. Our aim will be to learn more about any correspondences that may exist at a lower level of detail than what we have been referring to as the *segment*.

French
Lorsque les indicateurs de direction d'une ou plusieurs remorques sont connectés à la prise sept broches prévue à l'arrière du tracteur et que les indicateurs de direction sont actionnés, le témoin vert de remorque s'allume pour indiquer le bon fonctionement.

A substantially word-for-word translation might be somewhat as follows:

English word for word
When the indicators of direction of one or several trailers are connected to the socket seven pins provided at the back of the tractor and that the indicators of direction are activated, the green light of trailer lights itself to indicate the good functioning.

While almost word for word, even this is not an entirely mechanical translation. The word *témoin*, for example, is more often translated as *witness*. We translate it as *light* because this is one of the ways in which the word can be used and it is what makes sense in the context. We should clearly also have taken the context into consideration in deciding what we should allow to count as a word or lexical item. The sequence *les indicateurs de direction*, for example, should be rendered as *turn signals* in this context.The French word *broche* would be *spit* in a culinary context. It is only in an electrical context that we would normally expect it to be rendered as *pin*. The words (SEVEN-PIN SOCKET) constitute a pair of noun phrases that can be rendered properly only if it is realized that the second of them modifies the first. The kind of plug that on walls throughout a modern house is often referred to as *une prise de courant*. A phrase *la prise sept broches*, however, would not be generally understandable outside a very restricted technical context.

The word *pris* is the past participle of the verb *prendre* (TO TAKE) and *prise* is its feminine form. French *prendre*, like *take*, has many and diverse uses. Here, however, it is preceded by *la* (THE), strongly suggesting that it is being used as a noun. But this still leaves many translation possibilities open. It could be *purchase* in a sentence like *It is difficult to get any purchase on this*, or a *dose* of medicine. In a military context, it might be translated as *capture*. There are other possibilities in other contexts.

There is an interesting subtlety associated with the word *prise* even when restricted to an electrical context. It can, in fact, be used to refer either to a plug or a socket and while one is more probable in this context, socket is more likely. Why is this?. The reason seems to be the following. Tractors can operate independently of trailers, but a trailer is useless without a tractor to pull it. Therefore, trailers are provided with cables that are used to connect them to tractors. When there is no trailer, there is no cable. This is the main reason why the cable comes with the trailer and not with the tractor. If you have three trailers, you need three cables. If you have no trailers, you do not need any cables. That is the first part of the rationale.

The second part is as follows. When a cable is attached to a mobile object, it almost always terminates with a male connector, that is, with a plug. Think of a vacuum cleaner or an electric drill. The fixed object has a female connector—a socket. These are often found on the interior walls of buildings. If the situation were different in this case, we can be fairly sure that it would have been made explicit. So, to get an appropriate translation for this single word, it seems that we have to pursue a detailed line of argument, requiring a level of technical expertise than most people probably do not even realize that they have and which is not about words. The argument is about tractors and trailers.

The French word *plusieurs*, generally corresponds to the English word *several*, which is not the same as *more*. This is true at least in some abstract sense. Pragmatically, however, in a context like the current one, the meanings of these two words are exactly the same. Several things is more than one thing. The words *one or more* occur frequently enough to constitute essentially a set phrase—a lexical item in its own right—as does *un(e) ou plusieurs* in French.

The word *prévue* is the feminine form of the past participle of the verb *prévoir* which can be rendered in English in a variety of ways. It means *to foresee* or *anticipate* and also *to plan*. In this case, it means *to provide* or *to furnish*.The English phrase *the plug at the back of the tractor* sounds somewhat more natural than *the plug provided at the back of the tractor* whereas the reverse is the case in French. The nature of the semantic relationship between a noun and a phrase is often made more explicit in Romance languages by the addition of a word that need have no translation in English. Where the loudspeaker in an English speaking country might announce *Train 4321 to Marseille*, the French would probably say *le train 4321 à destination de Marseille*. A very literal translation of this back into English would be *Train 4321 with destination Marseille*. More natural would be *Train 1234 bound for Marseille*, but it is no better than simply providing no translation for *à destination de*. *Train 1234 from Marseille* would be *le train 4321 provenant de Marseille*. It is harder to find a word-for-word translation of this. We might perhaps say *train 4321 originating in Marseille*.

Some time ago, and perhaps still today, the announcers at the Gare de Lyon in Paris, when speaking English, would describe these trains as *Train 1234 going to Marseille*, and *Train 4321 coming from Marseille*. Apart from the fact that these are clearly unidiomatic English, they also invite somewhat misleading interpretations. The phrase *Train 1234 going to Marseille* suggests that train 1234 sometimes goes to Marseille, and sometimes somewhere else. This announcement concerns one that does go to Marseille.

Elsewhere in the station, there are arrows bearing the inscription *accès aux quais* (ACCESS TO THE PLATFORMS) which, in English would be simply *to the platforms* (or *to the trains*). Against other arrows are written the words *passagers munis de billets* (PASSENGERS EQUIPPED WITH TICKETS) where the English would say simply *passengers with tickets*.

Our final English translation of the tractor excerpt looks like this:

English
When the turn signals of one or more trailers are connected to the seven-pin socket at the back of the tractor and they are turned on, the green trailer light comes on to show that they are working properly.

We can summarize our decisions on the segmentation of the text, and the alignment of the segments in one language with those in the other in the form of a table like the one in Table 2.1. The last column gives the way in which the segments have to be rearranged to give the English translation.

TABLE 2.1 Segment alignments

	French	English	
1	Lorsque	When	1
2	les	the	2
3	indicateurs de direction	turn signals	3
4	d'	of	4
5	une ou plusieurs	one or more	5
6	remorques	trailers	8
7	sont	are	9
8	connectés	connected	10
9	à	to	11
10	la	the	12
11	prise	socket	14
12	sept	seven	13
13	broches	pin(s)	14
14	prévue		
15	à	at	15
16	l'	the	16
17	arrière	back	17
18	du	of the	18
20	tracteur	tractor	20
21	et	and	21
22	que		
23	les indicateurs de direction	they	21
24	sont	are	22
25	actionnés	turned on	23
26	le	the	24
27	témoin	light	27
28	vert	green	25
29	de remorque	trailer	26
30	s' allume	comes on	28
31	pour	to	29
32	indiquer	show	30
33	le bon fonctionement	that they are working properly	31

In many cases, the pairs of segments look like extracts from a bilingual dictionary. In some cases, the words are not in the canonical form that we should expect to find in a dictionary: they are in the plural (*indicateurs de direction* : *turn signals*); they are past participles (*actionnés* : *turned on*), possibly in the feminine or plural forms; they are finite verbs (*sont* : *are*). As in a standard bilingual dictionary, some of the entries are phrases rather then single words. A case might be made for allowing *when* as a possible translation of *que* in line 22. However, it is interesting to note that this allows a parallel, slightly different, interpretation of the sentence. The original, and presumably intended, interpretation is that the light comes on when two conditions are simultaneously met, namely some trailers are connected and the turn signals are turned on. With *que* rendered as *when*, we can also take it to mean that either condition is sufficient to cause the light to come on.

The only two entries in the list that do not fit the pattern are:

23	les indicateurs de direction	they	21
33	le bon fonctionement	that they are working properly	31

It would be strange indeed to claim that *les indicateurs de direction* means the same as *they* under any conditions. But, if we take the French version to be the original, it is not difficult to see what has happened. The translator recognized not only that *les indicateurs de direction* repeated a phrase that had been used before in this sentence and that this instance of it referred to the same thing as before. Repeating the phrase added weight to the sentence for no apparent reason and readers could be relied upon to interpret *they* as having the same reference. We shall argue extensively later that the first duty of a translator is to maintaining identity of reference between items in the original and the translation rather than the senses of the words, and that requirement has been maintained here.

The second pair is more disturbing. It would be a large bilingual dictionary indeed that would provide an entry for these two phrases because, if the notions of set phrase and sameness of meaning are to be extended to these, then the set of other pairs that would presumably have to be treated in the same manner would be vast. Furthermore, the phrases have altogether different grammatical properties so that the question of how to use the entries would be far from a simple one.

Presumably, we should regard a bilingual dictionary as the fundamental theoretical model of what a bilingual speaker knows about the vocabularies of his two languages that enables him to translate items in one into items in the other. But, do we really want to claim that someone who translates *le bon fonctionement* as *that they are working properly* must have encountered this pair before, and remembered it?

A pair of phrases like this last one, that can only be assimilated to the notion of a lexical entry with painful suspension of disbelief, will generally turn out to be a case of what we shall refer to as *pragmatic* translation. We contrast this with the more standard *syntactic* translation. Syntactic translation is based on the model of a bilingual dictionary made up of pairs of words or phrases, together with a grammar that reorders these and specifies their grammatical forms. The best model for pragmatic translation probably involves departing from the linguistic realm altogether. The translator comprehends the words in question in a much more abstract manner and then, assuming what is essentially the role an original author, looks for a way of expressing this in the other language. The French adjective *bon* might be said to correspond in some very loose way to the English *properly*, and the French *fonctionement* to the English *working*. But these cannot surely be correspondences that a translator has stored in his mental lexicon so that they can be called upon when required. We pursue what is going on here further in the next section.

2.4   Syntactic and Pragmatic Translation

The terms *syntactic translation* and *pragmatic translation* are not part of the standard terminology of translation theory but they make an important distinction that we shall frequently find useful. If each word and phrase in a segment of a translation is a translation of a word or phrase in the original, then we will say that we have a good example of *syntactic translation*. Somewhat more precisely, syntactic translation happens when lexical items in one language are translated by lexical items in the other language, and phrases in one language by phrases in the other. The distinction between a word and a lexical item is one we shall explore further shortly. To the extent that the translation does not fit this pattern, we have an instance of *pragmatic translation*. This distinction is, of course, an idealization and actual translations, and parts of translations, are located somewhere on a cline between them.

Let us return to the world of train travel. When a train reaches the end of its journey in France, an announcement is commonly made on the public-address system containing the sentence *Assurez-vous que vous n'avez rien oublié dans le train*. Sometimes, the announcement is repeated in English, with the sentence *Make sure that you have not left anything on the train*. This is a good syntactic translation because it can be accounted for entirely in terms of low-level correspondences between the two texts. The correspondences include those in Table 2.2.

TABLE 2.2 Correspondences

Make sure	Assurez-vous
that	que
you	vous
have	avez
not	ne
left	oublié
anything	rien
on	dans
the	le
train	train
the train	le train
on the train	dans le train
left anything on the train	rien oublié dans le train
have not left anything on the train	n'avez rien oublié dans le train
you have not left anything on the train	vous n'avez rien oublié dans le train
that you have not left anything on the train	que vous n'avez rien oublié dans le train
Make sure that you have not left anything on the train	Assurez-vous que vous n'avez rien oublié dans le train

To define syntactic and pragmatic translation precisely, one would need to tie them to a specific formal grammar that would determine just what was a phrase and what was not, and a lexicon for each language which would list lexical items. But we do not need a precise definition because all we are really trying to capture is the notion of words and phrases that the translator intuitively uses.

French railways sometimes translates the same sentence as *Make sure that you have all your belongings with you*, which is a largely pragmatic translation. We say that it is *largely* pragmatic because at least "Make sure" still translates as "Assurez-vous", and "that" as "que" and, of course, the sentence as a whole still translates the sentence as a whole. But nothing in the French corresponds to "belongings" or "have with you" in English. But the original makes only the most indirect reference to belongings and a considerable amount of inference is required to get from the negation of "oublié" (FORGET) to "have with you". But it is surely the case that, if you did not leave your belongings on the train, then you have them with you.

All other things being equal, syntactic is generally preferred to pragmatic translation. To render the words and phrases of the source by corresponding words and phrases in the target language, that add and delete as little information as possible, is to give the original author the greatest possible control over the the choices that have to be made, and this is as it should be, because the author owns the text and the translator should remain as anonymous as possible. This argument is particularly cogent in the case of religious texts, especially where what must be translated is taken to be the word of God. St. Jerome, the patron saint of translators who gave us the first Latin version of the New Testament was strong in his opposition to slavish, word-for-word translation, but insisted that it was the only option when the text in question was the word of God.

This is clearly also a central issue in legal translation and courtroom interpretation. The court should hear everything that is said, but no more, and the best way to insure this is generally to maintain a unit-for-unit correspondence between the two texts. However, this is not, by itself, enough to guarantee that the translation will have the desired properties.

We claimed that syntactic is generally preferred to pragmatic translation *all other things being equal*. We are therefore apparently advocating word-for-word translation, a practice that we have all been urged from an early age to hold in derision. However, the practice of syntactic translation should be avoided only when the result is inadequate on other grounds. And, indeed, it should not necessarily be avoided even then, as the example we have just considered makes clear.

We need to distinguish syntactic from from the narrower notion of word-for-word translation, and also to show when all other things are, and when they are not, equal. We also need to explore the nature of the relationship that exists between a passage in one language, and its pragmatic translation in another. After all, if the parts of the translation do not correspond to the parts of the original, then just what is it that does correspond to?

However much syntactic translation may constitute some kind of ideal, it is one that is achieved relatively rarely, especially by professional translators, and possibly for contrary reasons. On the one hand, professional translators take particular pride in a product that reads naturally enough that it cannot be recognized as a translation. On the other hand, when they are forced to work under pressure, they often find it easier to produce an adequate pragmatic translation than a more syntactic one.

Many instances of pragmatic translation could be characterized as *inferential* because the translation naturally invites the same inferences as the original and, to this extent, means the same thing. In many cases, one could formalize the rules necessary to show the equivalence so we can imagine that they, like the lexicon and the grammar, would be part of the equipment that the translator brings to his task.

Consider the French sentence *Je n'ai rien oublié dans le train* which translates straightforwardly into English as *I forgot nothing on the train* or *I did not forget anything on the train*. We can imagine there being a rule, somewhere between the dictionary and the grammar saying approximately that, whenever one can say *X Y nothing*, where *X* is a verb, and *Y* is a noun phrase, then one could also say *X does/did not Y*. So, instead of *John saw nothing*, we can say *John did not see anything*. We choose between *does* and *did* on the basis of the form of the original verb. Instead of *John remembered to buy milk*, we can say *John did not forget to buy milk*. The meanings of many verbs can be conveyed by negated forms of corresponding other verbs.

We take it that a truly pragmatic translation is generally an original creation. If it has been used elsewhere to translate the same word or phrase, the translator is almost certainly unaware of it. It presumably does not have the same sense as the original word or phrase because its parts do not correspond. The nagging question therefore remains: in what sense is a pragmatic translation a translation at all? The answer must be that it has the same meaning in the given context. On the one hand, this is satisfying because, just as we have somehow always known that word-for-word translation is bad, we have also always known that context is crucial and, finally, it has appeared on the scene. But what are we to make of it? How can one sequence of words mean the same as another if it does not have the same sense? Just what is this thing that we call "context" and how does it exercise its influence?

2.5 Context

We have already used the term "context" a great deal. We have talked about the electrical context, the culinary context; we have said that something was true of this context but not of that one. It is a common word that is treated casually in everyday parlance, and that is the way we have used it. Do we really need to make it more precise? The answer is "yes" because it is also useful in a more precise technical role, though one that is still very simple and intuitive. It means something very similar to what we have previously referred to as *mental image*, or *mental state*.

A text that does what its author intended carries the reader from state to state as it unfolds a story, an argument, a description, a proof or whatever. The state that is reached after the n-th sentence is the context for the $n + 1$-st sentence. It is not the sum of the items of information that the first n sentences have conveyed. It will almost always be more than that. Consider the following children's story:[5]

1. Once upon a time there was a little girl. Her name was Goldilocks. She had golden hair.
2. One day Goldilocks was walking in the forest. She saw a house and knocked on the door. She went inside. Nobody was there.
3. Goldilocks saw three bowls on the table. She was hungry.
4. "This porridge is too hot! This porridge is too cold! This porridge is just right!" Goldilocks ate all the porridge.
5. Goldilocks was tired now. "This chair is too big! This chair is too big, too! This chair is just right!" But the chair broke.
6. Goldilocks was very tired. She went upstairs. "This bed is too hard! This bed is too soft! This bed is just right!"
7. Soon, the bears came home. "Someone's been eating my porridge!" said Daddy bear.

---

5. LearnEnglish Kids. 2012. *Goldilocks and the three bears.* British Council. Accessed March 23, 2017. https : / / learnenglishkids . britishcouncil . org / sites / kids / files / attachment / stories - goldilocks - and - the - three - bears - transcript_2012_07_13_0.pdf

8. "Someone's been eating my porridge!" said Mummy bear. "Someone's been eating my porridge—and it's all gone!" said Baby bear.
9. "Someone's been sitting on my chair!" said Daddy bear. "Someone's been sitting on my chair!" said Mummy bear.
10. "Someone's been sitting on my chair—and it's broken!" said Baby bear.
11. "Someone's been sleeping in my bed!" said Daddy bear. "Someone's been sleeping in my bed!" said Mummy bear.
12. "Someone's been sleeping in my bed—and she's still there!" said Baby bear.
13. Goldilocks woke up and saw the three bears. "Help!" She ran downstairs and into the forest. She never came back again.

Let us try to imagine that we do not already know the story. From the first sentence, we learn that it is intended for very small children and is almost certainly fictional. *Once upon a time* is a formula that means just that. We learn that it is going to be about a little girl and that she is called Goldilocks. We know that the words *her* and *she* in the next two sentences refer to the little girl, Goldilocks, because it is a feminine pronoun and, in any case, there is nobody else around for a pronoun to refer to. So far, what we know is pretty much the simple aggregate of what is made explicit in the first paragraph. We have been introduced to a person who will have a role, probably an important one, in the story.

Paragraph 2 begins *One day Goldilocks was walking in the forest*. The phrase *One day* is almost entirely free of content. It is almost like *Once upon a time*. If it were simply omitted, however, the sentence would have an abrupt character that the author does not intend. If it had read simply *Goldilocks was walking in the forest*, the reader might be tempted to wonder if he had missed something. Should some additional context not have been provided? The phrase *One day* assures that reader that no additional contextual material is required. Like almost everything in the text, it functions as an operator on the context but, in this case, rather than adding something to the context, it acknowledges that some thing is missing, and that this is deliberate.

We know it was Goldilocks who saw a house, and that it was she who knocked on the door. The indefinite article in front of *house* tells us that this is a new thing that is being introduced into the story. But what about the door? This noun has a definite article, so surely we may ask what door Goldilocks knocked on? We search the context for a door and notice that the new item that has just been introduced into the context is of a kind that generally has doors. They have exterior and interior doors; they have front doors, side doors, and back doors, sometimes several of each. But we do not introduce gratuitous complexity into the story. That rule is especially important for stories intended for small children. On the stage in our head where this story is being played out, there is the simplest of houses, facing us, with a door in the middle, and probably one window on either side.

Goldilocks went inside. Inside what? Inside the house because the context provided nothing else for her to go inside and the house is the last thing that the spotlight shone on. Do we know how she got inside? Certainly we do. She went into the house through the door that she had just knocked on. That is why we were told about the door and that she knocked on it. These assumptions could be wrong but, if they were, then this story would be the work of a poor writer of children's stories.

The context required to interpret paragraph 3 needs to contain a table. It does not need three bowls. It actually supplies these. But the phrase *the table* needs as referent. We make the same kind of inference that has worked for us before. The interior of a house is the very kind of place in which one expects to find things like tables, especially tables with things on them that have to do with eating. One often eats out of bowls, especially bowls on tables. We are encouraged in this line of thinking when, in the very next sentence, we are told that *She was hungry.*

Up to this point, the inferences we have had to make in order to update the context and thus understand the story have simple and entirely effortless, as they should be in a story for small children. In paragraph 4, however, things change. As adults, we see quotation marks, strongly suggesting that we are receiving a report about some speech. But we are not told who is talking or whom they are talking to. Since the context strongly suggests that nobody else is around, it may well be that it is Goldilocks, and she is talking to herself. Maybe she is thinking these words rather than saying out loud. If we were reading this story to a child, we would have to find a way of distinguishing the words in this sentence that are reported speech. We might try to do this with a change in voice quality, or by pointing at a picture of Goldilocks, if one was available.

Goldilocks says three things to herself, all about something called *porridge*, that is not yet in the context. To make matters worse, what Goldilocks says is three contradictory things about the porridge. Somehow, we must update our context to accommodate this. Our only clue as to how to do this comes from the three bowls which, fortunately, are the most recent, and therefore the most salient, things in the context. We put the porridge in the bowls and then assume that Goldilocks considers each of them in turn to assess their utility. We know she is hungry, so utility means suitability for eating and we know that temperature is often relevant in that domain. If we happen to know that porridge is something that is eaten hot, this inference is easier to make. A child in America, where porridge is *oatmeal*, might need help with this.

Suppose that paragraph 3 had not been part of the story so that the reader would know nothing about three bowls on any table. This would make paragraph 4 very much more difficult to understand. The paragraph would be in a different context and its meaning would therefore also be different.

The last sentence in paragraph 4 is problematic because it does not give a clear interpretation for the sentence *Goldilocks ate all the porridge*. Since the first two bowls that she tried had something wrong with them, we may assume that she did not eat the porridge in these. But the matter is not really cleared up until the last sentence of paragraph 8.

Paragraphs 5 and 6 must be interpreted in the same way as paragraph 4. But paragraph 7 contains some more challenges. Many versions of this story start out by introducing the three bears, and saying that they went out for a walk, possibly in order to let their porridge cool. This makes the problem of how to keep the context updated much simpler. This version refers to some things as though they had been introduced earlier when, in fact they are quite new. It tells us the the bears came home, but does not actually say that there were three of them, or that they ever left.

The bears came home. So what home did they come to? Where is it and what is it like? Suppose that paragraph 2 of the story had read

> One day Goldilocks was walking in the forest. She walked past the hut where the three bears lived. Then she saw a house and knocked on the door. She went inside. Nobody was there.

This surely would have changed everything. Even though there are three of everything in the house, we would not suppose that this is where the bears live. Maybe each of the bears has a friend and this where the three friends live. Maybe there are three little boys live who love porridge just as keenly as the three bears dislike it. Just about any trio can live here *except* the three bears.

2.6 Pragmatic Translation and Context

We shall have a lot to say about the notion of *sense* in the next chapter. Roughly speaking, we shall conclude that it a property that words and phrases have independently of any context in which they are embedded. So, how can they have the same meaning in context if they have different senses out of context? As we have said, the answer must be that a reader will make substantially the same inferences from both forms in the given context. How can the translator arrange for this to happen? The answer is that he reads the original, observes the update that this brings about in the context, and constructs a sentence, or sequence of words in the target language that causes essentially the same update.

Goldilocks saw a house, knocked on the door and went inside. According to the text, *Nobody was there.* Suppose this was a translation from another language, perhaps French, in which case the original might have said *Il n'y avait personne.* The English translator could have translated this pragmatically by writing *She was alone* or *She was alone in the house* or *There was nobody but her in the house.* All of these carry the reader from the state he was in before encountering that sentence to the one he is in after he has read it without establishing a correspondence between individual words and phrases.

Consider paragraph 4 of the story, namely:

"This porridge is too hot! This porridge is too cold! This porridge is just right!" Goldilocks ate all the porridge.

Alternative translations from the original language into English might have been:

The porridge in the first bowl was too hot and the porridge in the second bowl was too cold. But the porridge in the third bowl was just right. She ate all the porridge in the third bowl.

or

The first bowl had porridge that was too hot and the porridge in the second bowl was too cold. But the porridge in the third bowl was neither too hot nor too cold and she ate it all.

Neither of these deviates radically from the syntactic version. The main things that have happened are that the quotation marks have been eliminated, and it had been made clear that the three temperatures mentioned map onto the three bowls. More pragmatic versions would, of course, be possible, such as:

She could only eat the porridge in last bowl because what was in the first bowl was too hot for her and what was in the second bowl was too cold.

or

She ate all the porridge in the last bowl because, of the others, one was too hot and the other was too cold.

It would, however, be difficult to justify so great a departure from the obvious, and simpler, syntactic alternatives. More importantly, they are gratuitously leading further and further away from the language of the child for whom the story is clearly intended. A more serious problem with the second of these is that it looses that relative ordering of the first two bowls which is needed for the rest of the story.

If I am in a group of people on a station platform who have just alighted from a train, and that group specifically is being addressed on the loudspeakers, then what is being said will very probably concern trains, the arrival of trains, and alighting from trains. When I hear *Make sure that you have all your belongings with you*, I therefore assume that, of all the belongings that I have in the world, the only ones that are relevant are the ones that accompanied me on this journey. If those belongings are with me now on the platform, then I did not leave them on the train. If I were asked if I had all my belongings with me after my house had just burnt down, a different set of belongings would clearly be in question. Notice that the word *all*, which seems quite unequivocal, must, in fact, be taken to refer to different sets of belongings in the two contexts.

It seems that we could now characterize some of pairs of texts we considered earlier for giving directions in Paris as examples of pragmatic translation run amok. Considerable creativity was invested in avoiding pairs of lexical items that even a small bilingual dictionary dictionary could be expected to contain. The question that therefore seems most urgently to require an answer is whether pragmatic translation is ever really needed and, if so, under what circumstances.

We shall pursue this question vigorously here, and the remainder of this book, but first, let us put it in its proper perspective. If pragmatic translation is a technique that professional translators sometimes use to good effect when an equally good syntactic translation is available, there is no *a priori* reason why the syntactic alternative should be preferred. Many people are familiar with syntactic translation from learning foreign languages in school or from reflecting on how machine translation might work. But, *a priori*, its use does not require special justification.

That being said, the following questions still remain: Are there situations in which this simply cannot be avoided? Are there situations where it can be avoided, but the pragmatic solution is still preferred? Is the distinction one of which translators are aware in their daily work or is it really only apparent to us who view the activity from the outside? Is there indeed a clear dividing line between syntactic and pragmatic translations?

Let us start with the last of these questions, which is surely the most important. On the one hand, the journeyman translator is probably rarely aware of the distinction between syntactic and pragmatic translation, and then only when the pragmatic component of the translation is large. When that component is small enough, we may conclude that there is really no distinction between the strategies. The following examples are all taken from the transcripts of debates in the European Parliament, a corpus of parallel texts and a large and growing number of languages that provides the basis for much contemporary work on translation, especially machine translation.

1. In the case of Turkey it is different.

   Le cas de la Turquie est différent.

2. When will the Commission appoint a Special Envoy for Tibet?

   Quand la Commission entend-elle nommer ce délégué aux affaires tibétaines?

3. The Commission, like others, has urged dialogue.

   La Commission, comme d'autres, a demandé qu'un dialogue s'établisse.

At first glance, sentence 1 appears to be almost word for word. Only the words *In* and *it* have no French correspondents. The structure, however is different. The material in the initial prepositional phrase in English becomes the subject in French. And just what is it that the English pronoun refers to? Apparently, the word *it* seems to be filling substantially the same function as it does in sentences like *It is raining* and *It looks to me as if we won't get any lunch*. The best solution in this direction would perhaps be *Dans le cas de la Turquie, les choses sont différentes* (IN THE CASE OF TURKEY, THINGS ARE DIFFERENT). In the second example, the English version is in fact the original. A French version that followed this more closely would be something like *Quand la Commission nommera-t-elle un délégué spéciale pour le Tibet?* or *Quand est-ce que la Commission nommera un délégué spéciale pour le Tibet?*. Replacing *nommera-t-elle* with *entend-elle nommer* adds a slight note of impatience to the question, as though the English had been more like *When does the Commission intend to appoint a Special Envoy for Tibet?*. Perhaps the translator had independent reason to believe that this properly reflected the speaker's state of mind. Maybe it reflected the translator's own state of mind. Ignoring the pressure under which translators work in the European Parliament, a purist might disapprove of this rendering.

The supposed correspondence between a *Special Envoy for Tibet* and a *délégué aux affaires tibétaines* is also one that turns on a particular set of views on the state of world affairs that were presumably understood by members of the Parliament at that particular moment. They were part of the context from the start. A special delegate from, to, or for, Tibet must have been part of the recent discussion in the house so that minor variants in the way that the person is referred to would presumably go unnoticed. What we have here does, however, contain an element of pragmatic translation.

One very minor feature in the sentence *Quand la Commission entend-elle nommer ce délégué aux affaires tibétaines?* that still needs to be accounted for is the word *ce*. The English version speaks of *a special envoy*, and not *this special envoy*. This reinforces feeling of impatience in this speech that we noted earlier. From the point of view of the standard model, it is information gratuitously added to the translation.

If we take a narrow view of what constitutes information, then the amount of it conveyed by a word or phrase is often different in an original text and a translation. As we shall see repeatedly, there are cases where this is difficult or impossible to avoid but, in others, it seems gratuitous. Consider the following examples:

4. Mr Berenguer Fuster, we shall check all this.

   Cher collègue nous allons vérifier tout cela.

5. Thank you, Commissioner Schreyer.

   Merci beaucoup, Madame Schreyer.

6. As people have said, the situation there is extremely volatile.

   D'aucuns l'ont dit, la situation en Indonésie est extrêmement explosive.

7. Thus, the Erika was refused access to American waters.

   C'est ainsi que les États-Unis avaient refusé l'accès de l'Erika à leurs eaux.

The English is the original, so what the translator has done is to is to replace a proper name by a quite different form of address. There is nothing surprising about this since a first and last name together does not constitute a standard form of address in French. The same is true in German and, indeed, in the present case, the German translator made an exactly parallel change, rendering the sentence as *Lieber Kollege, wir werden das prüfen.* The simplest way to avoid the problem would be simply to omit the first name. But forms like "cher collègue" and

"Lieber Kollege", which have no regular equivalent in English, constitute the most natural solution here.

Sentence 4 is similar. However, in this case, information is added in the translation. It would probably be more accurate, in cases like these, to say that information that is implicit in the original is made explicit in the translation because the information must clearly be recoverable from the original context. The translator presumably makes it explicit because he feels that it is less easily recoverable from the context of the translation as he is making it. Here again the German translator felt impelled to make this information explicit in the translation *Wie bereits festgestellt wurde, ist die Lage in Indonesien äußerst instabil.* The English word *people*, however, becomes implicit in the German. A word-for-word translation of the German back into English would be something like *As has already been established, the situation in Indonesia is extremely unstable.*

Sentence 7 is a classic example of pragmatic translation. The French version is the original. As in the other cases, the sentences mean essentially the same in the given context. It is not explicit in the English translation that it was the United States that refused access to American waters. But who else could or would have denied such access? A slavishly syntactic English translation would surely have said that the United States denied access to American waters rather than to *their waters (leurs eaux)*, but this would have been unnecessarily ponderous and, once again, it means exactly the same in this context.

Our aim in this chapter has been to make explicit a model of what translation is and how it works that is taken for granted, not only by lay people, but by many who are professionally engaged with translation and by virtually everyone engaged with machine translation. Most of the translations that are actually made depart from this model frequently in small ways, and sometimes very markedly. Many departures from the model are unremarkable and could have been avoided if there had been any good reason to do so. Others seem to be necessary in order to maintain a target text that reads naturally or in order to accommodate more or less radical differences in the languages or cultures.

3

Reference

3.1 Language as a Digital System

The very fact that there are different, mutually incomprehensible languages in the world, and that the possibility of translating among them arises at all, comes from the fundamentally digital nature of language. English, French and German contain the words *dog*, *chien* and *Hund*, all of which, as it happens, mean the same thing. But there is nothing about these three languages, or about dogs, that makes this necessarily so. The relationship of each of these to dogs, and to one another, is entirely arbitrary, and it is the digital nature of language that makes such an arbitrary system of relationships possible. The question, of course, is not so much why this is possible, but why it is important. Before we can approach that question, we must first get a clear idea of what a digital system is, and we will attempt to do that now, starting with a much simpler example than natural language.

A simple example of a digital device, though not a naturally occurring one, is an ordinary light switch. This device has one external movable part, called a *toggle*, which is normally in one of two positions, say *up* and *down*. One can try to put the toggle in some intermediate position but, as soon as one lets go of it, it will spring to one of these positions, presumably the one nearest to where it was when released. Let us suppose that the switch is off when it is up and that we move the toggle slowly downwards from this position. If we release the toggle after moving it only a short distance, it will spring back to the *up* position and the light will remain unaffected. But if we move the toggle beyond a certain point roughly half way to the *down* position, the light will suddenly come on and, if we release the toggle, it springs to the *down* position. The important point is that, although we can move the toggle to indefinitely many positions between fully *up* and fully *down*, these do not cause the light ever to be partly on. It is always either fully on or fully off.

What makes the common light switch a digital device is that there are only a certain number of clearly distinct states—in this case, two—in which the switch can place the light that it controls. The toggle can be forced into intermediate positions and we can imagine an arrangement in which the light would be capable of shining with various intensities depending on the current position of the switch. But the switch we have in mind is unable to do that. There are just two clearly distinct messages that the switch we have can send to the light. This makes the communication between the switch and the light a digital one.

Electric cooking stoves once routinely incorporated rotary switches with markings like *Off*, *Low*, *Medium*, and *High*. The knob could be moved to any position but, when released, would jump to whichever of these marked positions it was nearest to, and the heating element in the stove would adopt one of the four preset intensities. It would, of course, be more convenient to be able to set the stove to any position in the range of possible temperatures and, since modern technology makes that easier, it is now the way these controls usually work. So the older digital stoves have been largely replaced by analog ones. A minute analysis of one of the new stoves might reveal it to still be a digital device, but in which the number of states that the switch could be in was so many, and the differences between neighboring intensities so small, that it behaves essentially like an analog device.

Why do we therefore say that language is a thoroughly digital system? What is it about English that makes it like a light switch? The similarity is easiest to see in the written language, or, more specifically, the printed language. The symbols used to write English constitute a closed set, consisting of letters, digits, and punctuation marks. For some purposes, we put upper-case letters together with their lower-case counterparts, and think of them as one. This is not important. What is important is that similarities of appearance between one of these symbols and another are irrelevant to the way the system works. Two symbols on the page are either absolutely the same or absolutely different. In cursive script, it is not always clear where one letter ends and the next one begins, but the whole can be interpreted in the usual way only by mapping it onto a sequence of the agreed closed set of symbols.

It is the same with the sound system. We are able to make sense of the great variety of noises made by people with different voices and different dialects, calm or under stress, relaxed or hurried, tired or re-

freshed, only by mapping them onto a closed set of so-called *phonemes*.
The words *hill* and *heel* sound fairly similar. Only the vowel distinguishes them and there are dialects in the southern United States where
the word *hill* is pronounced much as northerners and speakers of British
English pronounce *heel*. A native speaker of English can naturally pronounce either of these words on demand. In addition, such a person
can, with a little practice, easily pronounce sounds that are intermediate between these two. So let us conduct a thought experiment in which
one person pronounces words from various places along this continuum,
and the other person says what word, if any, he thinks he is hearing.

We expect the results of this experiment to mimic those of our experiments with the light switch. So long as the utterance sounds sufficiently like *hill*, the hearer reports hearing *hill* (or *heal*, which is the
same in the present context). When it sounds more like *heel*, the hearer
reports hearing *heel*. Somewhere in the middle, the hearer may be confused and unsure what to say. But there is never a moment when the
hearer reports hearing a word that is intermediate between *hill* and
heel. There is no such word, and therefore no circumstance in which it
could be heard. There is never a moment at which the switch comes to
rest between *On* and *Off*.

We might expect things to go slightly differently if the hearer were
from an American Southern region where there is little or no difference
in the ways in which *hill* and *heel* are pronounced. Such a subject
would presumably report hearing either *hill* or *heel* when the stimulus
was *heel*. When the stimulus was *hill* the theory predicts that he would
be confused because his dialect contains no word that sounds like this.
In fact, he would almost certainly report hearing *hill* unless he has been
carefully kept isolated from the rest of the world from a very early age.

Let us now return from the technical world of writing, phonetics
and phonology to the more familiar one that translators and other
ordinary people inhabit. In this world, we encounter language in the
form of words and phrases, and the digital nature of these is every
bit as apparent. The words *dog* and *dig* are as close to one another
in sound and spelling as the *on* and *off* positions of any switch, but
their meanings are as far apart as one could easily get. The words
right and *write* sound identical, but they are different words and we
have therefore no reason to expect their meanings to be related in any
way. When a speaker of British English says *bomb* and *balm*, another
British speaker hears two words with unrelated meanings. When an
American speaker says the same two words, a hearer, whether British
or American, hears one of two different words or, if they happen to

notice that there are two possibilities, may wonder which of the two was intended. Such a hearer will, however, by no means try to create a meaning to correspond to the sounds that is somewhere between those of *bomb* and *balm*.

The importance of this complete dissociation between variability among the forms of words, and variability among the things words can refer to cannot be overestimated. Variability among written or spoken words is clearly immensely restricted. There are twenty-six letters in the English alphabet and we have well under a hundred phonemes in our language, whatever that language may be. The dimensions along which these letters and phonemes can differ from one another are therefore necessarily very limited. Vowels can be high, mid, or low; front or back; rounded or unrounded. There are one or two more dimensions for consonants. But the dimensions along which the things we can refer to differ are unlimited. A rich and flexible system of communication therefore needs to be one in which neither set of dimensions is systematically related to the other and this is achieved most completely if the relationship between the two systems is entirely arbitrary. In other words, there is no natural or systematic relationship at all between the two systems. The relationship is achieved, at least conceptually, by means of a dictionary—an arbitrary list of word-meaning pairs.

In a digital system, it is possible to make a clean and clear distinction between *types* and *tokens*, and our discussion of language as such a system so far has relied heavily on this distinction.[6] We have, for example, considered a given word in a variety of scripts or the various ways in which a person might pronounce a word. We have considered whether a given utterance might be heard as an instance of the word *bomb* or the word *balm*. To say that something is an instance of a letter, a phoneme, or a word, is to say that it is a *token* of that *type*. Each of the letters that make up an English text, however many of them there might be, is an instance of one member of the standard inventory of twenty-six types. It makes sense to say that only if the question of what type a given token is a type of is uncontroversial, and that is indeed the case. The ideal dictionary that relates the words in a language with their meanings contains an entry—or possibly several entries, depending on how we imagine it being organized—of each word type in the language. A text, on the other hand, is a sequence of items each of which is a token of one of these types. The relationship between what a person writes or says—already an immensely complicated one—would

---

6. Terminology due to Peirce 1931–1958. A distinction between tokens and *occurrences* is sometimes made but does not concern us here.

clearly be altogether more complicated if we were not generally able to agree on what type a given token belonged to.

So, language seems to require that speakers and hearers have in their heads substantially similar dictionaries made up of pairs of word types and meanings. There is no natural relationship between the items that make a pair, except in very unusual circumstances such as those involving phonaesthetics, or sound symbolism. The word types constitute a digital system. The meanings, however, are quite another matter, and one to which we will devote a considerable amount of space.

3.2 Meaning and Philosophy

Questions of meaning have been a major specialty within philosophy since the earliest times, with its own terms of art, such as *sense* and *reference, connotation* and *denotation, semantics* and *pragmatics, lexical* and *compositional* to name a few. Anyone who seriously tries to understand what translation is about must come close enough to the philosophical disputes about meaning to feel the heat, if not to see the light. The question is whether one can get this close without becoming hopelessly caught up in tribal battles and disputes with questionable relevance to the main concern. This is what, with no little trepidation, we embark on now.

Fortunately, linguists have a natural immunity to at least some of the perils of linguistic philosophy because, while a linguist takes on responsibility for the sounds of language, the forms of words, the construction of sentences and even some of the logical constructions that sentences contract with one another, he assumes no responsibility for the validity of claims people make in their language about the world outside. Language works the same way whether it is expressing lies or truths, and arguments that would make it seem otherwise are red herrings. But these red herrings are all over the place and we must learn to recognize them for what they are.

We will consider the two aspects of linguistic meaning that have been of most interest to philosophers. In English, they are generally referred to as *sense* (also known as *intension* and *cognitive* or *descriptive* meaning) and *reference* (also known as *denotation, extension*, or *denotative meaning*).[7] Roughly speaking, the sense of a word or fixed phrase is the information that we expect to find about it in a dictionary.

Reference is a property of individual word tokens. The question of whether all words have senses is open to debate. It is generally agreed

---

7. I maintain the convention of spelling the words *intension* and *extension* with an "s" when they are used with these technical senses.

that reference is not a property of all tokens. Still speaking roughly, if the property of reference is relevant to a token of a word, it is because there is something that that token *refers* to in this particular place, in this particular text. If someone says *the cat chased a mouse* to someone else, it is presumably because there is some particular cat, in this or some imagined world, that they both know about and which is the *referent* of the token of the word *cat* in that utterance. The utterance also contains an instance of the word *mouse*, but the situation here is different because it is preceded by the word *a* rather than *the*. This is a signal that the word *mouse* refers to something that the hearer is being introduced to for the first time. This new entity is the referent of the word *mouse*.

As we have said, the sense of a word is something we expect to find in a dictionary. Thus, it is part of the sense of the word *cat* that it can be used to refer to a small furry domestic animal, with sundry other well-known properties. This knowledge enables the hearer of the utterance to pick the proper referent out of the set of things that the context established by surroundings and the preceding conversation makes available. It is part of the sense of the word *mouse* that it can be used to refer to a small rodent with a long tail and this may be useful in referring back to this animal later in the conversation.

The distinction between sense and reference thus corresponds in a fundamental way to the distinction between word types and word tokens. The dictionary associates with a word type information about the kinds of things it can be used to refer to. The actual references themselves are made by the tokens in the text. Some tokens of a type refer to one thing, and some to another. One of the confusions in the philosophical literature comes from the fact that some words, like "God," "Mark Twain," and "Pegasus" may seem to have such restrictive dictionary entries that there is only one thing that they can refer to. In these cases, it therefore seems that the type, as well as its tokens, has a referent. We will return to this matter shortly and will argue that, even if the meaning could be so restrictive, which we do not believe, it would not imply that the token itself had a referent.

None of this should be taken as implying that language does not need mechanisms for handling unique referents in the world. Just as *Samuel Clemens* and *Mark Twain* can generally be assumed to refer to the same person, so too can Italian *Venezia*, German *Venedig*, and English *Venice*. A person who is attached to London, either by birth or residence, is a *Londonner*, but someone from Paris is a *Parisian*. *John* becomes *Jean* in France, and *Giovanni* in Italy. *Bill* is short for *William* and *Bob* is short for *Robert*. There are words that live on the border between common and proper nouns. For example, the gentleman's hat known in Britain as a *Trilby* is a *Fedora* in America. A Sam Browne is a leather belt worn by army officers with a strap that passes over the right shoulder to steady his sword when on horseback. Now there is something that every translator clearly needs to know!

Everyday conversation about the meanings of words tends to focus on what the dictionary has to say about them, and everyday contemplation of the difficulties that translation might entail therefore focuses on the senses of words, particularly their ambiguity and vagueness. Generally speaking, however, utterances are made in order to convey information about relationships among particular entities in the real or some imaginary world. If I say *the cat chased a mouse*, it is because I want to tell you something that you may not know, namely that a specific cat that we are both familiar with chased something that you may not have known about before, but which has the properties we associate with mice. The utterance will have served my purpose only if it establishes this relationship among these entities in the mind of the hearer. For this reason, we shall say that the primary responsibility of the language user, and therefore of the translator, is to the referents of the text and the relations among them. As we shall see, the association between the sense of a word and the set of its potential referents can also be a very slippery one.

It is not only words that have senses and referents. A person may know one hundred thousand words in his native language, but this is trivial in comparison with the number of phrases and sentences that a person can produce and understand. These also have senses and referents, but the association between a phrase and its sense cannot generally be established by a list or dictionary, because a speaker generally has no difficulty in understanding them when he encounters them for the first time. You probably have no difficulty understanding the sentence *My cat's mother, Priscilla, chased fourteen mice the week before last*. Even in the unlikely event that you have heard the sentence before, it is very unlikely that you remember it and, even if you do, the question still remains of how you understood it the first time you heard it.

We take it that the senses of phrases and sentences are computed on the basis of the senses of the words that they contain and the grammatical constructions that they are embedded in. The phrase *My cat's mother*, and the word *cat* both refer to cats, but not to the same cat. We find the cat that the phrase refers to by starting at the referent of the word *cat*, that we are presumably familiar with, and then looking for the mother of that cat. The French phrase *la mère de mon chat* (THE MOTHER OF MY CAT) works in the same way but we have to know that French grammar relates the words corresponding to *mother* and *cat* in a different way. For one thing, it puts them in a different order.

The sentence we have just proposed has an interesting property, that we will discuss at length later, when considered as a translation of our English sentence about cats. It has to do, not with differences in word order, but with the fact that French does not allow us to talk about a cat without giving the cat a gender. We can be pretty sure about the gender of my cat's mother, but there is nothing about English grammar that gives away the gender of my cat or that requires me to know it in order to formulate the sentence. Perhaps we could discover this by examining the surrounding context. In any case, the French language does not allow us to remain uncommitted. This is an example of a pervasive, and particularly troublesome problem concerning not just gender, and not just French, but a great many different kinds of information in a great many languages.

Later in this chapter, we will engage in a more or less technical discussion of the distinction between sense and reference and its importance for translation. First, however, we will look at it more informally against the background of translation in general, and the well known distinction between word-for-word, and other kinds of translation, in particular.

3.3 *Things* and the Cognitive Perspective

Sense and reference are clearly intimately bound up with one another. Later in this chapter, we shall concentrate on issues that relate particularly to sense. Now, we focus on reference, considering it from what we will characterize as the *Cognitive Perspective.*

We begin by considering an argument made by John Stuart Mill (1868) and others. It has to do with the observation that we made earlier that the senses of some words are apparently so restrictive as to allow them only a single referent. Proper names are used to refer to individuals. There are no properties, except possibly gender, that an individual needs to have in order to be the carrier of a name. In other words, a proper name has no sense beyond that of picking out that one individual, which is essentially no sense at all. Therefore, if it turns out that the individual that the name purports to pick out does not exist, then the name has neither sense nor reference. In this case, the name has no meaning at all, and neither does any phrase or sentence in which it appears. So, for example, the sentence *Santa Claus lives at the North Pole* is neither true nor false, because *Santa Claus* is a proper name and the meaning of a proper name, according to him and many others, is the person or thing that it refers to. Notice that this turns, not on whether you believe in Santa Claus or not, but on whether he actually exists.

This is a troubling line of argument, because it apparently claims that the sentence *Santa Claus does not exist* is meaningless precisely because it is true! Later philosophers gave more subtle accounts of proper names, but most of them continued to insist that the existence of particular people and things in the real world has a role to play in this argument. It therefore has a role to play in the way language works.

A similar kind of problem arises when two different names purport to refer unambiguously to the same entity in the world. The American author Mark Twain was known as Samuel Clemens in private life. In other words *Mark Twain* and *Samuel Clemens* are just two names for the same person. Consequently, if one of the names is replaced in a sentence by the other one, the truth of the sentence should be unchanged. The sentence "Samuel Clemens was born in Missouri" is equivalent to "Mark Twain was born in Missouri." But consider the sentence "My friend does not believe that Samuel Clemens was Mark Twain," which describes a situation that could surely arise. Apparently this is a sentence about the relationship between the historical figure Samuel Clemens and my friend's beliefs about him. In particular, it is about whether he is sometimes known by the name "Mark Twain." Since Samuel Clemens has two names, it should not matter which I use when referring to him. So it should be possible to say the same thing with the sentence "My friend does not believe that Samuel Clemens was Samuel Clemens," which is almost surely not what he believes.

One may reasonably ask what it is about proper names that makes them particularly susceptible to these difficulties? The answer surely has something to do with the distinction we referred to earlier between types and tokens. Notice that the argument turns on the simplifying assumption that there never was, and never will be, more than one person that can be referred to as either "Mark Twain" or "Samuel Clemens." This is certainly not necessarily the case, though it may be the case that a speaker or writer needs to take special measures to establish a situation in which they had different referents. Let us therefore go along with the assumption for the moment. So what is special about proper names is that, not only the various tokens of them that occur in speech and text all have the same referent, but that their type that occurs in an ideal dictionary also has that same referent? Our claim, on the other hand, is that types do not have referents—ever!

What is true of proper names, according to this argument, also carries over to so-called *definite descriptions*, that is, noun phrases, often beginning with the word *the* that purport to refer unambiguously to a single entity in the world. The most well-known example comes from Frege: the expressions *the morning star* and *the evening star* both refer to the same entity which, as it happens, is not a star at all in the astronomer's sense, but the planet Venus. I should also be able to claim that my friend does not believe that the morning star is the evening star by saying *My friend does not believe that the morning star is the morning star*, but this does not work for the same reason that it does not work for Mark Twain.

The intellectual journey that begins with considerations such as these gathered a considerable head of steam at the beginning of the twentieth century and has been carried forward, through papers and books and lectures, to the present day. The matter is considered to be important because it seems to underlie the very possibility of talking about the world in a reliable manner and therefore of using language as a tool in the quest for truth. According to one proposal, a proper name, for example is coupled in the mind of the language user with a description which is such as to pick out just one referent in the world. Different people may have different descriptions which, nevertheless, identify the same referent. This approach also runs into problems. How, for example, does it allow us ever to determine that two names do, in fact, refer to the same thing?

There does seem to be something of a trend in the way this discussion has been developing over the past century, and it is towards the view that the connection between words and phrases on the one hand, and the entities in the world to which they purport to refer on the other, must be considerably more remote than was earlier thought. As we have already hinted, we will embrace a strong version of this view with enthusiasm. A linguist, it seems, can hardly do otherwise because the question of whether the utterances he considers are a faithful reflection of reality clearly cannot have anything to do with their linguistic status. Consider the chaos that would reign otherwise. Before the 1960s, nobody had ever heard of the Higgs boson particle or much considered what such a thing might be. It was then speculated that the universe might contain such particles and that their importance for physics would be paramount. Not until 2012 was it possible to conduct the experiment that removed almost all remaining doubt about the particle's existence. Physicists in the world according to Mill must therefore have spent a particularly exciting half century wondering whether many of the sentences they were reading and writing in fact had any meaning. In the worlds of later philosophers, these or other worries about the workings of language would also suddenly strike. But one thing that linguists should surely be spared is the fear that experiments in a supercollider in Geneva could change the outcome of semantic computations already made years before.

We therefore think that, whatever direction these arguments take philosophers in, linguists will be justified in passing them by with an indulgent smile. It may be argued that the position of those whose concern is with translation may, however, be less secure. This is because of a fact that we shall stress repeatedly, namely that translation is not a purely linguistic matter. Teachers of translation, and others who theorize about the field, insist that a translator must be familiar, not only with the two languages involved in his work, but also with the subject matter of the texts that he works with, and the wider world that that subject matter is embedded in.

We will remain true to these principles, but also to the view that translators need not be nervous about the drift of philosophical investigations. We shall base our approach on what Ray Jackendoff (2012) calls a *cognitive perspective* on language. We will take it that an account of how language works that assumed a direct connection between words and phrases on the one hand, and objects in the real world, on the other, would be hopelessly complicated and would run up against endless anomalies like the one Santa Claus and the Higgs boson particle led us to. If the language is what we are interested in, then sanity comes from concentrating, to the extent possible, on what must go on in the head of a speaker or hearer for the system as a whole to work as it does. What goes on in the rest of the world is for other people and other times. This does not mean working on the level of synapses, and neurons, and electrical pulses. That would be another perspective—a physical perspective. The cognitive perspective enables us to abstract away both from the real or imaginary world that it is often used to talk about, and the physical mechanisms that enable it to work in the head, leaving an entirely stable and consistent basis for our investigations.

We take it that language is used to talk about *things*, and we will use the word *thing* as a somewhat technical term. In particular, not only will we say that language is used to talk about things, but that whatever language is used to talk about are things. Existence out there in the real world is a property that some things in the cognitive world may have, and others not. The words *Santa Claus* are used to refer to a thing and it is generally supposed to be the same thing on each occasion.

As a theory of the world, this makes no sense. It will be an immensely cluttered view unless there is some way of limiting the number of non-existent things that it recognizes, but maybe clutter will not be bothersome. On the other hand, it releases linguistics from the responsibility of keeping track of what does and what does not exist in the real world, a responsibility that it could only discharge if it encompassed the whole of physical science, at the very least. Even more importantly, it enables us to give a fairly straightforward account of sentences like the following: *Mary is excited about Santa Claus coming even though she is beginning to doubt if he really exists.* The pronoun *he* presumably refers back to whatever *Santa Claus* refers to. If *Santa Claus* does not mean anything, then it presumably cannot refer to anything and it therefore does not make much' sense to say that *he* refers to that same thing. But what is clearly going on here is that Mary is being claimed to be *beginning to doubt that he exists*, where *he* refers to whatever thing it is that *Santa Claus* refers to, real or imaginary, in whatever world.

Suppose, instead, that the text goes on like this: *This does not surprise her parents, because lots of her friends are also beginning to have doubts.* *This* is a pronoun that is used to refer to things. So what does it refer to here? Presumably to a fact, namely that Mary's friends are beginning to doubt the existence of Santa Claus. So this is also a thing. Suppose, again, that the text continues *It usually happens at about that age.* Here the word *It* refers to the fact of someone—anyone—doubting the existence of Santa Claus. This is also a thing.

We do not have to suppose that all these things are somehow always available, and catalogued in the minds of all English speakers, in case someone might want to refer to them. Santa Claus is a thing that has been known to many people for a long time, and the particular thing called *Mary* that is referred to here is presumably known at least to the circle of people around her. Other people know different Mary's— perhaps several of them. But most things are created on the fly as they are required at a particular moment in a communication. I say *she is beginning to doubt if he really exists* with the intention of creating a new thing in your head, namely the doubt that Mary has concerning Santa Claus.

As a speech, a dialog, or a text proceeds, already known things are referred to, and new ones are created. Some of these things are relations that tie other things together in some way. When each one is mentioned, it becomes salient. It is caught in the spotlight for a while, and then gradually fades into the background if neither it, nor other things closely related to it are mentioned again. It is as though the speaker, or writer, had a stage in his head on which the things he was talking about acted out their parts. With his words, he is trying to cause the listener, or reader, to create that same scene on a similar stage in his head. This is where the translator comes in. His job is to create a new text that will cause essentially the same scene to be played out on the stage in the head of a reader of another language.

So, where does this leave *Santa Claus* and other proper names? Mill says that a proper name is *a word that answers the purpose of showing what thing it is that we are talking about but not of telling anything about it* (1868, 1. ii. 5). If you believe me when I say *I saw a dog*, you not only believe that I saw a thing, but that it was animate, had four legs, probably had a tail, and so forth. A common name is associated with a set of properties that I can use to decide whether the word is appropriate for a new thing I want to refer to, or how to pick something you are referring to from the available candidates. If a proper name has any associated properties, they are minimal, rarely including more than number and gender. The advantage of the proper name as a way of referring to things is that we assign them to things in an essentially arbitrary manner so that the likelihood of there being much doubt about what is intended on any given occasion is very small. We return to this later.

Philosophers have generally been happy to dispose of proper names quite summarily. They have treated them as though there was a single individual that each of them identified, while they clearly know that this is not true. They have also treated proper names as something quite different from common nouns of which it is clear from the outset that they can be used to talk about a great variety of individuals. But the difference is actually very small if, indeed, there is one at all. A common name is used to refer to a class of things that the community has agreed to associate in a more or less arbitrary way with that name. We know the names of things we want to refer to often and the arbitrariness of the association provides some robustness to the system.

We can also talk about the whole class of shoes, ships, cabbages, and kings, as though the classes were single entities. We can say things like *The set of kings in the world is small, and it is rapidly getting smaller*. The thing that *it* refers to in this sentence is the set of kings. In the sentence *shoes are usually made of leather and that is why many people cannot afford them*, the word *them* refers the members of the set of shoes. The second part of the sentence can be paraphrased approximately as *Whatever member of the set of pairs of shoes you pick, many people could not afford it.* In English, the question of whether a noun phrase refers to a set of things is a notoriously tricky matter. The sentence *cabbages contain glutamine* refers to every member of the set of cabbages. *Cabbages are used to make borsht* asserts the existence of a subset of the set of cabbages, here referred to simply as *cabbages*, that are used in making borsht. The sentence can be paraphrased as *The making of borsht requires some cabbages.*

Pronouns, like *he*, *she*, and *it* are usually used to refer to things.[8] In *She took his wallet. I saw it in her hand*, the word *it* presumably refers to the wallet or, at least, to the corresponding thing in the minds of the speaker and hearer. In *She took his wallet. I saw her do it*, on the other hand, *it* refers to the act of taking his wallet. In *She took his wallet. I could not believe it*, *it* refers to the fact that she took his wallet rather than either the wallet or the act of taking it. The fact that something can be referred to with a word like *it* strongly suggests that it is the kind of thing we are talking about.

We can conveniently think of a large class of things as inhabiting a world with the familiar three dimensions, plus a fourth dimension for time, because present things apparently have no priority over past and future things with respect to the ease with which we can talk about them. As of this writing, England has no king, but this in no way impedes my talking about an English king of a bygone age as, for example, *the king that led the English to victory at Agincourt.* or speculating about whether Prince Charles will ever become what I can felicitously refer to as *the king of England.* In other words, I can speculate whether there will become a time when the phrase *the king of England* will come to have the same referent as *Prince Charles*, not only in my head and my interlocutor's but also in the real world. Prince Charles is, after all, not that different from Mark Twain or the morning star.

It is, of course, also possible to talk about entirely fictional things that do not share our space and time at all. Suppose I read a story about a zebra, and that I have no reason to suppose it is anything but true. Now, suppose I read a story that is identical except that the zebra has been replaced by a unicorn. I am sure that this one is false, but it is not more difficult to understand nor apparently do I bring any different mental mechanisms to bear in understanding it. I can keep the main unicorn character separate in my head from its brothers and

---

8. The last of these is sometimes used differently in utterances like *it is raining* and, arguably, *I find it surprising that he would say that*

sisters and from the other members of the herd just as I could with the zebras who, but for the assurance I was given, may also not have been part of the real world.

I learnt to count and to do arithmetic long before I was ever confronted with the question of whether numbers exist. But people took numbers very seriously and they are things about which some propositions are provably true, and others false. The question of whether the thing called *five* that all instances of the word seem to refer to exists did not arise, and did not even seem to be a very good question. For our present purposes, five is surely a thing, if only because of the complete transparency and, indeed, banality, of utterances like *Five is an odd number. Indeed it is a prime number.* The pronoun in the second sentence presumably refers to a thing which is also referred to by the word *five*. The word *five* can, of course, refer to other things, as in the sentence *There are three fives in my telephone number*, where it presumably refers to a *numeral*, that is, a graphic shape of a kind that is particularly useful for referring to numbers.

This can be confusing because we also use the term *number* to refer both the abstract objects and the corresponding, arguably somewhat less abstract, graphic shapes. Numbers constitute a class of abstract entities that are familiar to everybody and that we have frequent cause to refer to. Other abstract entities, such as propositions and relations among things, may be introduced briefly into the discourse, and disappear again moments later. We have seen the first of these in the example *She took his wallet. I could not believe it.* The second is equally easy to illustrate, as in *The difference between Hindi and Urdu is very small, but it is significant.*

We are not taking a position against the possibility of things that actually inhabit space and time. This is the reality-based, as opposed to the cognitive perspective. Scientists, policemen, and ordinary people need to be assured that the things they are talking about are real so that, for example, when they reason about them using ordinary language, they can expect their conclusions to apply in the real world. Indeed, as we have already suggested, this connection between language and reality has seemed so important as to lead many philosophers to using it as a starting point when considering the relationship between words and things. In this view, things are real, and fiction is a secondary, and somewhat embarrassing, problem.

The class of what we are calling *things* is clearly very large, embracing anything capable of being referred to in the past, the present or the future, in the real as well as in indefinitely many fictional worlds. It includes physical objects, abstractions like numbers, sets, times, propositions and situations. If someone sees me carrying a book, and says "That is a good book. I just finished reading it," he is probably referring to the abstraction—the text—that is printed in this and many other copies of this text. But he might be referring to this actual copy from which he read before I got my hands on it. These are two *things*. In "The book took on a new importance with the invention of the printing press," we have a reference to another kind of thing. This is what we call a *generic* use of the word.

3.4 Given and New

The following simple story will be familiar to even casual opera goers:

> At night, outside a Commendatore's$_1$ palace, a young man$_2$ grumbles about his$_3$ duties as servant$_4$ to a dissolute nobleman$_5$. Soon the nobleman$_6$ appears wearing a mask, pursued by the Commendatore$_7$'s daughter$_8$, whom he$_9$ has tried to seduce. When the Commendatore$_{10}$ answers his daughter$_{11}$'s cries, he$_{12}$ is killed in a duel by the nobleman$_{13}$, who$_{14}$ escapes. The daughter$_{15}$ now returns with her fiancé$_{16}$. Finding her$_{17}$ father$_{18}$ dead, she$_{19}$ makes her fiancé$_{20}$ swear vengeance on the assassin$_{21}$.

The author appears to make the usual assumption that the reader knows nothing about the story before beginning to read his text. He therefore takes it as his job to construct a more or less complex *thing* in the head of his reader, namely, a moving picture of what happens as the story unfolds. The writer invites the reader to first construct images of simpler things, giving each at least enough properties to be able to distinguish it from the others. He builds more complex things out of the simpler ones until, eventually, the whole story comes together. Each time he refers to a thing, he must make it clear whether it is a new thing that is being introduced for the first time, or a thing that has already been introduced and about which more is now being said.

For the sake of simplicity, we will restrict our attention to the human participants, namely:

1. the Commendatore
2. a young man
3. a dissolute nobleman
4. the commendatore's daughter
5. the daughter's fiancé

In what follows, an unparenthesized number between 1 and 5 will refer to an entry in this list. Some of the words in the story itself, those that refer to one of the five characters, have subscripts to make it easier to refer to them in the discussion. There are twenty-one references to people in the story all together, and they are listed in a second table below. Each reference takes the form of a one of the tags *Given*, *New*, or *Given/New* followed by a number which refers to one of the characters, and can be decoded by reference to the list above and the subscripts in the text. The Commendatore is 1, the young man is 2, and so on. In what follows, a number in parentheses will refer to a subscript in the text, or the corresponding entry in the second table.

(1) New: 1	(12) Given: 1
(2) New: 2	(13) Given: 3
(3) Given: 2	(14) Given: 3
(4) Given/New: 2	(15) Given: 4
(5) New: 3	(16) New: 5
(6) Given: 3	(17) Given: 4
(7) Given: 1	(18) Given: 1
(8) New: 4	(19) Given: 4
(9) Given: 3	(20) Given: 5
(10) Given: 1	(21) Given: 3
(11) Given: 4	

The Commendatore is introduced with the phrase *a Commendatore* (1). Most of us will not know what a Commendatore is, and it will turn out that it does not matter.[9] The indefinite article *a* or *an* generally serves as an invitation to the reader to create a new mental entity—a new thing. In this case, the new entity corresponds to a person. The reader calls him *the Commendatore* and places him in the mental model under construction. Entry 1 in the above table, which corresponds to word (1) in the text, is "*New*: 1" because it is this word that establishes a new mental entity corresponding to person 1. The next reference to one of the characters is *man*, or *young man* (2). It is also introduced with an indefinite article and establishes a new character in the reader's mental space—"*New*: 2."

The word *his* (3) refers back to the young man, someone that is already given, so the corresponding table entry is "*Given*: 2." The word *servant* (4) also refers back to the young man, but unlike (3), it also provides an additional description of him, to wit, that he is a servant. In other words, there are both given and new aspects to this token. For the moment, we represent this is the table as *Given/New*.

---

9. In modern Italy, "commendatore" is an honorary title awarded by the government in return for extraordinary service to the country.

Word (5) introduces a third character to the scene, namely the dissolute nobleman. Words (6) and (7) refer to given entities, and (8) introduces the Commendatore's daughter. The remaining references are to given characters, except for (16) which introduces the Commendatore's daughter's fiancé.

Our story is in fact a modified version of a synopsis of the first act of the opera *Don Giovanni*.[10] The original reads like this:

> At night, outside the Commendatore's palace, Leporello grumbles about his duties as servant to Don Giovanni, a dissolute nobleman. Soon the masked Don appears, pursued by Donna Anna, the Commendatore's daughter, whom he has tried to seduce. When the Commendatore himself answers Anna's cries, he is killed in a duel by Giovanni, who escapes. Anna now returns with her fiancé, Don Ottavio. Finding her father dead, she makes Ottavio swear vengeance on the assassin.

It is natural to concentrate on the human characters in the story because they are the natural source of its dynamism. We are humans and are interested in the exploits of other humans. It is also natural to distinguish humans from one another by using names which presumably came into existence to serve just this function.

Our modifications of the original synopsis consist essentially in removing the proper names. We have, of course, been at pains to deny any special status to proper names. Why, then, this heavy-handed tampering with the story? The answer is simple, and altogether innocent. The only remarkable property of proper names is that the association between them and the things they refer to is, as we have already remarked, largely arbitrary. There are some that are almost always used for males, others for females, and others that can be used for either. The writer of a piece of fiction has great liberty in choosing names and therefore naturally uses different names for different people, or things, to avoid unnecessary confusion. We removed the names from this story simply in order to highlight some of the more general mechanisms that are used to refer to things and to distinguish given and new references.

Needless to say, it is misleading to treat human characters as the only things in our story. There are, for example the night on which the events take place, the Commendatore's palace, Leporello's grumbling, and his duties as a servant that he grumbles about, not to mention the existence of these things and their relations to one another. If, towards the end of the story, a sentence occurred saying *the nobleman removed his mask*, this would contain a reference back the mask first

---

10. John W. Freeman. n.d. "Don Giovanni Synopsis." *Opera News* ()

introduced in the phrase *soon the nobleman appears wearing a mask*. In place of this, the original version of the story has *Soon the masked Don appears*, in which the mask is obliquely referred to by an adjective, but it nevertheless serves to introduce a new potential referent.

The truth of this, like the other stories we are telling about the workings of language, are simplifications, but we are at pains to minimize the extent to which this compromises their validity. For the case of distinguishing given from new, for example, consider the following: "Sally arrived at the house around noon, and introduced herself to the owner. Harry arrived at almost the same time, but to the back door." The last five words, and especially the word "but," encourage the belief that Sally arrived at the front door. Is it given or new, and where shall we say that it is introduced into the story?

When an adjective, or other modifier, is used to distinguish among given things, linguists say that it is being used *restrictively* because it restricts the set of possible referents of the noun phrase in which it occurs. When it adds new information, it is said to be used *nonrestrictively*. This is a distinction that is sometimes reflected in the grammar of a language. The sentence "The essays of Montaigne, which changed my whole outlook, are collected in this volume," refers to a volume that contains all the essays of Montaigne, and volunteers the additional information that these essays changed my whole outlook. The relative clause is used nonrestrictively. The sentence "The essays of Montaigne that changed my whole outlook are collected in this volume" is more likely to refer to a book that contains just those essays that changed my outlook. Here the relative clause is used restrictively.

In the early stages of learning French, English students are taught that some adjectives precede the nouns they modify, and others follow. But this is true only when the adjectives are used in the commonest way, which is restrictively. When an adjective is used nonrestrictively, it usually precedes the noun. The sentences *J'ai été enchanté de faire la connaissance de votre charmante fille* and *J'ai été enchanté de faire la connaissance de votre fille charmante* can both be translated as *I was delighted to meet your charming daughter*. However, the first can also be paraphrased as *I was delighted to meet your daughter, whom I found charming* whereas the second means something closer to *It was the charming one of your daughters that I was delighted to meet*.

The difference between restrictive and nonrestrictive use of modifiers is largely a matter of reference. A restrictive modifier is used to reduce the potential referential ambiguity of the term it modifies. You have two daughters, both salient in our conversation. I wish to restrict what I have to say so that it refers to a particular one of them. You know that I consider only one of them to be charming, so I use the word as a restrictive modifier. If I use it nonrestrictively, then only one daughter is in question, but a new thing is introduced, namely the charm I ascribe to her.

We have seen that a *text* is a sequence of word and phrase *tokens* which tell a *story*. The story may not be what we would normally call a story, but it is intended to evoke a set of *things*, some of which are simple, elementary things and some of which are relations among other things. The Don Giovanni story contains some elementary things which are people, times, and places, and some relational things like a pursuit of one person by another, a duel and the relationship that a woman has with a man when she is his fiancée. A recipe tells a story about some ingredients, the relationships they contract in the course of becoming a dish, and how a cook can bring those relationships into being. A maintenance manual tells a story about a thing that is composed of other things and what a person must do—which are also things—to maintain a desirable set of relationships among them. The things are the referents of the tokens in the text and the connection of a token to the corresponding thing exists by virtue of the sense of the *type* to which the token belongs. Some tokens—particularly those occurring earlier in the story—introduce *new* things into the story. Others refer to *given* things that the reader is presumed to be already familiar with.

It is generally easier to refer to given than to new things. This is because, if it is clear from the context that we intend to refer to a given thing, then it is sufficient to distinguish it from other given things that have already been introduced. When introducing a new thing, a writer may choose among all the things that one might possibly refer to. Of course, this is a simplification. Referring to given things is actually easier than we have suggested because the thing that is being referred to has, in all likelihood, not only been placed on the mental stage where the story is being played out, but is at the moment in the spotlight, or close to it. Referring to new items is not quite as difficult as we have said because we know enough about the stories people tell to be able to guess what kinds of new things are likely to be introduced once the story is under way. However, it remains true that, when a given reference is made to a thing we have become fairly familiar with, there are generally many different subsets of its properties, all of which would pick out that thing. In the above story, we could replace (6) by *the latter*. Likewise (10) could be replaced by *the father*. (17) and (18) could be replaced by *the Commendatore* and still pick out the same thing. Similarly, (21) could be replaced by *the murderer*, or *the nobleman*. It could not be replaced by *the man*, because there is more than one man in the limelight.

Here now is the key observation. The words and phrases that we claim could replace one another, without doing any violence to the story, do not have to have the same senses. Their senses simply have to involve enough of the already established properties of the thing they are used to refer to to distinguish it from other things in the story. The senses of words that are used to introduce new things, or to ascribe new properties to things that have already been introduced, are clearly much more narrowly constrained. This is because the set of properties they can assign to the new thing are largely open. Instead of *a young man*, we might have found *an old man*, *a young woman*, but this would have made it a different story.

What is given, thereby making several very different senses essentially equivalent, clearly concerns not only the actions of the principal players which constitute the driving force of the story, but also quite minor properties of the situation or the cultural context. A person who picks up the telephone and discovers that the call is for someone else in the vicinity, may say *Just a moment*, or *Hang on*, which have entirely different senses but evoke the same prototypical thing, namely the brief wait while the desired person is located. The receptionist in a place of business my have been taught to say *one moment please*, or even *Please hold*, but what is important, namely the things that are referred to, are the same. In France, the person picking up the phone will probably say *ne quittez pas*, the sense of which is literally *Do not stop*, or even more literally *Do not leave*, but, in this context, something closer to *Do not hang up*. It is a given thing because it belongs to the prototypical telephone-call story.

If a bus that would normally operate on a regular route is being driven from one place to another without passengers, then the sign that would normally declare its destination may well be replaced by something like *Not in Service*. In German, the sign would probably say *Betriebsfahrt* or *Sonderfahrt*—literally *Service Journey* and *Special Journey*. The sign on a German train would be more likely to be *Nicht Einsteigen* (*Do not get on* or *Do not board*). In French, it might say *ne prend pas de voyageurs* (DOES NOT TAKE PASSENGERS). While these all have manifestly different senses, they all evoke the same prototype and therefore the same referents. In other words, in these contexts, they mean the same.

As we have said before, the first responsibility of the writer and the reader, and therefore translator, of a story is to keep track of the referents in it. Keeping track of the things that are being referred to is paramount. Words and phrases that introduce new things in the translation, must have substantially the same sense as the words and phrases they translate, but the same requirement does not apply´to words and phrases that distinguish given things from one another.

Here is another synopsis of the first act of Don Giovanni, this time in French, with an English translation. There is no way in which the French could be a translation of the earlier English version because, while we may take it that both tell a story that is consistent with the opera's libretto, the stories that they tell are not the same. The writer of a synopsis aims to retain only what is most important from the original text, suppressing a great deal of detail. But writers will invariably make different decisions as to what is important and what can be suppressed. Furthermore, we have adopted a very restrictive view of what it means for the stories to be the same. What the stories evoke on the mental stages of readers, whether of the original or of the translation, must be the same down to a very low level of detail and our commitment to ontological promiscuity commits us to recognizing large numbers of details.

Leporello monte la garde devant la maison dans laquelle Don Giovanni s'est introduit afin de séduire Donna Anna, la fiancée d'Ottavio. Soudain, Donna Anna apparaît avec Don Giovanni. Elle veut savoir qui il est et appelle à l'aide ; lorsque le Commandeur survient, il provoque l'agresseur en duel. Il est frappé à mort par Don Giovanni, qui prend la fuite sans avoir été reconnu. Donna Anna est choquée, et Don Ottavio jure vengeance.	Leporello is standing guard outside the house that Don Giovanni has entered in the hope of seducing Donna Anna, Ottavio's fiancée. Suddenly, Donna Anna appears together with Don Giovanni. She wants to know who he is and calls for help; when the Commendatore arrives, he challenges Giovanni to a duel. Giovanni kills him and gets away without being recognized. Donna Anna is devastated and Don Ottavio swears vengeance.

The first version told us at the outset that Leporello is Don Giovanni's servant and that we find him grumbling about this as the opera opens. The second version says nothing about any of this. We don't know who Leporello is, or that he is anything but entirely happy with his lot. We do, however, know that he is standing guard outside the house, a fact that is missing from the first version. From the first version, we learn that Giovanni suddenly appears accompanied by Donna Anna, but not that they appear from inside the house, or that she is pursuing him. In short, the stories are not the same, in large measure because the things that the stories contain are not the same. There is no reference in the first version to Leporello's standing guard or Donna Anna's pursuit. The thing that is Leporello's grumbling, and the fact that he is Giovanni's servant are absent from the second version.

Now, let us concentrate on the second version of the synopsis and its translation into English where substantially that same set of things is to be found on both sides. The phrase *monte la garde* has been rendered as *stands guard*, a phrase with a very similar sense, which is important, because it names something that is being introduced into the story for the first time. The set of things that these two can refer to is very similar, but not quite identical.

Now consider the sentence "Suddenly, Donna Anna appears together with Don Giovanni." which refers to two people, both of whom have already been introduced to the reader. Many alternatives suggest themselves. Preserving the words *suddenly* and *appears*, which name new things, we have at least the following:

1. Suddenly, she appears together with him.
2. Suddenly, Don Giovanni appears together with Donna Anna.
3. Suddenly, the two of them appear.
4. Suddenly, they appear together.
5. Suddenly, they both appear.
6. Suddenly, he appears together with his fiancée.

We cannot refer to Donna Anna as the Commendatore's daughter because this refers to a fact that has not yet been established in this version of the story. We could also have moved *suddenly* to other positions in the sentence, or replaced it with other words or phrases. In 5, we used *both* to fill the role of *together* in the other versions, and we could clearly have done this in the other versions as well. We concentrate on references to the characters in the drama because these are references to *given* things and they allow far greater variation. And the reason why they allow greater variation is that the senses of the words and phrases that fill these roles can vary greatly so long as they continue to pick out the required member, or subset of members, of the currently salient things.

The sentence *Elle veut savoir qui il est* (SHE WANTS TO KNOW WHO HE IS) refers to its two human participants by pronouns so that the information provided about the intended referents is minimal. But it is sufficient under the circumstances because only one man and one woman are currently in the limelight. The situation is quite different in the followings sentence, *lorsque le Commandeur survient, il provoque l'agresseur en duel.* (When the Commendatore arrives, he challenges the aggressor to a duel) because we have not met the Commendatore before and the attempt to refer to him with a pronoun would fail, because this could succeed only in referring to someone already on stage. But, once the arrival of the Commendatore has been established, we can say *he challenges him to a duel.*

There is a subtlety in this last sentence, resulting from the fact that it contains both the word *he* and the word *him*. These are the nominative and accusative singular of the same English pronoun *he.* Only a single verb intervenes between them so that, other things being equal, we should expect them to refer to the same thing. Two different, though closely related, facts about the sentence prevent the reader from becoming confused.

The first fact is simply that people do not, nor did they ever, challenge themselves to duels. This is not a logical conclusion or a rule of grammar. It is simply common sense. The second fact, however, does have to do with a rule of grammar for, if the subject and the object of a sentence have the same referent, and it is being referred to with pronouns, then the second of these must be in a special form, called the *reflexive*. Specifically, the sentence would have had to be *he challenges himself to a duel*. Rules governing reflexives do not operate in the same ways in all languages so that they can lead to problems for the translator.

While we expect an interesting or useful text to be constantly introducing new material, and therefore new things, in our sense, we also expect these new things to be related to previously introduced, or given, things. As we have seen, reference to given things can generally be achieved with a great variety of words or phrases that may have quite different senses. The choice can therefore often be based on what might normally be thought of as secondary considerations such as euphony and rhythm. This is therefore a very natural source of what we have been calling pragmatic translation.

4

Sense

If what we have been claiming is correct, the power and utility of language comes in part from the great variety of real and imaginary things that it can be used to refer to. We have said relatively little, however, about how this connection between words and things that we call *referents* is actually achieved. How is it that, if I say *Please pass me the hammer* to you, you will know that I am referring to a particular kind of tool which, under appropriate circumstances, you will be able to pass to me? In many situations, probably including this one, the question does not seem particularly problematic. You and I both know about a class of tools the members of which are referred to as hammers. We know that they are designed principally for hitting things, prototypically nails. Something else we know about them, which is especially important in the present context, is what they generally look like. So, when I say *Please pass me the hammer*, you know what kind of thing to look for.

The properties that hammers share, by virtue of which you know what I am likely to be referring to when I use the word, constitute the *sense* of the word *hammer*. If you are able to pass me the tool I have in mind, it may, in part, be because of additional information in the context. There may, for example be two hammers that you could pass me with equal ease. Since I asked for *the hammer*, rather than *a hammer*, I hope to establish a reference to a particular given thing—something that I expect to be on your mental stage. There is nothing unusual about this. You may be fairly sure which hammer I want because you know that only one of those available is suitable for what I am doing, or there is one that I have been using frequently, and the other not at all. In other words, it is in the spotlight, or more so than any others. If I wanted to override these assumptions, I would presumably ask for the *big hammer*, the *claw hammer*, or simply the *other hammer*.

As well as knowing two languages, a translator clearly also needs to be familiar with the subject matter of the text, and the particular senses that words like *hammer* and *claw hammer* can have when used in that domain. This is particularly clear in the case of technical subjects where many terms, and many of the notions that the terms might refer to, would be recognized only by specialists. These specialized parts of the vocabulary of a language are referred to as the *terminology* of a field. Once the translator has become familiar with the terminology of the field, it generally presents fewer problems than everyday vocabulary because the two languages usually have closely corresponding terms for the objects and operations that are important in the field. There are, of course, exceptions to this, as in the case of the British and American words *wrench* and *spanner* discussed earlier.

There is no hard and fast boundary between terminology and the general vocabulary. Native speakers of a language are just as particular about subtle distinctions in the meanings of everyday words as are the practitioners of specialized fields. A waiter serving breakfast in an American coffee shop might ask the client if he would like some jam with his toast. If the client said *yes*, he might very well bring him some orange marmalade. A British client might find this strange because, for him, what would otherwise be called *jam* must be referred to as *marmalade* if it is made with citrus fruit.

A similar situation involves the British *biscuit* and the American words *cracker* and *cookie*. A cookie is sweet, and a cracker is not. The notions are quite separate. But this is not to say that there could not be a particular thing, or kind of thing, that was hard to classify as one or the other.

A kitchen tool consisting of a flat piece of metal attached to a handle and useful, for example, for removing fried eggs from a pan is called a *spatula* or a *cake turner* in America, but a *fish slice* in Britain. These, and many other, words belong to the terminology of everyday life. They attach to very well-defined notions in a way that outside observers of translation all too often imagine almost all words do. Observe that such tools of the culinary trade are not in fact usually referred to as *tools*, but rather by another special piece of terminolgy, namely *utensils*.

Dictionaries that are published in book form are presumably a pale reflection of the dictionaries that the native speakers of a language have in their heads. The definition of *bachelor* referred to earlier apparently applies to celibate monks, but many native English speakers are uneasy with calling such people *bachelors*. What about a man who has lived with the same woman for thirty years and has two children with her? Any English speaker who would be unhappy calling these bachelors presumably has a mental dictionary in which the entry for the word is more nuanced.

An obvious way to think of the sense of a word is as a set of the properties that a thing must have if the word can be felicitously used to refer to it, together with the subsets of these properties that are sufficient to establish that a thing is one of those that the word can refer to. In other words, it must give the *necessary conditions*, every one of which the thing must meet, as well as the *sufficient conditions*, beyond which no others need be sought to determine that the word can refer to the thing. For a thing to be a bachelor, it is claimed that a thing must be (1) human, (2) male, (3) of marriageable age, and (4) unmarried. These are the necessary conditions. If one of them is not met, then we cannot be sure that we have a bachelor, so that the set of four also constitutes the only sufficient set.

This notion of the sense of word as the necessary and sufficient conditions for applying it to a thing breaks down fairly quickly. In the first place, the set of things covered by many word senses can be hopelessly difficult to tease out into discrete, verifiable conditions. Consider the word *school* in the following list of examples, which could be considerably extended:

1. We live right opposite the school
2. The school makes quite a lot of noise
3. The school usually invites us to its major functions
4. The school is (are) all rooting for its (their) team
5. Emma left school at 16.
6. Emma left school around 3.30.
7. They go to school at age six.
8. They go to school at six in the morning.
9. Tyler goes to school at home
10. I usually go to school to pick Tommy up
11. The university has a very good law school
12. She finds school very difficult
13. French schools are more difficult than American ones.

We deliberately leave aside the Flemish school, schools of porpoises, various schools of thought, and so forth. In our restricted set of examples, a school is apparently sometimes a building, sometimes a collection of students, and sometimes a set of administrators, sometimes a type of activity, sometimes collections of these things, and sometimes other things. To say that each corresponded to a different sense, each with its own necessary and sufficient conditions for referring to something, would be to dismiss as irrelevant the obvious commonality that they all clearly have.

As another often cited example, consider the properties of *roastingn* that distinguish it from *baking*. There presumably are some, because one does not roast ham, and roast and baked potatoes are different. Various properties come to mind. When applied to meat, roasting typically changes its color whereas the color of ham, when it is baked, stays substantially the same. Historically, roasting was usually done on a spit in a fire whereas baking required a dry oven. It may be, therefore, that we speak of roasting when the result is substantially similar to that we should get with the spit, and baking when the result looks as though it came from an oven. This is borne out in the case of potatoes, for a roast potato is cooked in the juices from the meat whereas a baked potato is cooked in a dry oven.

In English, we make a distinction between a door and a gate. In a given context, English speakers rarely have any difficulty deciding which word to use, and there are relatively few situations in which both are equally acceptable. In most cases, the decision as to which word to use turns on whether the wall, fence, or other structure in which the door, or gate, is embedded continues not only to the left and right of the opening, but also above it. If somebody says that there is a door between the Rose Garden and the Orchard, we take it that these two places are separated by a wall or a fence which is not interrupted by the door. If, however, they say that there is a gate between the two, then we take it that the wall, or the fence, is interrupted at that point. The situation is essentially as depicted in Figure 4.1. There are obvious cases that are not covered by this prescription. It does not, for example, apply to the departure gates at airports or to the entrances to medieval towns and castles. We may have to admit that separate senses are involved, especially in the case of departure gates.

What is the difference between a cup and a mug? *Merriam-Webster On Line* provides the following definitions:

cup: An open usually bowl-shaped drinking vessel. [11]
mug: A cylindrical drinking cup.[12]

---

11. https : // www . merriam - webster . com / dictionary / cup, accessed March 28, 2017

12. https : // www . merriam - webster . com / dictionary / mug, accessed March 28, 2017

Door

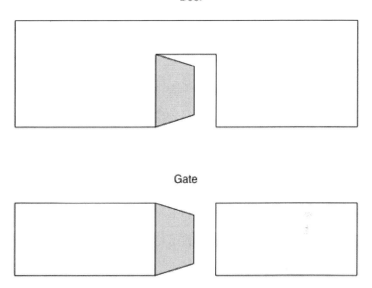

Gate

FIGURE 4.1 Doors and Gates

To make sense of the first of these definitions, we need to know what the shape of a bowl is. The dictionary defines it as *a concave usually nearly hemispherical vessel.* In other words, it is considerably wider at the top than at the bottom—just like a teacup! Mugs apparently constitute a subset of the class of cups. The class is presumably quite small since, to qualify for membership in it, an object must be both spherical and cylindrical.

The Random House dictionary gives the following definitions:

cup: A small, open container made of china, glass, metal, etc. usually having a handle and used chiefly as a receptacle from which to drink tea, soup, etc.[13]

mug: A drinking cup, usually cylindrical in shape, having a handle, and often of a very heavy substance, as earthenware. [14]

Here, mugs are also taken as constituting a subset of cups. However, whereas cups are used chiefly for drinking, mugs are invariably used for this purpose.

Here are the definitions from the Oxford Advanced Learner's dictionary:

---

13. http://www.dictionary.com/browse/cup, accessed April 6, 2017

14. http://www.dictionary.com/browse/mug, accessed April 6, 2017

cup: A small container shaped like a bowl, usually with a handle, used for drinking tea, coffee etc.[15]

mug A tall cup for drinking from, usually with straight sides and a handle, used without a saucer.[16]

Here it is clear that

1. a mug is a cup;
2. a cup is shaped like a bowl
3. a mug has straight sides.

In fairness to the lexicographers, we should note that they are responsible only for giving a reasonably good idea of what a cup is and what a mug is. They are not generally required to distinguish the meaning of the word they are defining from those of all other words that can be used to name similar things. Let us, however, undertake that exercise just for the case of cups and mugs.

The following properties seem to be more typical of cups than mugs:

1. has thin walls
2. tapers towards the bottom
3. has a saucer
4. has no cover
5. has a small handle admitting at most two fingers
6. keeps company with teapots

The parallel list for mugs would contain the negations of the first three items from this list, and modifications of the next two, so that it would be somewhat as follows:

1. has thick walls
2. does not taper towards the bottom
3. has no saucer
4. may have a cover
5. has a large handle admitting four fingers

Clearly none of these is either a necessary, or a sufficient, condition for being a cup or a mug. Indeed, we could follow the lead of the professional lexicographers and hedge each one of them with words or phrases like *usually, chiefly,* and *etc,* thus leaving open the possibility of there being objects which were both cups and mugs. These are properties

---

15. http : / / www . oxfordlearnersdictionaries . com / us / definition / english / cup_1, accessed April 6, 2017

16. http : / / www . oxfordlearnersdictionaries . com / us / definition / english / mug_1, accessed April 6, 2017

that would make us more inclined to call a thing either a cup or a mug. The more properties it had from one, and the less from the other list, the greater our inclination would be to call it a cup or a mug.

There are certain properties that an object we might otherwise call a mug could have that would override the ones in these lists. For example, if it was made of silver and clearly intended to be awarded as a prize in some competition, then we should have to call it a cup, and not a mug. If it was made of paper, or cardboard, then we should have to call it a cup however close it was to being cylindrical in shape, or otherwise similar to a mug. There is simply no such thing as a *paper mug*.

For the philosopher Wittgenstein the word *game* was a particularly striking counterexample to the theory based on necessary and sufficient conditions:

> Consider for example the proceedings that we call 'games'. I mean board games, card games, ball games, Olympic games, and so on. What is common to them all? Don't say, *There must be something common, or they would not be called 'games'* –but look and see whether there is anything common to all. For if you look at them you will not see something common to all, but similarities, relationships, and a whole series of them at that. To repeat: don't think, but look! Look for example at board games, with their multifarious relationships. Now pass to card games; here you find many correspondences with the first group, but many common features drop out, and others appear. When we pass next to ball games, much that is common is retained, but much is lost. Are they all 'amusing'? Compare chess with noughts and crosses.[17] Or is there always winning and losing, or competition between players? Think of patience.[18] In ball games there is winning and losing; but when a child throws his ball at the wall and catches it again, this feature has disappeared. Look at the parts played by skill and luck; and at the difference between skill in chess and skill in tennis. Think now of games like ring-a-ring-a-roses;[19] here is the element of amusement, but how many other characteristic features have disappeared! And we can go through the many, many other groups of games in the same way; we can see how similarities crop up and disappear. And the result of this examination is: we see a complicated network of similarities overlapping and criss-crossing: sometimes overall similarities, sometimes similarities of detail. (Wittgenstein 1953, 66)

The distinctions between wrenches and spanners, jam and marmalade, roasting and baking, doors and gates are, on the one hand,

---

17. American English: *tic-tac-toe*

18. American English: *solitaire*

19. Ring around the rosie.

remarkably subtle and difficult to tie down and, on the other, quite arbitrary and apparently unmotivated. It would therefore be quite surprising if we were to find exactly parallel distinctions in other languages. Indeed, we have already observed that some of them do not even carry over between British and American English. As expected, we look in vain for a pair of French words that distinguish cups and mugs just as they are distinguished in English. English distinguishes a pen from a pencil, and French makes a largely parallel distinction between a *plume* and a *crayon*. French recognizes at least three kinds of things among those that are routinely referred to with the word *book* in English. A printed book, designed to be read, is a *livre*. A book intended primarily to be written in, such as a school exercise book, is a *cahier*, and a book of pages intended to removed one by one, such as a book of tickets, is a *carnet*.

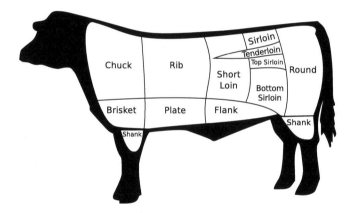

FIGURE 4.2 U.S. Beef Cuts,
https://commons.wikimedia.org/wiki/File:US_Beef_cuts.svg, access 28 March 2017

There are areas of semantic territory that some languages divided up in altogether different ways from others. A good example concerns cuts of meat. These differ radically even between America and Britain. Wikipedia supplies the diagrams in Figures 4.2 and 4.3 to show the differences. According to the accompanying articles, the cultural anthropologist Margaret Mead wrote in the American Anthropological Journal of the American Anthropological Association, "cultures that divide and cut beef specifically to consume are the Koreans and the Bodi tribe in East Africa. The French and English make 35 differenti-

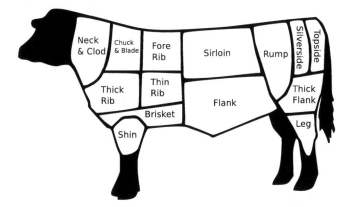

FIGURE 4.3 British Beef Cuts,
https://commons.wikimedia.org/wiki/File:British_Beef_Cuts.svg,
access 28 March 2017

ations to the beef cuts, 51 cuts for the Bodi tribe, while the Koreans differentiate beef cuts into a staggering 120 different parts."

4.1 Prototypes

Considerations like these cast considerable doubt on the proposal that senses should be equated with necessary and sufficient conditions. Instead, the list of properties should be thought of as characterizing an ideal, or prototypical referent for the given word. It is almost as though the territories in the semantic grid each had a capital somewhere near its center and living close to the capital correlated with a word's claim to citizenship. Countries, however, do not overlap and crucially, our regions do. A word can be used to refer to a thing if that thing is sufficiently like the word's prototypical object. An obvious, canonical example of a cup will not be called a mug because it shares significantly more properties with the prototypical cup. A thing that shares approximately the same number of properties with both prototypes will cause hesitation as to what to call it.

The psychologist Eleanor Rosch, who formulated prototype theory (Rosch 1973), argued that prototypes have varying status in a given culture. She points out that, if I ask what you are sitting on, and you are in fact sitting on a chair of some kind, then you are likely to respond *I am sitting on a chair.* You are a great deal less likely to say that you are sitting on a *kitchen chair*, which would be more specific, or a *piece of furniture*, which would be less so. Notice that a chair is something that it is very easy to construct a mental picture of. We can create a mental image of a simple, canonical chair very easily. This is more difficult for a kitchen chair and just about impossible for a piece of furniture. Basic categories are relatively homogeneous in terms of sensori-motor affordances—a chair is associated with bending of one's knees, a fruit with picking it up and putting it in your mouth, etc.

Examples of this kind can be multiplied many times over. In American English, the word *school*, referred to earlier, can be used to refer to an educational institution at any level whereas, in British English, a university is not a school. Famously, in America, a public school is indeed a school that is open to the public whereas, in Britain, it is private. However, a British public school is not just any private school. For example, a prep school, which is also private, is not a public school. The prep school accepts pupils that are less than thirteen years old whereas the public school accepts them starting at age thirteen.

Not only can the university be a school in America, but it can contain other schools within it, for the next level of organization above that of the department in a university is the level of the school. Thus, there is a school of engineering, a school of medicine, possibly a school of arts and sciences, and so forth. In other places, these are sometimes referred to as *faculties*. On the basis of this fact, we may wish to argue that the word *school* has at least two separate senses, one for an institution of higher education as a whole, and another for its major components, but the criteria for doing this are far from clear.

Words with several senses are, of course, commonplace. Indeed, words sometimes apparently have conflicting, but closely related, senses. Consider the word *give* in the following context. Suppose that I ask John *Who gave you that book?*. He may reply *nobody gave it to me. I bought it from Mary*. But what does it mean to buy something? If John buys a book from Mary, then John gives Mary some money and Mary gives John the book in return. But then, surely, Mary does indeed give John the book. German has the verb *schenken* for giving when nothing is expected in return so that the apparent anomaly would not arise in that language. When desperate to express just this notion in English, some people press the word *gift* into service as a verb.

A writer is, of course, someone who writes. In the twentieth century, many writers gave up the pen in favor of the typewriter. In other words, they did their writing with a typewriter. Nowadays, most of them doubtless do it with a computer. So, when writers write, they do not actually write, they type. To make sense of this, we would presumably have to assume that the word *write* has two senses. One has to do with the composition of text and the other with making marks on paper with a hand-held device.

The properties that define a prototype do not have to be inherent properties of the object. By far the most important class of non-inherent properties have to do with the use to which the object is put, or is intended to be put. The definitions of mugs and cups considered above almost all contained phrases like *drinking cup, from which to drink tea, used for drinking tea*, and so forth. A spoon is *intended for* preparing or eating food. A bookcase is a set of shelves *intended to* accommodate books. Spoons and bookcases may, of course, be used for other purposes, or left unused altogether.

The use to which an object is intended to be put is part of the context in which the object is embedded, and other aspects of that context can also influence the prototype that we attach to it. The person who controls what the members of an organization do may be called the *director* if the organization is of certain kinds, such as a laboratory. The person is the *captain* if the organization is the crew of a ship, the *chief executive officer* if the organization is a company. A person who drives a car is a *driver*. But, if that person is employed by someone else to do this job, he may be referred to as a *chauffeur*. The person who brings food to the customers in a restaurant is called a *waiter* and, so that he knows what food to bring, he engages with the customer in an activity known as *taking an order*. At the end of the meal, he presents the customer with an invoice which, in a British restaurant, is called a *bill* and, in an American restaurant, is called a *check*. In no restaurant is it called an *invoice*. A person who is admitted to a society is said to *matriculate* if the society is a university, to be *called* or *admitted* to the bar, if it is the legal profession, to be *inducted* into a sports hall of fame, and so on.

Family relations constitute an important class of non-inherent, potentially defining properties. An *uncle*, for example, is a man who stands in a particular family relationship to another person—his *niece* or *nephew*. A *suspect* is someone who is suspected of something by at least one other person. A *goal* is a state of affairs which someone hopes to achieve. A *sum* is a number that you get when you add other numbers together.

Prototypes are part of the language. Each language has its own set of them though many of them may correspond almost completely, especially in languages spoken by members of related cultures. The prototype most readily evoked by the English word *school* is nearly identical to those corresponding to *école* in French, and *Schule* in German. But these languages have no prototype corresponding to the British *public school*, presumably because the notion is as foreign to their cultures as it is to the American. The words *give* and *write* generally correspond to *donner* and *écrire* in French, and *geben* and *schreiben* in German, and both words correspond to a pair of prototypes which are close to the English pair.

Clearly prototypes can be associated with expressions of various kinds, and not just words. The prototype associated with the idiom *kick the bucket* is similar to, or identical with, the prototype for *die.* There are prototypes for the idioms *take for granted, find fault with, over and above, a clear and present danger* (but probably not *the clear and present danger*), *by and large,* and so forth. But just as our ontology contains a large number of things, with those in the real world constituting a relatively small subset, the number of prototypes recognized by language must be larger than our vocabulary, and larger even than the set of senses that the words in our vocabulary have.

Expressions that behave like words in that they have idiosyncratic meanings that are not inferrable from the words that make them up are what we generally refer to as *idioms*. The line that separates these from nonidiomatic expressions is not entirely clear. This is because of expressions that mean what one expects them to mean even if one had not heard them before, but which are used often enough that they have become conventional, almost ritualistic. They include:

> any friend of yours is a friend of mine
> gimme a break
> love conquers all
> no money down
> name, rank, and serial number (US)
> sign on the dotted line
> take it or leave it
> we're doing everything humanly possible

and foreign phrases like:

> ab initio
> persona non grata
> sine qua non
> ceteris paribus
> a propos
> au contraire
> c'est la vie
> de rigueur
> savoir faire

Notice that the words that make up an idiom do not always have to occur next to one another. In the phrase *as my son's teacher would have it*, the words *my son's teacher* can be replaced by any other phrase that designates an entity that can have an opinion, such as *As the Boston Globe would have it*. Likewise, the word *clear* in the phrase *as clear as can be* can be replaced by a great many other adjectives. Similar examples include

the brunt of *someone's* anger
the force of *someone's* personality
for *someone's/something's* sake
in *someone's/something's* stead

Where else but in these expressions do you find the English words *brunt* and *stead*?

The material that can fill the hole is required to be a noun phrase in many idioms. Consider the following examples:

the top of *one's* form
the end of *one's* tether/rope
the time of *one's* life

Furthermore, its meaning must be related to that of the idiom as a whole in a specific way. The term "discontinuous idiom" is therefore perhaps misleading. They might more accurately be referred to as idioms with a variable filler.

The placeholder *one's* can be replaced only by a possessive pronoun which usually refers back to the subject of the sentence. In *Martha Graham was at the top of her form*, the word *her* refers back to Martha Graham. We cannot say *She was at the top of Martha Graham's form*, or *She was at the top of somebody's form*. We cannot ask *Whose form was she at the top of?* For the same reason, we cannot say *John was having the time of my life* or *I was having the time of John's life*. We can, of course, say *this all happened during the time of his life*, but this is not an instance of the idiom. Almost every instance of this particular idiom is the object of the verb *have*, but we might also say something like *He expected this to be the time of his life*.

By far the largest class of idioms seems to have a verb at their core. Consider the following examples:

bend *someone's* ear
clip *someone's* wings
cramp *someone's* style
get under *someone's* skin
drop *someone* a line
take *someone* to task
take *something* for granted

A common part of the standard curriculum for teaching English to foreigners is based on so-called *phrasal* verbs. These have also been the subject of many papers by linguists in learned journals. They are verbs that can have an idiosyncratic meaning when they are followed by a verbal particle or a phrase headed by a particular preposition. The verbal particle does not necessarily follow them immediately. Here are some examples:

put up	They put up the visitors for the night
	They put the visitors up for the night
put off	We should put off the meeting until next week
	We should put the meeting off until next week
write up	You need to write up the experiment
	You need to write the experiment up
write down	You need to write down the whole thing
	You need to write the whole thing down
write off	They had to write off the whole house
	They had to write the whole house off
write out	He wrote out the whole poem in longhand
	He wrote the whole poem out in longhand
set down	They set down a list of conditions in the document
	They set a list of conditions down in the document
set up	They set up an organization to handle these cases
	They set an organization up to handle these cases
set off	this is what set off the revolt
	this is what set the revolt off

It is by no means the case, in any of these examples, that any arbitrary sequence of words can intervene between the two parts of the idiom. It must be a single syntactic unit—a word or phrase. Furthermore, it must be the object of the verb that the idiom represents. So, *They put up the visitors for the night* is a sentence with *They* as its subject, *put up* as its verb, and *the visitors* as its object. In the alternative form, the object comes before the particle *up*. But we cannot put anything else in that place. We cannot, for example, say *they put for the night the visitors up* or *they put willingly up the visitors for the night*. If the object is a pronoun, then it must precede the particle, so, *We put up them for the night* is impossible.

It is well known that these verbs have close parallels in German, often called *separable verbs*. They are referred to in this way because, in some of their forms, notably the infinitive, or *citation* form, the particle is attached to the rest of the verb as a prefix. In finite forms, it is separated and moved to the end of the clause. The German sentence *Du muß dein Paß vorzeigen* contains the infinitive form of the verb *vorzeigen*, meaning *show*. In the sentence *Er zeigte sein Paß vor* (HE SHOWED HIS PASSPORT), the prefix *vor* is separated and moved to the end of the sentence. In these simple examples, the two parts of the verb are separated be a single noun phrase which is the object of the verb, much as they would be in English. However, in *Du muß dein Paß in solche Unständen oft mehere Mals vorzeigen* (IN SUCH SITUATIONS, YOU OFTEN HAVE TO SHOW YOUR PASSPORT SEVERAL TIMES), everything except the subject of the sentence appears before the verb and the particle.

We observed that a visit to a restaurant involves the ritual that is established as part of our culture. The ritual involves being taken to a table, given a menu, placing an order, having food brought to the table, and paying the bill. The ritual is nearly identical in every country of Europe and so are the corresponding prototypes. However the choice of the prototypes for which there is special terminology differ slightly from one language to another. When the English or French diner has finished eating and would like the bill brought, he constructs a request using the everyday facilities of the language and directs it to the waiter. In English, he might say *Can I have the check, please, I guess I'd like the bill, when you have a moment*, or simply *The check please*. German and Italian speakers can do the same thing, but they have the additional possibility of framing their requests using the verbs *zahlen* and *pagare*. They can say, for example, *Zahlen, bitte* or *Pagare, per favore*. The words *zahlen* and *pagare* each have a sense which corresponds to this part of the restaurant ritual, or the restaurant *script*. The English word whose senses are closest to those of these German and Italian verbs is *pay*. But the conventions are such that it would, at least, be strange to say in English something like *I would like to pay, please* or *May I pay now*. It would be distinctly more strange to say *Pay please*, or just *Pay!*, whose direct equivalents in German and Italian are quite acceptable.

It may, in fact, be possible to trace the differences between the restaurant terminology of English and those of German and Italian to something more than convention, though it is not clear whether anything of linguistic interest would turn on this. It is standard practice in English-speaking countries for a waiter to serve as a messenger between the customer and the cashier. The cashier issues the bill; the waiter carries it to the customer; and then returns to the cashier with the money. In Germany and Italy, a different model is common. The waiter computes what is owed and conveys this to the customer, who pays him directly. The waiter keeps the money in his own wallet and settles with the cashier at the end of the day, or the end of the week. According to the second model, it is frequently the case that no bill is presented, and the interaction between the customer and the waiter is indeed one of direct payment.

At first sight, there may seem to be something of a contradiction in the way in which semantic categories operate. On the one hand, the distinction between cups and mugs seems extremely fluid with each category interpenetrating the other. On the other hand, jam and marmelade, although they share all but a very small number of attributes, are strictly distinguished. As senses, *cup*, *mug*, *jam* and *marmelade* all belong to the digital world of language and each is strictly distinct from the others. In discussing what distinguishes a mug from a cup, we were attempting to clarify the relationship between two of these categories and the kind of object in the analog world that they can be used to refer to. The analog world exists outside language and it would clearly be hopeless to expect the infinite variety of things that it contains to fall conveniently into some finite set of predetermined boxes.

One of the principal problems that arises, even in the most pedestrian kinds of translation, comes from the fact that, while both texts must refer to the same things, the categories that the two languages make available for this purpose do not always correspond to one another. French, for example, does not contain the word that corresponds to *mug* in English so that, in many cases, it would be quite appropriate to translate it in the same way as *cup*. The word *chope* refers only to a beer mug.

One way to think of semantic space is as a multidimensional map that the speakers of a language lay down on reality, as in Figure 4.4. The solid lines enclose the territory covered by the English words *door* and *gate*. The dotted lines show the territory covered by the French words *porte* and *sortie*. We show a small part of the English territories as overlapping because we take it that there are things that could be doors but that could also be gates. Likewise with the French words. A lot of the territory of *sortie* covers that of neither *door* or *gate*. Much of it doubtless covers that of *exit*. The territory of porte covers much of both *door* and *gate*.

It is not the case that every language has a prototype in every region of the space. This can make it difficult to translate a word or phrase corresponding to that prototype in another language. If you want a strong espresso coffee, made with very little water, you can use the phrase *café serré* in French, or *ristretto* in Italian, but there is no word that

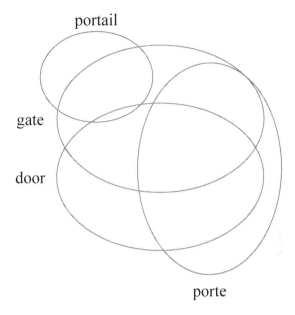

portail

gate

door

porte

FIGURE 4.4 The semantic grid

corresponds exactly to this notion in English or German. The French word *délai* pinpoints a notion very similar to that of a *period of time* in English, but associated with the notion of waiting or postponement. It is often used where no word at all is required in English, as in *dans un délai de trois semaines* (WITHIN THREE WEEKS), *dans les meilleurs délais* (AS SOON AS POSSIBLE; *literally:* IN THE BEST TIME PERIODS.).

Before boarding a main-line train in France, one must feed the end of one's ticket into a slot in a special machine that will stamp it with, among other things, the current date and time. The purpose of this is to ensure that, even if the conductor somehow does not manage to check the ticket on the train, it will nevertheless not be reusable at a later time. This act with the ticket and the machine is referred to with the verb *composter*. The act has no precise counterpart outside France, and there is therefore no corresponding verb. The Collins dictionary suggests translating *N'oublie pas de composter ton billet avant de monter dans le train* as *Remember to punch your ticket before you get on the train*. We ignore the unfortunate fact that today, at least, the machine stamps the ticket rather than punching it. Otherwise, this would be entirely adequate under almost all circumstances because the operation does indeed lead to the ticket being stamped and the default way of causing this to happen to it is by completing the operation the French call *composter*.

An operation that is logically parallel to *composter* is carried out in many parts of Europe with bus tickets. The French verb most often used for this operation, however, is *valider*. This is a much more general word than *composter*, but it is entirely reasonable word to use because the operation is required if the ticket is to be considered *valid* for the journey that is about to begin. The corresponding German word is *entwerten* which literally means *invalidate*. Although this apparently means exactly the opposite of the French word, there is a perfectly reasonable story one could tell to justify its use. The purpose of the operation that is performed on the ticket is to make it impossible to reuse it after the completion of the current journey. In other words, the purpose is to cause the ticket to become *in*valid after the journey. In Italy, the verb *validare* is used in some provinces, and *invalidare* in others.

The stories one may be inclined to tell to justify the apparent contradictions in the uses of these words doubtless have some truth to them, but they have little to do with the way the words function in the modern language. There is a ritual—a script—that is followed when boarding a bus in places where one of these systems is in operation, and there is an operation in that particular script that has an agreed name. These words may also have other uses, including some in which notions of validation or invalidation are prominent, but these notions have no more than a historical and anecdotal relevance in the present situation.

In places like Europe, where a great deal of cultural background is shared, prototypes in one language that have no correspondent in another are less common than single prototypes in one language that correspond to more than one in another. Almost everybody has encountered some of the more celebrated members of this class, such as the English verb *know* corresponding to *savoir* and *connaître* in French, *wissen* and *kennen* in German.

The crucial observation about examples of this kind from the translator's point in view is that, when a single prototype in the source language corresponds to two or more prototypes in the target language, the translator is forced to make information explicit in the translation that was implicit, at best, in the original. The inverse of this situation is clearly less problematic because it is generally easier to let information remain implicit in the translation that had been explicit in the original.

The English word *chair* corresponds to two prototypes in French corresponding to the words *chaise* and *fauteuil*. The latter has arms whereas the former does not. The interesting question concerns whether English has a single prototype, or something very similar to the French pair. Consider the French sentences *Il était assis sur la chaise* and *Il était assis dans le fauteuil*, which can be translated into English as *He was sitting on the chair* and *He was sitting in the chair*. The same noun is used in both English sentences. Notice, however, that different prepositions—*on* and *in*—are used with it in the two sentences. It is as though a chair with arms was suggestive of a box—a more enclosed space—and therefore one to which the preposition *in* is more appropriate.

Suppose, now, that we are planning a dinner party. In particular, we are trying to decide where each of the guests should be seated. We exchange remarks like *Let's put aunt Agatha in that chair*, and *Cousin Jimmy always sits in that chair*. Although the chairs involved very probably have no arms, are not particularly well padded, and would clearly qualify as "chaises" in French, it is out of the question that we should say *Let's put aunt Agatha on that chair*, or *Cousin Jimmy always sits on that chair*. What is involved here is a subtle and seldom remarked upon distinction between what we can only regard as two meanings of the word *chair* with different prototypes. In this scenario, we are not referring directly to articles of furniture, but to positions around a table at which—incidentally—there are usually chairs. In this situation, the appropriate preposition is always *in* and never *on*.

It seems that we choose between *on* and *in* with the word *chair* in the sense of French *chaise* depending on whether the reference is to a specific piece of furniture or to a position in a larger structure. We find the distinction again in references to words like *bus* and *train*. I say *I go to work on the bus* when I use the public bus service to get to work. But, if my colleague, John, owns a Volkswagen bus, and he picks me up and takes me to work, then I may say *I go to work in John's bus*. It would be unacceptable to use *on* in this case. It does not turn on the fact that I characterize the bus as *John's* because there are other circumstances in which *I go to work on John's bus* would be entirely natural. This would be the case if, for example, John always takes the 8:15 bus rather than the one at 8:45 and I do this also. The 8:15 bus is John's bus. Notice the difference that the alteration between *in* and *on* makes in *Cynthia has been in/on the original Orient Express*. With *in*, the train need not have moved while Cynthia was there.

4.2 Scripts and Lexical Functions

The great American linguist Kenneth L. Pike used to delight and instruct audiences with demonstrations of how much he could learn about a language in half an hour from a native speaker of it, without recourse to any language that he shared with the person. Someone who fills this role for a linguist is often called an *informant*. In order to put the informant at ease, and perhaps with the aim of distinguishing statements from questions, he would say things in a language called Mixtec, an Oto-Manguean language of which he was a fluent speaker but of which the informant could be counted on to know nothing. He used a large number of props—leaves, stones, stuffed animals—chosen to be culturally neutral to the extent possible.

Pike first established names for a few objects by holding them up, or pointing to them, and asking, in Mixtec, what they were called. After a few minutes, he would hold up two or three objects of the same kind, thus rapidly establishing the names of the first few numbers and the means, if any, of pluralizing at least some nouns under at least some circumstances.

It is easy to imagine that the procedure by which children begin to acquire their first language is not very different from this. Out for a walk in the stroller,[20] a dog appears on the scene and the mother says *doggie*. A person rides by on a bicycle, and the mother says *bicycle*. Two dogs appear, and the mother says *brown doggie* while pointing to one, and *white doggie* while pointing to the other. At first, the child can't be sure that *bicycle* means the conveyance or the person on it, or whether *brown* and *white* are colors, but practice has its just reward.

This is the most primitive way of establishing the senses of words. It is known as *ostensive definition*. Hitherto, we have taken the sense of a word to be a property of the word that enables us determine what kinds of things it could felicitously be used to refer to. Ostensive definition works the other way round, inferring the sense from a sample of felicitous references. As many philosophers, notably Quine, have pointed out, this is a process that does not have to work. When the dog appears, or Pike holds up a leaf, there are numerous things that could, in principle, be the associated reference if, indeed, any references are being made at all. But babies are apparently less obtuse than at least some philosophers and rapidly catch on to what is happening. Just how they do this need not concern us, as long as it works.

Simple ostensive definition, based on the most primitive of assumptions, namely that classes of things have names, gets things started. However, it breaks down when it encounters things that have certain names in certain contexts. For the most part, dogs are dogs. But colors can be surprising. It is easy to see what it is that white dogs and white

---

20. *pram* in British English!

birds and a white house have in common. But what of white wine? A piece of white paper fits the pattern, but what about the Churchill white paper of 1922 and such statements of government before they are voted upon? In French, a *carte bleue* (BLUE CARD) is a credit card of any color. The books in which American university students write the answers to examination questions will doubtless continue to be called *blue books* even if some reason is found to change the color of their covers. Whether or not this is the case, to use the term *blue book* in the context of an American university examination is specifically to refer to the book in which the responses to examination questions are written. To run a red light is a very specific kind of action and a red-light district is a very special kind of place. A referee in association football issues a red card to a player under very special circumstances. In French, this is a *carton rouge* and not *une catre rouge*. A foreigner allowed to take up residence in the United States is issued a *green card*—which, as of this writing, will turn out to be blue!

Roger Schank used the term "script" to refer to a prototypical scenario inside which a sense of a word may locate a referent (Schank 1991; Schank and Abelson 1977). The most well known of the scripts that he discussed is the restaurant script. Talk of a restaurant brings to mind not just a static image of a room full of dining tables with customers and waiters but also a ritual that is typically enacted in such a place. One enters a restaurant because one wants a meal. One is met be an employee that Americans often call a *Maitre D* (with a very special, very unFrench pronunciation). If no such person is waiting, then one waits for him or her to arrive. One is taken to a table, and is given a menu, either by the maitre D or by a waiter. One orders; one is served; one asks for the bill; one may leave a tip and one pays either directly to the waiter or at a place appointed just for this purpose.

Once it has been established that we are talking about going to a restaurant, this script, together with its associated vocabulary, is activated. Now one can talk of being *shown to a table*. A private person who invites you to dinner may ask you to sit in a certain place, but you are unlikely to say that he *showed you to a table*. If the person who will attend to most of your needs in the restaurant is male, then he will be referred to as the *waiter*, even as *your waiter*. If this person is female, it used to be customary to refer to her as a *waitress*, but using this term these days counts as an infraction against the rules of political correctness. Those who prize political correctness above linguistic sensitivity may blithely use *wait person* for both male and female. Others seek a circumlocution like *the person who served us* or

...*waited on us*. Notice that the two-part verb *wait on* has almost no uses outside the restaurant script.

The meal is a drama with some number of established acts, known as *courses*.[21] In its most prototypical form, Americans refer to these as the *entrée*, the *main course*, and the *desert*. In Britain, they would probably be referred to as the *starter*, the *main course*, and the *pudding* or *sweet*. Variants are of course possible. The first course can, for example, be referred to as the *appetizer* on either side of the Atlantic.

The restaurant script is relatively large and complex. A simpler one is the standard commercial transaction. It has four participants: a buyer, a seller, some merchandise, and some money. Linguistically, it is organized around a set of verbs which differ most strikingly in the way the script's participants are distributed among the syntactic arguments of the verbs. For example, the buyer is the subject of the verb *buy*, but the indirect object of *sell*. The merchandise is the direct object of both of these verbs. The merchandise is the subject of *cost*. Some of the verbs that are associated with this script are listed below, together with the ways in which the participants map onto their arguments, and a sentence or two to illustrate each.

Participants
> buyer
> seller
> merchandise
> money

Verbs
> buy   subject: buyer
>   direct object: merchandise
>   PP(to): seller
>   PP(for): money
>   *John bought the car from Mary for $600*

> sell   subject: seller
>   direct object: merchandise
>   indirect object: buyer

---

21. These practices were not imported into western Europe from Russia until the early nineteenth century, the previous practice being to set out all the food at the same time.

PP(for): money
Mary sold the car to John for $600
Mary sold John the car for $600.

pay subject: buyer
   direct object: money
   PP(for): merchandise
   indirect object : seller
   John paid $600 to Mary for the car.
   John paid Mary $600 for the car.

cost subject: merchandise
   direct object: money
   indirect object: buyer
   The car cost John $600.

charge subject: seller
   direct object: money
   indirect object: buyer
   PP(for) merchandise
   Mary charged John $600 for the car.
   ?Mary charged $600 to John for the car.

give subject: seller
   direct object: merchandise
   indirect object: buyer
   PP(for) money
   John gave Mary $600 for the car.
   John gave $600 to Mary for the car.

get subject: buyer
   direct object: merchandise
   PP(from): buyer
   PP(for) money
   John got the car from Mary for $600.

Needless to say, terms like *subject* and *direct object* refer to active sentences and need to be adjusted appropriate for othere constructions, such as the passive.

We write "PP(for)" to indicate a prepositional phrase with the preposition *for*, and likewise for other prepositions. The term "indirect object," as we use it here, can show up in a particular sentence either as the first of two noun phrases following the verb, like *John* in the sentence *Mary sold John the car* or as the object of the preposition *to* in a sentence like *Mary sold the car to John*. We place a question mark before the example *Mary charged $600 to John for the car* because it strikes us as somewhat unnatural.

In some of these examples, only a subset of the syntactic arguments, and consequently only a subset of the script's participants, are required to be present. Subjects must always be there, and direct objects almost always. But indirect objects and prepositional phrases can usually be omitted. This is a matter that is specified by the grammar and we therefore do not set out the details here.

It should be clear that this list is at best a sketch of the commercial transaction script. To start with, several other verbs clearly need to be included, such as *purchase, spend, trade, dispose of*, and *acquire*. More importantly, two aspects of scripts and their interactions with lexical items need to be explored. One concerns how broadly we should interpret the notion of syntactic argument for these purposes, and the other concerns the specific situations under which a script should be invoked. They are not entirely separate issues. They are both fascinating and important questions, but their detailed exploration is beyond our present scope. We limit ourselves to the following remarks.

Consider the sentence *John bought Mary's car for $600*. It clearly invokes the commercial-transaction script. What is not clear is whether Mary is one of its participants. If she was indeed the seller of the car, then she is a participant. But suppose that some of Mary's possessions were being sold as a result of a court judgement or after her death. In such a case, she did not receive the money involved in the transaction, and was not a willing participant in it. So we take it that sentence is ambiguous in this respect.

There are many scripts which, like the commercial transaction, relate a set of verbs, assigning different participants in the script to their grammatical arguments. The verbs may assert the enactment of the script on some occasion. Some of them may serve to deny that there was such an enactment, or that one was started, continued, or completed. There is a script for knowledge, prominently involving the verb *know*. It presumably also involves the verb *learn* to designate the inception of a state of knowledge, and the verb *forget* to designate its termination. To learn something is to come to know it and to forget it is no longer to know it.

In Igor Melčuk's *meaning-text* theory, synonymy and antinomy are the simplest of a set of around fifty so-called *lexical functions* that relate lexical items through the scripts they invoke (Melčuk 1996). What we are referring to as scripts, he calls *lexical units*. A lexical function is a mapping from scripts of words and phrases that are used to name their prototypical participants onto actors in the script. The lecturing script involves a *lecturer* who *delivers*, or *gives* a *lecture* to an *audiance* on a *subject*. A French lecturer also gives (*donne*) a lecture. But, in German, the verb is not *geben* (GIVE) but *halten* (HOLD).

It can be useful to think of scripts and lexical functions as being organized in a hierarchy in which more specific members are the children of less specific members. There is doubtless a script for *movement* or *displacement* involving verbs like *move*, *leave*, and *arrive* as well as prepositions like *from* and *to*. More specific scripts, below this one in the hierarchy, are used for *travel* or, perhaps, different modes of travel—by car, ship, air, etc. The script for air travel may be further specified to distinguish a script for *commercial air travel*. To see that such a script as this is indeed part of the English language, one need only consider the highly specialized English vocabulary items for which it provides the only natural home. They include the verbs *take off* and *land*, and the nouns *take-off* and *landing*. French has the corresponding nouns *décollage* and *atterrissage*. The very form of these words suggests something that happens on land. But, in English, a sea plane lands on water. French has a separate word for this, namely *amerrissage*. Also attached to this script are the words *boarding card*, *cabin attendant*, *business class*, *aisle seat*, *exit row* and many others. A historical version included *stewardess* in place of *cabin attendant* and the term *passenger* seems to be in the course of replacement by *customer*. The terms *arrival* and *departure* in the English commercial air travel script are presumably inherited from the parent travel script. But German has *Anflug* and *Abflug*, and corresponding more specialized verbs.

Lexical functions may involve pairs of scripts that are closely related to one another. To grant permission to do something is to *permit* or *allow* it to be done. Not to do this is to *forbid* or *disallow* it. The scripts are related in that the assertion of one is the denial of the other. Not to forbid is to allow, and conversely. The verbs *allow* and *forbid* are antonyms of one another and the lexical function called *antinomy* carries each onto the other. The pairs *accept* and *reject*, *like* and *dislike*, *remember* and *forget* stand in this same relation to one another.

Another lexical function relates verbs that can refer to the same events but which assign the participants in the events to different syntactic roles in the sentence. The verbs *buy* and *sell* are such a pair. If

Mary sells her car to John, then John buys the car from Mary. If a follows b then b precedes a. It is not only verbs that can participate in this relation. If a is longer than b, then b is shorter than a. If b is shorter than a, then either a is longer than b or a is taller than b. Since *longer* and *taller* have different senses, then this presumably means that *shorter* has at least two senses.

We have already remarked that there is a lexical function that relates many verbs to their prototypical subjects—*escape* to *escapee*, *guarantee* to *guarantor*, *receive* to *recipient*. Another relates verbs to their objects—*give* to *gift*, *know* to *knowledge*, *drink* to *drink*. We are, of course, not claiming that whenever verbs like these are used, it is appropriate to refer to the object of the action by the corresponding noun. We are claiming only that this word is the canonical, default designator of such an object. In fact, the inference is more reliable in the reverse direction: a gift is something that is given, a drink something that is drunk, and so forth. A speech is something that is spoken, though something that is spoken is not very often a speech. A loan is something that is lent, but only if it is money.

According to Melčuk, there are more than fifty standard lexical functions. Another imprtant one he calls *magn*. It carries a noun onto an adjective that is used to intensify the sense of the noun. For example, one talks of heavy rain or snow, a strong drink, a powerful argument, great affection and need, high hopes and intense heat. Something that is very simple to do is *dead easy*. To put great reliance on something or someone is to rely *heavily* on them. When coffee and tea are not weak, they are not powerful; they are *strong*. Desire and hope are perhaps the only things that can be *fervant*.

4.3 Classifiers

In English, if one wishes to talk about a specific number of cattle, one can use an expression like *fifteen head of cattle*. This is perhaps the most frequently quoted example of a so-called *classifier* in English. The word *cattle* is a mass noun and thus does not have a plural form. Furthermore, one says *a lot of cattle* and *they raise cattle*, using the singular form with a clearly plural referent. However, classifiers are also sometimes used with plurals as when a florist speaks of *twelve stem of roses*. Their typical use is to distinguish individuals from the mass that the noun refers to so that, in particular, they can be counted. Other English examples are *three head(s) of lettuce, an ear of corn, a blade of grass, a rasher of bacon* (mainly British).

Many languages, notably those of East Asia, always use classifiers, when a specific number of items is being referred to. In some cases, the classifier that must be used with a given noun corresponds to some coherent class of objects but, as with genders in Indo-European languages, there are generally large numbers of objects whose position in the classification makes little semantic sense and is thus is quite arbitrary.

Classifiers are not nearly so common in European languages. Here are some French ones, together with their English equivalents:

une pincée de sel	a pinch of salt
une mèche de cheveux	a lock of hair
une touffe de cheveux/poils	a tuft of hair
une goute d'eau	a drop of water
une tranchée de pain	a slice of bread
une grappe de raisins	a bunch of grapes
un morceau de sucre	a lump of sugar / a sugar cube
une noix/noisette de beure	a knob of butter
une tête de bétail	a head of cattle
	(usually only plural in English)

German has the word *Stück* which means *piece* as in *a piece of paper* (*ein Stück Papier*). However, it is also used as a kind of generalized quantifier, as in the following interchange:

A: Ich hätte gerne einige Eier, bitte.	I would like some eggs, please.
B: Wieviel?	How many?
A: Sechs Stück	Six

The most prominent classifier in English is doubtless *pair* as in articles of clothing like *a pair of pants*, *trousers*, and *pajamas*, and tools like *chop sticks*, *tongs*, *scissors*, *pliers*, *shears* as well as a *pair of glasses*. The rationale for this classifier is fairly clear in examples like *chop sticks* and *glasses*, but considerably less so in the case of *trousers*, *pajamas*, *pliers*, and *scissors*.

The articles of clothing are bipartite at least to the extent of having legs. One probably could not have *a pair of jacket* or *a pair of skirt*. With pajamas, it is less clear but English speakers are not in complete agreement that one should use *pair* with these. Pliers and scissors have two almost separate but similar parts that are loosely joined to constitute the complete tool, but it is ludicrous to talk of a *plier* or a *scissor*.

Needless to say, other languages cannot be relied upon to use a special classifier for articles that we have somewhat arbitrarily decided to think of as pairs. French does indeed use the term *une paire de ciseaux* (*a pair of scissors*). A *pair of pliers*, however, is *une pince*.

4.4 Doing Things with Words

Earlier in this chapter, we included one of the most frequently quoted passages from Wittgenstein's *Philosophical Investigations*. In it he discusses what it is about an activity that makes it appropriate to refer to it as a *game*. Foreshadowing Rosch's prototype theory, he concludes that there are no necessary or sufficient conditions that an activity must satisfy to count as a game and that the best we can do is to rely on *family resemblances* of various kinds among the members of the set. Each game has its own set of rules that its players must follow if their activities are to count as an instance of the game. For Wittgenstein, language itself is an instance of the kind of rule-governed behavior that he called a game. Words and phrases can be used in a variety of ways to make moves in a game just so long as they obey the rules.

He also draws a parallel between language and the kind of activity that goes on in a carpenter's shop. The words and phrases in a language are like the tools in a carpenter's shop; some are good for making some kinds of moves in the language game and some for others. Screwdrivers are good for driving screws, hammers for driving nails, pincers for extracting nails, and so forth. These are the purposes for which the tools were designed. But they can also be pressed into service for other purposes—screwdrivers for prying things apart, hammers for driving a mortise into a tenon, pincers for opening soda bottles. It is the same with words and phrases. They have more or less conventional uses that lexicographers catalog, and others that can be quite unexpected when they first occur.

The practice of applying old words to new purposes is so common that we have developed a terminology for the commonest forms that it takes. Perhaps the commonest is metonymy which is the use of a word to apply, not to its established kinds of referent, but to other things related to these in ways that are generally fairly obvious. We use the names of the capitals of countries to refer to the governments, or the rulers of those countries, as *It is unclear what is behind this move by Pyongyang*, or *Washington and London are standing firm on the matter*. This last example is a move that might be made in the American version of the game. In Britain, the second of these governments would doubtless be referred to as *Westminster*. If we see less sentences like *The president has made his views known to Tegucigalpa*, it is doubtless in part because of the relatively minor role that Honduras tends to play in our news stories, but also because newspaper editors do not entirely trust our nation's geography teachers. This last remark is not entirely flippant. Notice that you may still see references to *Paris, France* in

American newspapers, but never in Britain, and this cannot be ascribed entirely to the existence of towns called Paris in Texas and Tennessee.

If someone is asking a lot of questions for reasons that are obscure to those listening, they may be inclined to say that he is *just fishing for information* or that he is *on a fishing expedition*. Notice that both of these phrases are well on their way to becoming standard members of the tool kit. But someone might also say something like *He may have gone fishing for the weekend, but we should check his net on Monday*. This is more than an appeal to the current trendy way of saying things. It engages the reader in that game, and translating it into another language could pose corresponding real challenges.

Metonyms are presumably used sometimes to add variety and color to a text, and sometimes new referents have appeared in the world, broadly construed, that call for vocabulary with corresponding senses. The word *dish* can be used to refer to a certain kind of container used for the serving of food. Over time, certain assemblages of food in a dish became liked so that they were repeated frequently and a name was therefore needed for such assemblages. The word *dish* came readily to hand and remained in service for that purpose. Over time, countless words enter our language in this way and continue to do so.

Wittgenstein's application of the tool metaphor to words and phrases goes beyond using them in new and unaccustomed ways. The metaphor becomes more compelling in the work of the philosopher J. L. Austin, especially in his highly influential book *How to do things with words* (1962). He points out that, while the sentences that attract most attention from linguists and philosophers are used with the principal purpose of stating facts, this is by no means the only use to which they can be put. Consider, for example, the following:

1. Write your name on this line.
2. Don't you ever do that again!
3. Look out!
4. Time to get started!
5. What do you want me to do?
6. Please turn the light on.
7. Would you please turn the light on?
8. I call the meeting to order.
9. So that is how it works for adults. Now what about children?
10. Don't you find it cold with that window open?

The first three have a particular grammatical form that we call imperative and they are consequently commands. The canonical purpose

of commands is to incite some kind of action in the listener. If they are
negated, however, their purpose is to inhibit an action in the listener, as
in 2. Example 2 is a particularly insistent form of imperative, using both
you and *ever*. In modern English, the form of the imperative with *you*,
which is commoner when when it is negated, is restricted to situations
where the prohibition is very insistent and where the person making it
sees themselves as having considerable authority in the matter.

Some might not even think of 3 and 4 as sentences at all, but the
first is in every English speaker's tool box and, if the second is a tool,
then it is like a drill into which various bits can be inserted to adapt
it to one situation or another. After all, we can also say *Time to wrap
this up!*, *Time to move on!*, or *Time for some tea!* and so forth.

Example 5 will stand in for the essentially infinite set of sentences
whose syntactic form marks them as questions but that are otherwise
unremarkable. They have the obvious purpose of eliciting a response
from the hearer, typically in the form of an utterance that will supply
the information the current speaker is looking for. But questions can
also be designed to elicit other kinds of response as in 6 and 7. The
word *please* makes the analogy between words and tools particularly
compelling because by far the best way of explaining its meaning is to
describe how it is used. The *New Oxford American Dictionary* describes
it, for some reason, as an adverb, whose meaning it then goes on to
characterize as follows:[22]

- used in polite requests or questions: *please address letters to the
  Editor: what type of fish is this, please?*
- used to add urgency and emotion to a request: *please, please
  come home!*
- used to agree politely to a request: *"May I call you at home?"
  "Please do."*
- used in polite or emphatic acceptance of an offer: *"Would you
  like a drink?" "Yes, please."*
- used to ask someone to stop doing something of which the
  speaker disapproves: *Rita, please—people are looking.*
- used to express incredulity or irritation: *You cleaned out the barn
  in only two hours? Oh, please!*

Example 8 is a sentence that certainly does not express a proposition
but which is used to bring about a definite, if intangible, change in the
state of the world. It is understood by all that the meeting in question is

---

22. http://www.oxfordreference.com/view/10.1093/acref/9780195392883.
001.0001/m_en_us1278753, accessed April 6, 2017

deemed not to have started before these words are said and that it has started once they have been said. Only when they are said by an appropriate person do they have this effect. Other examples are *I pronounce you man and wife*, and *I condemn you to prison for three years*.

Example 9 is a canonical example of a so-called rhetorical question. It does not differ in form from a question intended to elicit information from the hearer, but it is used in a situation where the speaker or writer actually intends to provide that information. Its use is probably clearest in written text. The writer has reached a point where he thinks the reader should be expecting a certain piece of information to be provided next and makes this clear by asking a question to which the information would be an appropriate answer. It is a device commonly used by writers of expository text that allows the reader to verify that he has understood what was intended.

Sentences like 10 are of a kind that has received considerable attention from Grice (1975) and consequently from many linguists. It could easily serve simply to elicit information. In this case, however, it could also readily be used as a suggestion that the hearer turn the light off. At the center of Grice's theory of language is that it is a cooperative enterprise between the speaker and the hearer. If a speaker contributes something that does not appear to be cooperative according to the generally accepted rules of conversation, the hearer will seek a different and possibly more elaborate way of interpreting what was said that makes it seem more so. He tried to capture some of what he thought cooperative language use might consist of in the following so-called *maxims*:

Maxim of Quality: Be truthful
Maxim of Quantity: Say what needs to be said, but not more
Maxim of Relation: Make your contribution relevant
Maxim of Manner: Be clear

It is easy to imagine sentence 10 being uttered in the midst of a conversation that had nothing to do with the temperature. It therefore seems like a clear violation of the maxim of relation. One way to make sense of it is as a suggestion that the window be closed. That at least makes it relevant to the physical situation that the parties to the conversation find themselves in and thus a collaborative remark. For Grice, there was an important distinction to be made between the literal meaning of an utterance—what he called its "timeless meaning"—and what the speaker *implicates*. This latter is what a collaborative hearer understands.

This view of meaning is reminiscent of Wittgenstein's claim that *the meaning is the use*. He repeatedly urged anyone with an interest in words to spend less time reflecting on them, and more on watching how people actually put them to use. As it stands, however, the exhortation to take the meaning of a word or phrase as simply the way it is used is at best insufficient and, at worst, incoherent. There must be something about these tools in the language user's toolbox that is stable and which makes them suitable for some purposes and unsuitable for others. If someone is unfamiliar with a word or phrase, it must sometimes be justifiable to take what they do with it as misuse. The primary use of a screwdriver is for driving screws and the primary use of the word *dog* is to refer to dogs. This, for Grice, is the word's timeless meaning.

Grice argues for language as a tool that enables two or more people of good will to collaborate in constructing a common context. It is a convincing view, especially when applied to spoken language, where the process starts from a common context and every move in the construction is the result of negotiation. Its application to the translator's world of written language, there is an obvious asymmetry resulting from the passive role that the reader must take. Nevertheless, the process works only to the extent that the writer succeeds in second guessing the reader's reactions to what he writes. In other words, the process can succeed only if the writer and the reader have largely compatible contexts when the text begins and they are able to make largely parallel updates to them as it proceeds.

According to Grice, what a speaker means by an utterance can be divided into what the speaker "says" and what the speaker thereby "implicates" (1961). An author who writes "She was poor but she was honest," for example, says that she was poor and she was honest, but also expects his reader to agree that there is an important contrast of some kind between poverty and honesty. If he writes "He is a professor, but he writes programs," he presumably expects his reader to agree that, by the time one becomes a professor, one no longer indulges in the mundane activity of writing programs. If he writes "He had only a high-school education, but he is a good writer," expects you to find the conjunction of these properties in one person surprising. If the overt, surface meaning of a sentence does not seem to be consistent with the Gricean maxims, and yet the circumstances suggest that the speaker is nonetheless obeying the cooperative principle, the reader and the translator must look for other meanings that could be implied by the sentence.

4.5   Word-for-Word Translation

If there is one thing about translation that everybody agrees on, even if they know only one language and have otherwise devoted almost no thought to the subject, it is that word-for-word translation is often— almost always—bad. But we start out uncommitted as we consider more carefully just how the term *word-for-word* is, or might usefully be used in reference to translation.

Suppose you had to get an extremely important message across to a person whose only language was one of which you had not the slightest knowledge. Maybe the person is the chief of a ferocious band that is holding your anthropologist friend because they are convinced that he has hidden or destroyed their most precious idol. As it happens, you know where the idol has been hidden, and think they will release your friend if you can send them this information by the evening. But you must communicate the information in their language and your only hope for doing this is the dictionary that your anthropologist friend compiled after his last trip and of which you have a copy. In desperation, you compose a message in English, and then write down what you find listed in the dictionary against each of the words that it contains.

If the leader of the ferocious band is intelligent and endowed with a modicum of good will, this desperate attempt at translation might actually secure your friend's release. A lot would clearly turn on just what was in the dictionary. You might, for instance, be surprised that you were unable to tell them to turn right at the tree with the yellow flowers because the dictionary, generally reassuring in its size and coverage, contained no entry for *yellow*. But now you remember your friend once telling you that these people in fact have no word for yellow, and that is not all that unusual. There is another problem about telling them to turn right because, while the dictionary lists a number of words in the other language against the English word *right*, it does not make it clear which of them corresponds to *right* as opposed to *left*, and which to *right* as opposed to *wrong*. You do not even think of having a *right* to something, or to do something. Oh, that he had had time to get out a second edition!

The English text that you wrote, and are now translating, contains a sentence that begins *In order to get the idol back*. On second thoughts, you are tempted to rephrase this because you realize that *get* can mean something special when the word *back* occurs soon after. Maybe, instead of *get...back*, you should use *recover*. But you certainly do not want to sound condescending to these people and a word like *recover* sounds just a little snooty. But, this time, the dictionary turns out to be more helpful than you had even hoped. In the entry for *get*, it has a section on *get...back*, relating it to a particular word in the other language.

It seems that *get...back* can constitute a single construction with its own paragraph in the dictionary, even when *get* and *back* are separated by other words. It is what we referred to earlier as a "particle verb." This is welcome news, but it leaves open the question of where the single word that is offered as a translation should go. Should it be in the place of *get* or of *back*. But this is just a version of a problem that occurs everywhere because the dictionary provides no information on how the words in the other language should be arranged. We know that this is a matter that can vary widely from one language to another. For information on this, we would need a grammar in addition to the dictionary and we would have to study at length before we could assemble sentences that we could count on to be comprehensible. So you keep your sentences short, hoping that the reader's good will, which you are counting on heavily in any case, will enable him to see through the grammatical chaos to the intentions beneath.

We do not need to pursue this improbable story further. A number of points are already clear. Important among them are the following:

1. We should probably not be too literal minded in our interpretation of the term *word*. The sequences of letters that appear between spaces are generally words, but perhaps not the second member of the sequence *a priori* or the last member of *to and fro*. Some groups of space-bounded letter sequences should probably be allowed to count as words even if they are broken up by other words, as in the case of *get...back*, *take...into consideration* and *write...down*. Let us take it that it is the dictionary itself that determines what a word is. If a string is in there, it is a word.

2. Translating word for word, with this liberal notion of what a word is, by no means entails that the dictionary supply only one corresponding word in the other language. A word that has a variety of interpretations can have a corresponding variety of translations, accompanied by notes on the circumstances under which each of them would be appropriate. Where there are synonyms, some groups of corresponding words may remain undifferentiated.

3. We may think of a word-for-word translation as one that maintains too slavishly the word order or other grammatical features of the original. This is an important, but surely an independent matter. One who offers *Is it that this is the book that you seek*

as a translation of the French *Est-ce que c'est le livre que vous cherchez* is guilty, not of word-for-word translation, so much as gross grammatical subservience.

This leaves us with an interpretation of word-for-word translation that is arguably too liberal to be of much use. A translation is word-for-word if it can be seen as having been produced by selecting the appropriate words listed against those in the source text in a comprehensive bilingual dictionary, giving them suitable grammatical forms, and arranging them so as to produce sentences that preserve the meaning of the original. It is, in other words, a translation that fits too well what we have referred to as the "standard model" of translation.

4.6 Situation and Context

It is a commonplace that finding a good translation for a word, phrase, paragraph, or collection of books, must take its context into account. Less clear is just what we should really have in mind when we talk about context. Strings of words are generally embedded in other, longer, strings, and the longer strings are often thought of as constituting the *context* of the shorter ones inside them. But the term is also used to refer to the nonlinguistic situation in which the string is found. A word or phrase uttered during a parliamentary debate, or scrawled on a sign in a street demonstration, must be interpreted in the corresponding context. Let us consider some examples.

The word *book* has several meanings and belongs to several grammatical categories. In the sentence *Have you read the book*, our knowledge of the grammar of English tells us that it is functioning as a noun whereas, in *I will book a table for four*, we know that it is a verb. In the first sentence, we generally expect it to be referring to reading material consisting of pages that are bound together in a certain way. In the second, we take it as a synonym of *reserve*. In the sentence *They decided to book Henry for speeding on the High Street*, we know that the word is also functioning as a verb, but the context tells us that, here, it refers to a formal police procedure that Henry had to undergo. It has nothing to do with reserving anything. In each case, the surrounding words give us information about how to interpret the word *book* over and above what we could learn by looking it up in a dictionary. This is information that comes from the context.

On other occasions, the information we need in order to determine how a word like *book* should be understood comes, not from how the word is embedded in a larger text, but from how that text is embedded in the world. Imagine two doors in a library with signs over them that say *Books* and *Periodicals*. A patron of the library presumably can be relied on to know that the word *book* is a noun in this context and that it is being used to tell readers which of the two doors they should go through depending on whether it is books or periodicals that they are looking for. There seems to be some difference in the meaning of the noun in this context because libraries often bind all but the most recent issues of periodicals into volumes for ease of handling. In other words, they turn them into books. In this situation, however, the positioning of the words *books* and *periodicals* over a pair of doors invites the library user to seek a contrast between them, which presumably will normally happen quite readily. Such a person will go through the *books* door only if the books they are looking for are not expected to be bound collections of periodicals.

Let us suppose that a library patron goes through the *Books* door, and then asks a librarian for help in locating a particular item. He gives the librarian a slip of paper on which is written

```
Bloomfield, Leonard (1925). "Why a linguistic society?".
Language 1: 1-5
```

Perhaps the visitor to the library came through the *Books* door because he knew that Leonard Bloomfield did indeed write a book called *Language*. In any case, the librarian looks at the slip and says, "This is not a book. You need to go to periodicals". It begins to look as though the word *book* has more meanings than we had previously thought. We now know that it can mean something like *A bound volume not containing issues of a periodical*. This is disturbing, however, because it seems to leave us on a slippery slope. Suppose there was a third door in the library labeled *Government Documents*. It is a fair bet that many, if not most, of these would also be bound into volumes but would, nevertheless, be distinguished from books by the library's classification scheme. It seems that we would now have to allow the word *book* the additional meaning *A bound volume not containing government documents or issues of a periodical*. This is a meaning that most people would encounter very rarely, if ever. Maybe they would encounter it only if they visited this particular library.

This story would presumably have developed quite differently if, instead of *Books*, the third door in the library had been labeled *Other Books*. The only trouble with this, of course, is that it supposes that the three sections of the library contain only bound volumes. The phrase *Other Books* establishes a contrast between the things it designates and other things that are also books.

The moral of the story is that the interpretation we give to words, phrases, and other pieces of text are determined only in part from the kind of static information recorded against them in dictionaries. It is determined also by the situations, linguistic and nonlinguistic, in which they are used. A particularly striking way in which this happens is through the contrasts that the situation establishes among various words and phrases. In our highly contrived example, a visitor to the library is invited to interpret the word *Books* in such a way as to make it contrast with *Periodicals*, or with *Periodicals* and *Government Documents*. This person does not have to have contemplated these contrasts before, still less to have learnt any special meanings for the word *book* based on them.

Now, let us consider a similar story which takes place in a university bookstore rather than a library. Like the library, the bookstore has various signs to direct shoppers to the section of the store most likely to contain what they are looking for. One sign says *Books* and another says *Exercise Books*. This time, a contrast is set up between books and exercise books. In this situation, the invitation is to take the word *books* as not referring to exercise books, whether or not it would do this in a more neutral situation. Maintaining the parallel between this situation and the one in the library, we can argue that there is no reason to contemplate different meanings for the noun *book*.

In this case, however, there is a difference because there are languages, notably French and German, where the word on the first sign— *book* by itself—could not be used on the second sign. In French, a bound volume of printed text intended to be read, is a *livre*. A set of blank pages intended for a student to write in, is a *cahier*. In German, they are a *Buch* and a *Heft* respectively. An English-French or an English-German dictionary would therefore surely have to recognize these as separate meanings and provide separate entries for them.

Presumably, the question of whether a word or phrase in one language, say English, is ambiguous should not be allowed to turn into one whether some other language, say French or German, uses different words for it in different contexts. Suppose a school teacher says *If you find any examples of this in the book, then copy them into your books so that we can discuss them next time.* If we take it that the first instance of the word *book* is intended to refer to a printed book, and the second to an exercise book, then how are to decide, on evidence entirely internal to English, whether the word has been used with one or two meanings?

In French, the door that gives access to a room, building, or cupboard is a *porte* whereas, if it gives access to a car or a train, it is a *portière*.

Presumably this is not evidence that the word *door* in English has two corresponding meanings. In most situations the French sentence *Je vais faire une petite promenade* could translated as *I'm going for a little x*, for some *x*. But what should *x* be? It could be *walk, ride*

Now consider another situation. A sign outside a theater says:

OPENING NIGHT September 28
BOOK NOW!

The use of the word *now* encourages us to take *book* to be the verb. Our familiarity with signs of this sort and, in particular, the words *opening night*, leave little doubt about how the word *book* should be interpreted.

Observing phenomena like these, theoreticians have concluded that there are two quite different kinds of context that translators must attend to. They have even sought different names for them, calling one *context*, and the other *cotext*. The view we will take here is that they are substantially the same and that attempting to distinguish them can be a source of confusion. To be sure, textual context is a richer source of grammatical information, but information on the senses of words and phrases, and the meanings of larger segments of a text is derived from both sources, and in essentially the same way.

Consider the following extract from an imaginary narrative.

> Mary was intimidated by the size of the library at first and was unsure which of the big oak doors she should go through. But then she noticed that one was marked "Books" and the other "Periodicals". This gave her some confidence.

On reading this we interpret the word *books* just as we would if we were in the library, standing in front of the two oak doors. In other words, it matters little whether we find ourselves physically in the situation that gives some words their interpretation, or whether we are placed in that situation by the text itself. Indeed, this is just what presumably happened earlier when I first invited you to imagine doors in a library with signs over them.

In the remainder of this chapter, I will frequently invite the reader to imagine a situation in which some piece of language is used. This will generally simply be a convenient way of suggesting some surrounding text that places the reader in that situation without being specific about the particular words and phrases that have this effect.

Imagine a public, or semi-public, building—say an office or a hotel—with a short flight of stairs up to the front door. A sign by the front door says *Entrance*. At the bottom of the stairs, on one side or the other, is a sign bearing the words *Accessible Entrance* with an arrow pointing to the left or the right. To many people, the primary meaning of the word *accessible* is "capable of being reached" as in *accessible by car* and, by extension of this, *at accessible prices*. These could be rendered in French by *accessible* and *abordable*. But the situation we are considering is one in which the most obvious way of entering the building, and the one that is explicitly marked as the entrance, is by a route that contrasts with the one marked as being *accessible*. Fortunately, we recall that the word *accessible* has recently acquired a new meaning—something like *reachable by a handicapped person*. So we would probably translate it as *aménagé*.

The meaning we have arrived at as being the most plausible one for the phrase *accessible entrance* would be quite a reasonable guess even in the absence of the nonlinguistic clues that we have imagined. But it becomes entirely more appealing in a situation where the accessible entrance is pointedly contrasted with something else that is marked as the default entrance. And this contrast becomes salient because of a mental image that has been established in the mind of the reader in a linguistic or nonlinguistic manner.

5

Linguistics

A translation is a linguistic artifact and translating is a linguistic activity. We should therefore naturally expect the study of translations and translation to fall within the field of linguistics. That is the perspective on translation that we take up in this chapter. Linguistics is a large and complex field comprising numerous, sometimes incompatible, theories even on quite fundamental issues. There is general agreement, however, that utterances have a hierarchical organization, with sound structure placed, by convention, at the bottom, various aspects of meaning at the top, and grammar, also in several forms and varieties, in between. The field of linguistics as a whole therefore has this same hierarchical organization.

Language naturally makes contact with the greater world in which it is embedded at the top and the bottom of the hierarchy. At the top are the things it is used to talk about, and at the bottom are the sounds and symbols that carry its messages. There is much in between, and that is the subject matter of linguistics. Sometimes language is used purely internally so that the sounds are not physically realized and sometimes the things that are referred to are imaginary and are nowhere to be found in the real world.

We tend to give more attention to language as it is used externally for communicating among two or more people. This is not so much because external language use is more important. After all, most of us are speaking to ourselves whenever we are awake, conscious, and not talking or listening to someone else. But public language use is more open to public scrutiny so that, where it is concerned, it is easier to at least agree on what the phenomena are.

Figure 5.1 is a sketch of the hierarchical structure of the simple sentence *The dog chased the cat* as a linguist might see it. At the very

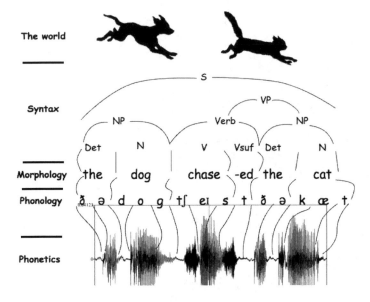

FIGURE 5.1 Linguistic Levels

bottom is the physical stream of sound itself. We show it as a wavy line such as one might see on the screen of an oscilloscope or a sound spectrograph. This is the subject matter of *phonetics.*

The level above belongs to *phonology* and we have shown the utterance with symbols from the international phonetic alphabet. On the level of morphology, the sounds have been collected into *morphemes,* which are the shortest units of language that have their own meanings. Notice that we represent the second syllable of the word *chased* as a separate morpheme because it makes its own contribution to the meaning of the word by giving it the past tense.

Syntax, on the next higher level of abstraction, can impose very different kinds of structure on the sentences, the differences depending on the theoretical stance adopted. At the very least, morphemes and words are collected into phrases, and these into larger phrases, and so on up to the level of the sentence. In the example we have used labels, like familiar parts of speech, from Table 5.1.

How many levels should be distinguished above that of syntax is a matter for debate. But at the highest linguistic level, language once again makes contact with the world outside. Here, however, the situation is altogether more complicated than at the level of speech sounds. As we shall argue in greater detail later, the things that

TABLE 5.1 Parts of Speech

S	Sentence
NP	Noun Phrase
Det	Determiner (or Article)
N	Noun
VP	Verb Phrase
V	Verb
VSuf	Verbal suffix

language can be used to talk about embrace not only those that make up the real world, but also those that inhabit limitless imaginary, contradictory, theoretical and entirely abstract worlds. They include the persons and objects in those worlds and also assertions, theories, and questions about those things.

Languages differ from one another on all the levels that linguists recognize, and possibly in other ways also. A complete characterization of a language therefore involves descriptions of its characteristics on each of the various levels. Taken together, these descriptions constitute a *grammar* of the language. All of them play a crucial role in translation, though some more centrally than others. The lowest levels—those concerned with the sound and writing systems—usually do not play a central role. To be sure, translators have sometimes to deal with rhyme and rhythm in poetry or advertising material. They may sometimes be confronted with passages purporting to represent atypical pronunciations or foreign accents. These are problems that translators might very well discuss at length among themselves, because they are unusual and particularly challenging. We, on the other hand, will give them little attention for that very same reason. They are not among the everyday concerns of the journeyman translator, and these are our principal concern.

We will, however, consider some aspects of the sound and writing systems of language, not because of any specific relevance that they have to translation, but because they provide a particularly clear example of a characteristic property of language, namely that of being a digital, as opposed to an analog system. This is a characteristic that goes largely unnoticed, but it is one that is of particular interest for translation.

5.1 Inflectional Morphology

In the days when English gentlemen were taught Latin, and often also Greek, while steadfastly avoiding all contact with other foreign languages, many of them thought of grammar as being about declensions and conjugations because these were the aspects of the classical languages that had the greatest effect on their lives. A true gentleman could translate the *Aeneid* at sight but all of them could reel off the principal parts of any irregular verb and provide the rarest entries in its conjugation. In Latin and Greek nouns and adjectives, but especially verbs, had such a rich set of *inflectional* forms, and many people thought of these as constituting the entire grammar of the Language. I knew a Frenchman who had studied Latin and English in school and who said he found English easier because it had no grammar.

The way in which words are constructed from smaller parts is called *morphology* and it is true that there is much more to it in some languages than others. There is virtually no morphology in Chinese, but a huge amount in Turkish and Finnish. In English, there is very little of the kind of morphology that is so prominent in Latin and Greek, though there is another kind, called *derivational* morphology, in which English is quite rich. French verbs have a rich morphology, and German nouns and adjectives interact with one another morphologically in ways that can be quite perplexing.

Inflectional morphology has two distinguishing features. First, it is not optional. Every noun *must* be inflected, which usually means that it must have an affix, or some other way of showing certain properties that every noun must have, such as number, gender, or case, when it appears in a text. Something similar may be required of adjectives, verbs, pronouns, and so forth. In English, every noun must be singular or plural; every verb must be in the present or the past tense. Every present-tense verb must also carry a marking that shows the number of the subject, even though this is exactly the same information as appears on the subject itself. The -s suffix in *dogs* marks it as plural and the same suffix on *runs* marks it as singular. This perversity is very minor by comparison with what inflections can do in some languages.

The second characteristic of inflectional morphology is that it is generally *fusional*. What this means is that the affixes and other devices that show that a textual word has certain properties typically ascribe more than one property to the words they are applied to. Appending -s to a noun like *dog* seems to do little more than mark it as plural. Appending it to *run*, on the other hand, marks it as singular, and also as being in the present tense.

It may seem that English, unlike Latin, violates the requirement that inflection is obligatory. Latin *canis* is marked as singular by the suffix -is, while *canes* is marked as plural by the suffix -es. In English, *dogs* is marked as plural by the suffix -*s*, but there is no suffix that marks *dog* as singular. However we can tell that the word is in fact singular if we find it a text because it is only the singular form that can appear without and inflectional suffix. Notice that we must say *the dog chases the cat*, and not *the dog chase the cat*. So, one of the ways of marking a word has having certain morphological properties, is by abstaining form adding a suffix.

As we have said, the most common way marking a word morphologically is with an affix—a prefix or suffix. The stems of words, as well as the affixes that combine with them are referred to as *morphemes*, which are characterized as *minimal meaningful units*, that is, items that convey some kind of meaning and are not composed of smaller units that also have this property.

There is an aspect of the way morphemes combine to form words that we take note of in passing, but will not pursue at length because it is of minimal concern to translators. It is called *morphophonemics* in the spoken language, and spelling rules in the written language (Cummings 1988). Spelling rules account for the following kinds of phenomenon: Adding -*s* to *try* gives *tries* and not *trys*; adding -*ing* to *run* gives *running* and not *runing*, and adding -*ing* to *love* gives *loving*, and not *loveing*.

Morphophonemics can become quite complex in some languages, notably Sanskrit and Finnish, but they are not a major concern for translators who can generally be counted on to have mastered them long before they could claim to be translators. They are, however matters of considerable concern for the designers of machine translation, and other language-processing, computer systems.

5.1.1 Gender

A native English speaker is struck in his first few French lessons, that every noun is either masculine or feminine. The same is true of the other modern Romance languages. In Latin and German, there are three genders and every noun belongs to one of them. Generally speaking, if a word refers to a class of objects that have a natural gender, then that is also the gender of the word. But even this is not true all the time. The German word for *girl* is *Mädchen*, which is neuter. For the most part, the assignment of words to genders is arbitrary, and it can differ even in closely related languages. The word for bill, or account, is masculine in French (*compte*), Italian (*conto*) and Portuguese (*conto*), but feminine in Spanish (*quenta*).

It is true that the shape of a word sometimes provides clues as to its gender. An Italian noun that ends in -*o* stands a very good chance of being masculine, whereas one ending in -*a* will probably be feminine. But when Don Giovanni sings *La ci darem la mano* (THERE I'LL GIVE YOU MY HAND), he is not only trying to seduce Zerlina, but reminding the linguistically sensitive among us that the Italian word *mano* (HAND) is feminine. The large class of Italian words that end in -*e* give no clue as to their gender. The point, however, is not that there are occasional correlations between the gender of a noun and some other property that it has, but that there is rarely any correlation with semantic properties that would be helpful to a non-native speaker trying to learn the language.

German has a number of derivational suffixes resulting in a noun which is generally feminine. One such is -*ung* which is added to certain verbal stems to yield a noun that refers to the state of affairs as a result of carrying out the action referred to by the verb. The verb *einladen* means *to invite* and *Einladung* is an *invitation*. The verb *erinnern* means *to remember* and an *Erinnerung* is a *memory*; *übersetzen* means *to translate* and an *Übersetzung* is a *translation*.

Several other derivational suffixes work the same way, and the gender of the resulting noun is feminine more often than not, though some of these suffixes yield neuter nouns. Another example is -*schaft*, which forms nouns often denoting collections of people from other nouns. From *Freund* (FRIEND) it gives *Freundschaft* (FRIENDSHIP), and from *Meister* (MASTER, CHAMPION) it gives *Meisterschaft* (*championship*).

Similar correlations to these are found in almost all languages with gender systems. Thus, French words that end in -*ation*, such as *la station* (THE STATION) are generally feminine, and a parallel regularity is found in the other Romance languages. The French suffix -*eur*, corresponding to the English suffix -*or*, when used to derive from a verb a noun referring to the person or thing that does the action named by the verb, is masculine, as in *contrôleur* (CONDUCTOR) and *directeur* (DIRECTOR). But, when it is used to derive from an adjective a noun that names the property that adjective predicates of the nouns it modifies, it is feminine, as in *largeur* (WIDTH) from *large* (WIDE) and *rougeur* (REDNESS) from *rouge* (RED).

Even though most of the things that nouns can refer to have no natural gender, there are sometimes regularities that have no apparent motivation in the modern language that a language learner can use as a crutch. The names of the seasons and the months are masculine in German as are wines and spirits. The names of trees and many flowers are feminine, and chemical elements are generally neuter. French trees are usually masculine, whereas their fruits are feminine.

Native speakers of French have learnt the genders of even small and remote countries, states and provinces, and the knowledge is important because it has an unexpected influence on the preposition that is used with these names. Thus *She is from France* is *Elle est de la France* where *de* is a very common preposition corresponding much of the time to English *of*. On the other hand, *She is from Portugal* is *Elle est du Portugal*, where *du* is an amalgam of that same preposition and the definite article *le*. The sentence *She is going to France* must be translated as *Elle va en France* whereas *She is going to Portugal* must be *Elle va au Portugal*. The word *en* is one of the prepositions that correspond approximately to English *in* and *du* combines *de* and *le*. The names of most countries are feminine, but several, including Portugal, Belize, Cambodia, Mexico, and Zimbabwe are masculine and must be given the appropriate prepositions corresponding to *in* and *to* in English.

Quebec, Nevada, and Texas are masculine. British Columbia, New York, and California are feminine. *He was born in California* is *Il est né en California* whereas *He was born in Texas* is *Il est né au Texas*.

Occasional correlations between the gender of a noun and some property of its sound or spelling are vestiges of an earlier stage in the history of the language when words with a certain form could almost always be counted on to have a certain gender. As we noted, this is still generally the case with words ending in *-o* and *-a* in Italian. The German endings *-ung* and *-schaft* may have once been separate words whose gender was feminine.

When conflicts arise between the forms of a word and its semantic properties, as is by no means uncommon, the grammar generally wins. A word like *mano* in Italian, which is feminine despite the fact that it ends in *-o* is quite unusual. German has a number of ways of forming diminutives. One of these is to add the suffix *-chen*. The resulting noun is invariably neuter. The common word *Mädchen*, the diminutive form of *Magd*, has become the standard word for *girl*, but is neuter. Exactly the same is true of the Czech word *děvče* (GIRL). There are some diminutives in Dutch, like *jongetje* (LITTLE BOY) and *vrouwtje* (LITTLE WOMAN) that are semantically masculine or feminine, but grammatically neuter.

When a German pronoun is required to refer back to a person that was introduced into the discourse with the word *Mädchen*, semantics would dictate that one should use *sie* (SHE) whereas grammar would seem to require *es* (IT). Generally, if the pronoun follows very closely after *Mädchen*, then *es* is preferred, otherwise *sie*. It has also been suggested that semantically based agreement is preferred when the reference is to an older woman, but this does not have the status of a *rule*. Thomas Mann's novel *Der Zauberberg* (THE MAGIC MOUNTAIN) contains the sentence *Ein Mädchen stich dicht an Hans Castorp vorbei und es ihn fast mit dem Arme berührte, und dabei pfiff sie* A GIRL BRUSHED PASSED HANS CASTORP, AND SHE ALMOST TOUCHED HIM WITH HER ARM, WHISTLING AS SHE WENT. The first instance of *she* translates the German *es*, which is neuter, and the second *sie*, which is feminine.

Anomalous genders cannot always be blamed on grammar. The English word *wife* is cognate with the German word *Weib*, which still retains its neuter gender from an earlier age. It is, however, a word that is enjoying its declining years, having been generally replaced by the very feminine word *Frau* in the meanings both of *woman* and *wife*.

Needless to say, a person who becomes a professional translator has long since left behind the frustrations occasioned by internalizing genders in a second-language learner. He knows the genders of almost all the words he encounters and he simply looks up those he does not know. The problem that grammatical gender presents to the translator is quite different. In fact, it arises precisely in the situations that are unproblematic for the language learner, namely where the grammatical gender straightforwardly reflects the natural gender.

If two people focus on someone on the other side of the room, one may say to the other *Is that your cousin?* If they are speaking French, however, they must say either *Est-ce que c'est ton cousin?* or *Est-ce que c'est ta cousine?* A choice must be made between *cousin* and *cousine* depending on whether the intended reference is to the man or the woman. The problem for the translator who finds this in a written text is that the information on the intended reference may simply not be available or may, at least, be hard to find. Now consider the inverse situation. The text is in French. What we know is that two people on this side of the room are looking at a man and a woman on the other side of the room. One member of the first pair says *Est-ce que c'est ta cousine?*. A natural translation into English would seem to be *Is that your cousin?* The trouble is that, unlike the French, this does not make it clear which of the two people is being referred to. Assuming this is important, the inventive translator must come up with something like *Is that woman your cousine?* And, of course, even this will not work if the female on the other side of the room is a girl and not a woman.

The example we have just been considering might become considerably more problematic if pursued one sentence further. Suppose the response to *Est-ce que c'est ta cousine?* were *Non. Je n'ai pas de cou-*

sine. No, I do not have a (female) cousin. The English translation certainly cannot be *No. I do not have a female cousin,* not only because it is highly unidiomatic but because, in the unlikely event of anyone actually saying it, it would imply that the speaker did, in fact, have a male cousin. We leave this problem as an exercise for the reader because we, in fact, have no good solution to propose.

The great Czech linguist Roman Jakobson put his finger on the problem we are facing here. He observed that the difference between languages consists not in what each one empowers its speakers to express, so much as in what each one forces its speakers to express. When speaking of many things that have a natural gender in French, and many other languages, I simply do not have the option of leaving the gender unspecified. In English, I not only have this option, but it is one I exercise very frequently.

On occasion, morphological categories, and particularly gender, can cause more subtle problems. A famous example of this, which attracted Jakobson's attention, is provided by Heinrich Heine's untitled poem consisting of the following two verses:

> Ein Fichtenbaum steht einsam
> Im Norden auf kahler Höh';
> Ihn schläfert; mit weißer Decke
> Umhüllen ihn Eis und Schnee.

> Er träumt von einer Palme,
> Die fern im Morgenland,
> Einsam und schweigend trauert
> Auf brennender Felsenwand. (*Buch de Leider,* 33, 1827)

The most well known of many translations into English, by the Scottish poet James Thomson (1834–82) is as follows:

> A pine-tree standeth lonely
> In the North on an upland bare;
> It standeth whitely shrouded
> With snow, and sleepeth there.

> It dreameth of a Palm Tree
> Which far in the East alone,
> In mournful silence standeth
> On its ridge of burning stone.[23]

---

23. Heinrich Heine. 1887. *Poems Selected from Heinrich Heine.* Edited by Kate Freiligrath Kroeker. Translated by James Thomson. London: Walter Scott, 67

Jakobson points out, as many others had before, that the contrast between the genders of the words *Fichtenbaum* (PINE-TREE or, more strictly, SPRUCE), which is masculine, and *Palme* (palm tree), which is feminine prompt an erotic symbolism. Since these associations are lacking in English, Jakobson judges that "English renditions of these lines make an insipid, rhetorical impression." In Russian, a language with grammatical gender, both words are feminine (сосна *sosna* and пальма *pal'ma*). This elicits from Jakobson the observation that "even by such an artist of Russian verse as Lermontov, native readers feel a peculiar, let us say, sugary tinge." Finally, he remarks that "French readers and listeners are amused or bewildered by Heine's octet when translated in their mother tongue, which calls both trees by masculine nouns : le pin and le palmier" (cite[109]jakobson).

In a less well known English translation, American poet Emma Lazarus (1849–87) confronts this problem directly and offers the following translation:

> There stands a lonely pine-tree
> In the north, on a barren height;
> He sleeps while the ice and snow flakes
> Swathe him in folds of white.
>
> He dreemth of a palm tree
> Far in the sun-rise land.
> Lonely and silent longing
> On her burning bank of sand[24]

As we shall see, the problem of what a language forces its speakers to express is pervasive. There are many grammatical categories other than gender where it arises in one language or another and limitless situations where it arises in the choice of words. The part of the grammar where the problem is most striking is morphology, and especially inflectional morphology. This is presumably because inflection is that part of morphology that is concerned with the various forms of a word that the grammar makes available to speakers. It is not possible to use the word except in one of these forms and choice entails some substantive semantic commitment. In translation, the information required by this semantic commitment may not be explicit in the original and has therefore to be inferred with varying degrees of confidence, by the translator. Before considering other common grammatical categories, we consider inflectional systems more generally.

---

24. Emma Lazarus, trans. 1881. *Poems and Ballads of Heinrich Heine*. New York: R. Worthington, 161

5.1.2 Tense

We have seen that it is important to distinguish word types from word tokens. This particular distinction is important enough that some languages have two plural forms for *word*, one of which is used for types, and the other for tokens. The German word *Wörterbuch* (literally WORD BOOK) refers to a dictionary, and the plural of *Wort* (WORD) when it refers to types is *Wörter*. But the sentence *He described it in a few words* would be *Er hat es mit wenigen Worten beschrieben* (HE HAS IT WITH FEW WORDS DESCRIBED) uses the plural form *Worte*, in its dative variant *Worten*, because it refers to tokens.

The term *word* also has other ambiguities. We say that *chase* and *chased* are different *forms* of the same word. We would say this also of *sing* and *sung*, or even of *am* and *be*. Referring to French, we would say it of *reçois*, *recevons*, *reçues*, and many other *forms* of the verb *recevoir*.

The intuition behind this usage is presumably the following: a speaker wishes to construct a sentence about one thing pursuing another. He chooses the phrase *the dog* to refer to the first of these, and *the bird* for the second. Actually, however, he wants to say that more than one bird was involved, and so he uses the plural for *birds*, to make this clear. For the verb he chooses *chase*. He wants to say that the pursuit happened some time ago. To express this, he chooses, not another word, but a particular form of one of the words already chosen. He chooses the form *chased*. So the sentence he produces is *The dog chased the birds*. The point is that the choice of the verb, and of the form that it will take, are largely independent.

Now consider the following variant of this story. Suppose the speaker wishes to say, not that a particular pursuit of some birds by a dog took place at some past time, but that it is something that happens regularly. The same three words are chosen, but now the present tense is selected instead of the past. Given that the instigator of the chase is a single dog, *chases* is chosen as the form of the verb. If there was to be more than one dog, or if it were the birds that were chasing the dog, then the appropriate form would have been *chase*.

The moral of these stories is twofold. First the factors determining the choice of a word, and of the form of that word that will be used, can be largely independent. Second, the form of the word that is used may not be an independent choice on the part of the speaker but may be required by the grammar of the languages, given the other choices that have been made. The distinction between present and past tense corresponds to a difference in meaning and reflects the speaker's choice. Crucially, however, the speaker is obliged to choose present or past;

leaving this open is simply not an option in English, as it is in Chinese. The distinction between singular and plural is determined automatically once the choices concerning the subject of the sentence have been settled. Once again, the speaker does not have the option of leaving the number unspecified.

The grammars of English and many other languages require that a verb in every sentence have the form associated with either its present or its past tense. This does not mean that one can always tell which of these tenses it has, because forms are often ambiguous. Thus, the verb *let* in *They let it happen* is consistent with either the present or the past tense. It also does not mean that that present and past are the only tenses provided for in English grammar. It means only that these are the two tenses for which verbs can have differing forms. Verbs in the Romance languages have a larger variety of morphological forms. In French, *recevrons* is one of several forms for the future tense, and *recevrions* is one of the conditional forms. English can make these same sense distinctions, but it does it not with different forms of the verb but by adding so-called *auxiliary* or *modal* verbs. So, where the French would say *Nous recevrions*, English speakers might say *We would receive*.

We have seen that the inflection that is used for a word in a particular context is determined in part by the intended meaning, and in part by the larger grammatical structure in which it is embedded. Tense, for example, generally reflects how the state or event being described is situated in time relative to some understood reference time, usually the time at which the utterance is being made. I would say *I wrote the letter* if I wanted it to be understood that the writing of the letter was completed before this utterance is made. If it more or less overlaps the time of the utterance, then I would normally say *I am writing the letter*. This is the so-called *progressive* form of the English present tense. The simplest form of the present tense, *I write the letter*, is usually used, not for this situation, but for the one in which I am in the habit of writing a letter under the circumstances we are discussing, or if I would be the one to write the letter, should the appropriate circumstances arise. There are many verbs in English, however, that do not admit a progressive tense,[25] notably those like *know* and *like* that refer to states rather than events.

We have noted that English verbs do not manifest future tense with different word forms, but through the use of auxiliary verbs. Because

---

25. Strictly speaking, the term *progressive* refers to an *aspect* and not a *tense*. However this usage is common when referring to the morphology of verbs

they are manifested in this way, these tenses are referred to as *periphrastic*. Thus, we say *I will write the letter* or *I shall write the letter*, the latter being less common in American English. The British prefer *shall* for the first person, and *will* for the other two persons. Both sets of dialects use *shall* in the third person to add a component of obligation to the simple future tense. This form is common in rules and laws, as in *The secretary shall then read the minutes* and *There shall be no smoking in the library*. It was not always so. Mr. Bennet, in *Pride and Prejudice*,[26] says to Mrs. Bennet of their daughter Elizabeth *Let her be called down. She shall hear my opinion.* [Ch. 20].

A special use of first-person *shall* occurs in offers, as in *Shall I get to the station before you do?*, which is an offer, as opposed to *Will I get to the station before you do?* which is a question about what the future holds. This is a peculiarity of English which tends not to have a standard equivalent in other languages. Seeking a French translation of *Shall I meet you at the station?*, we might settle on *Veux-tu que je te cherche à la gare?* (DO YOU WANT ME TO LOOK FOR YOU AT THE STATION). However, since *shall* is the standard form for the first person, at least in British English, this could also be simply a question about what the future holds, in which case it would be more appropriate to say *Est-ce que je te retrouverai à la gare?* (WILL I SEE YOU AT THE STATION). Notice the present tense in the first case, where the question is really about a decision that is being made now, but the future tense in the second case where the question is really about the future.

A translator who was called upon to render a text into English would doubtless be familiar with these, and numerous other subtleties concerning the use of the words *shall* and *will* in the relevant dialect and would very rarely give them any thought. It would only be if the original was a period piece, say from the nineteenth century, that he would, of course, consider corresponding departures from standard modern usage. In that period, one frequently finds second-person questions formulated using *shall*. *Pride and Prejudice* contains the following examples:

Where shall you change horses? [Ch. 37]
Shall you like to have such a brother? [Ch. 59]
Shall you ever have enough courage to announce to Lady Catherine what is to befall her? [Ch. 60]

and *Emma* contains two instances of *What shall you do?*[Ch. 7 and 10].

On March 18, 1980, Governor Robert F. Kennedy of Massachusetts endorsed Senator Martin Luther King Jr.'s presidential bid during a

---

26. Jane Austen. 1813. *Pride and Prejudice*. Whitehall: T. Egerton

rally in Boston, Massachusetts, with the words, *The dream lives on, and the hope shall never die.* The choice of *shall* is surely problematic. It is more striking because it is used with the third-person, and is therefore not canonical. So we take it that the governor is either making a decree which he expects the world to abide by, or that he is giving a personal assurance that the dream will be immortal. The effect that would have been achieved with *will* might have been more striking because it would have invited the interpretation that the immortality of the hope was somehow written in the sky.

There are, in fact, many commonly used ways of expressing the future tense in English and, once again, it is beyond our scope to explore them in detail. The following variants of a simple sentence are among those that can be interpreted as referring to future time in some context:

1. *I shall/will leave for Chicago at four o'clock.*
2. *I shall/will be leaving for Chicago at four o'clock.*
3. *I leave for Chicago at four o'clock.*
4. *I am leaving for Chicago at four o'clock.*
5. *I am going to leave for Chicago at four o'clock.*
6. *I am going to be leaving for Chicago at four o'clock.*

Version (2) can reasonably be called the future progressive which is typically used to situate the action referred to relative to a period of time that has been established in the context. So the above example might be expanded as follows: *I cannot meet at the end of the afternoon because I shall/will be leaving for Chicago at four o'clock.* A variant of this is exemplified in *We will have to finish early every Thursday because I shall/will be leaving for Chicago at four o'clock.* This is an event that will be happening routinely, every Thursday at four o'clock. Version (3) is appropriate when something is ordained or set down as in a schedule. In this case, it suggests that when and whether I go to Chicago is a matter that is out of my hands. Versions (4) and (5) are similar, except that they suggest that I am indeed the person responsible for the plan that has been made. I am going to leave for Chicago at four o'clock because that is what I have determined to do. The shorter utterance *I am leaving* strongly suggests a future time that is very close to the present—I am leaving right now. *I shall/will leave* suggests a more remote time. Version (6) is also similar, but suggests even more determination on my part.

Some of these possibilities exist in other Indo-European languages, but those involving progressive tenses generally do not. But, French *Je pars pour à Chicago à quatre heures*, Italian *Vado a Chicago domani*, German *Ich gehe nach Chicago morgen*[27] etc. correspond in essentially all respects to version (3).

The simple future tense with *will* is sometimes used in situations where the temporal reference is clearly to the present. Suppose the door bell rings. Someone may say *Oh, that will be Mary now.* Consider also:

> *Do you know where I can find Mary?*
> *I think she will be at home now.*

Tenses are normally thought of as belonging to the grammar of a language to the extent that they are expressed by morphological devices, such as suffixes, or are accompanied by other kinds of idiosyncratic grammatical phenomena. More importantly, languages that have tenses generally do not give the speaker the option of not using them. The distinction between present and past tense in English is expressed by suffixes in so-called *weak* verbs in English (*walk/walked*), and by changes in the stem vowel in strong verbs (*swim/swam/swum*). Some verbs are *suppletive*. In other words, they have completely different forms where more regular verbs add affixes. Examples are *catch/caught*, and *have/had*. The simple future tense does not involve changes to the form of the verb itself. It does, however, involve two members of a small class of so called *modal* verbs, namely *shall* and *will*, which have limited and special distributions. Modal verbs only have finite forms—they have no infinitive and no participles. In the third person singular, they take no *-s* suffix. They are typically used with the infinitive of another verb following, with no intervening *to*.

We have seen that the forms we commonly associate with future time can also be used in other circumstances. The same is true of the so-called *past tense.* Consider the following sentences:

> *If he went to the station, he probably met Mary.*
> *If he went to the station, he would probably meet Mary*

The first is a clear reference to past time. It means approximately *If it is the case that he went to the station....* The second, however, refers to present or future time. It means something more like *If he should go to the station* or, using another so-called past tense form, *If he were to go to the station...* or *Were he to go to the station....*

Translating these sentences into German, we would also have some decisions to make. Obvious renderings would include

---

27. Whether *gehen* is the appropriate choice for the verb, rather than, say, *fahren* or *fliegen* is, of course, a separate issue.

Wenn er an den Bahnhof gegangen ist, hat er wahrscheinlich Maria begegnet
Wenn er an den Bahnhof gegangen wäre, hätte er wahrscheinlich Maria begegnet

A more literal translation of the first sentence back into English would be *If he has gone to the station, he has probably met Mary*. The second sentence is just the same except that the verbs are in the subjunctive mood. The subjunctive is also sometimes called the *irrealis* mood because the situation referred to is not claimed to actually exist in the present, or any other, real time. In the present situation, we contemplate the possibility of someone's having gone to the station whereas, in reality, he may not have.

As we have seen, the grammars of English and some other languages require the use of a past tense verb in some clauses beginning with *if* or *when*, even though the reference is clearly to present time. They also require use of the present tense to refer to future time, as in *If/When he goes to the station, he will meet Mary*. The constraints placed on these so called *sequence of tenses* phenomena (*concordance des temps* in French) differ even among closely related languages so that some time must be devoted to them by language teachers. The English sentence *I will leave when he gets here*, for example, would be rendered in French as *Je partirai quand il sera arrivé* (I WILL DEPART WHEN HE WILL HAVE ARRIVED), and not *Je partirai quand il arrive* (I WILL DEPART WHEN HE ARRIVES).

Many languages are like Chinese in having none of these requirements on numbers and tenses and would do nothing to mark them in sentences like these, where they make no semantic sense, or in many other sentences where they can be easily inferred from the context. English makes a distinction between progressive and non-progressive tenses that is not made in a great many languages, including most European languages. Those that do allow such a distinction, like Spanish and, to a lesser degree Italian, use the progressive variant much more sparingly than English.

In verbs, a distinction between singular and plural is made in present, but not past, tense forms. Thus, we say *The dog runs* and *The dogs run* but *The dog ran* and *The dogs ran*. In most other languages where there is number agreement, it covers a greater proportion of the potential cases.

Translation from a language like Chinese into a language like English frequently gives rise to one of the classic translation problems in which substantive information that is needed to choose the appropriate tense or number must be supplied when it is not given explicitly in the source text. A similar problem arises when translating into English from, say, French with respect to the progressive, from Russian or Arabic with respect to aspect and so on. Usually, only one of the alternatives is possible in the given context. The French *Il écrit un article sur la traduction* could only be *He is writing a paper on translation*, unless this was an activity he repeated at regular intervals. On the other hand, *Il écrit un article dans chaque numéro* would have to be *He writes a paper in each issue.*

A similar problem faces the translator from English into French because the distinction between progressive and non-progressive in English reflects very poorly that between the the imperfect and perfect tenses in French. Thus, the simplest translation of *We went to the market last Monday* would presumably be *Nous sommes allés au marché lundi dernier*, whereas *We went to the market every Monday* would be *Nous allions au marché tous les lundis.* This leaves the question of how to translate simply *We went to the market on Monday.* One must assimilate its meaning to one of the other two on the basis of the context, which may be more or less helpful on the matter.

The distinction between perfect and imperfect is, of course, strictly one of aspect rather than tense. In other words, it is concerned with whether the event referred to is bounded in time, rather than where it is located in time relative to the present or to some other temporal reference point. In the languages of Western Europe, essentially every sentence makes a distinction in tense, while distinctions of aspect arise more rarely. In many other languages, this situation is reversed. After a moment's reflection, it should be clear that the problems that distinctions of aspect present to someone formulating a sentence in Russian arise most frequently in the past tense, because it is only for past events that the question of whether they have been completed or are still going on can be settled.

Russian is a language in which aspect distinctions are prominent. The English *I wrote a letter* would be rendered either as Яа писал письмо (*Ja pisal pis'mo*) or as Я написал письмо (*Ja napisal pis'mo*). The former would be appropriate in a context where I wrote a letter, say, every month, and the latter where only one letter and one writing event was in question.

As we have already remarked, the distinction between perfective and imperfective turns on whether the action referred to is complete, so that it could only apply with difficulty to the present tense because anything that is going on now can hardly already be complete. The morphological verb forms appropriate for the present tense are therefore regularly used for the future in Russian. Thus Я пишу (*Ja pishu*)—the imperfective form—means *I write* or *I am writing*, but Я напишу (*Ja napishu*) means *I will write*. This latter form is perfective; it cannot be used to translate *I will be writing* or *I will write* with reference to repeated events. For this, a periphrastic form, analogous to the form with *shall* or *will* in English, is used. Thus, the Russian for *I will be writing* is Я буду писать (*Ja budu pisat'*).

5.1.3 Mood

The great majority of sentences, especially in written text, state facts and are therefore in the *indicative mood*. By contrast, a sentence that expresses a command is generally in the *imperative* mood. *Give me the hammer* differs from the simple indicative sentence *You give me the hammer* in that the initial *You* is omitted. This is the way imperatives are typically formed in English.

We take the deleted word to be *you* because the implied subject is invariably the person addressed, that is, the person for whom the second person pronoun *you* is reserved. Other languages with similar structures to English also have imperatives that differ from indicatives by the omission of a pronoun, but the verb retains the form it would have had if the pronoun had been the equivalent of the English *you*. So, in French, we have *Donnez-moi le marteau* (GIVE ME THE HAMMER). In the more familiar form, *Donne moi le marteau*, the parallel is somewhat less clear because the written form of the word *donne* does not carry the suffix *-s* that it would have in the indicative and which is, in any case, not pronounced.

German imperatives are a minor variant of those in English and French, especially in the familiar forms. *Give me the hammer*, in the singular familiar form is a word-for-word translation of the English: *Gib mir den Hammer*. In the so-called polite form, however, the second-person pronoun is retained, but it is placed after the verb as in *Geben Sie mir den Hammer*, where *Sie* is the pronoun in question.

In real life, these grammatical forms, which are canonical imperatives, are probably not the commonest way of giving commands in English, and many other languages. A more peremptory way of telling someone to do something parallels the German polite imperative, though no one would call it polite in English. Examples are *You give me the hammer*, and *Don't you ever say that to me again*. More common are less peremptory forms like *Would you (please) pass me the hammer*, *Would you be so kind as to...*, and so forth.

Categories like tense, aspect, and number, that are often manifested through inflectional morphology, have obvious semantic correlates and this is clearly true of imperatives. Some may wish to quibble about examples like the French *Les petits oiseaux sont arrivés fatigués* (THE LITTLE BIRDS ARRIVED TIRED) on the grounds that what is semantically plural is the word *oiseaux*, the plural forms of the other words being dictated by the rules of agreement. But there are other morphological forms for which it can be argued much more strongly that no semantic correlate exists. The subjunctive mood in French is a case in point. The following are examples such as one might find in an introductory textbook for foreigners learning the language:

1. Je veux qu'il le *fasse* (I WANT HIM TO DO IT)
2. Je ne crois pas qui'il *puisse* le faire (I DO NOT BELIEVE THAT HE CAN DO IT.)
3. Je le laisse tranquille pour qu'il *puisse* le faire (I'LL LEAVE HIM ALONE SO THAT HE CAN DO IT.)
4. Il est la seule personne qui *puisse* le faire (HE IS THE ONLY PERSON THAT COULD DO IT.)

However, the English *He is the only one that can do it* would probably be rendered in French as *Il est la seule personne qui* peut *le faire*.

The words *fasse* and *puisse* are subjunctive forms of the verbs *faire* (DO, MAKE) and *pouvoir* (BE ABLE) respectively. The subjunctive form in these examples does not alternate with the indicative form to convey contrasting meaning. It is true that these are all *irrealis* contexts, but this fact is conveyed systematically by the verb in the main clause. We can therefore simply say that the subjunctive is obligatory in certain constructions such as *vouloir que...* (TO WANT THAT...) when negated, *pour que...* (IN ORDER THAT...) and in a relative clause associated with a superlative. Examples of these kinds present no problem to the translator because they are automatic and do not rely on any substantive information from the source language.

English has a vestigial subjunctive mood whose forms fall together with the ordinary indicative forms. The word *come*, for example is used for the present indicative tense except for the third person singular, where the form is *comes*. The third person singular of the present subjunctive, however, is also *come* as in *They insisted that he come immediately.*

The English subjunctive survives in a number of set phrases, such as *come what may, so be it*, and *suffice it to say*. Otherwise, it is much commoner in the usage of conservative speakers. Typical examples are *If I were you, I wouldn't do that, If he saw her, he would call me.* It is not entirely the syntactic frame in which the verb appears that determines the choice of the indicative or the subjunctive mood, as it more frequently is in French. Consider the pairs *He insisted that he had seen the pictures* and *He insisted that he be shown the pictures.*

The forms *I be* and *I were* are generally referred to as the present and the past subjunctive respectively, though they do not in fact reflect a difference of tense. While we use the present in *I insist that he be here*, we use the past for the expression of a wish, as in *I wish he were here.*

German verbs also have a pair of subjunctive paradigms corresponding to the present and the past tense but, as in English, they are not semantically present and past. Also, German usage of these forms largely parallels English, but there are additional common usages in which the German subjunctive has clear semantic force such as in reported speech. In the sentence *Der Minister sagt, er habe den Bericht nicht gesehen* (THE MINISTER SAID HE HAD NOT SEEN THE REPORT), the subjunctive *habe* enables the writer to remain strictly uncommitted as to whether the minister has seen the report. The indicative *hat* would also be possible in this sentence, but would not express the same level of doubt about what the minister had seen. A translator of an English into a German text would have to decide whether what the minister said was self evident or, at least, whether the author, whom he now represents, would take that view. In any case, he must choose between indicative and subjunctive; leaving it open is not an option.

5.1.4 Evidentials

Consider the following sentences:

1. Jerry won the game.
2. Jerry did not win the game.
3. I saw Jerry win the game.
4. I heard that Jerry won the game.
5. Jerry seems to have won the game.
6. It seems to me that Jerry won the game.
7. It seemed to me that Jerry won the game.
8. It seemed to me that Jerry would win the game.

They all involve a proposition about Jerry winning a game. All but the first also involve a second proposition giving some information on how the writer assesses the truth value of the first proposition. Example (2) simply rejects it as false. (3) supports the main proposition by claiming that the writer actually saw the event that it speaks about. Example (4) also supplies some supporting evidence, but rather less solid than in (3) because it rests on hearsay. Example (5) reflects some doubt on the part of the speaker as does (6). (6) however is more complex because it also makes explicit the idea that other people may have other opinions. Example (7) says nothing about the speaker's current view of who won the game, but does say that he once held the opinion that it was Jerry.

The differences illustrated in these sentences have to do with *evidentiality*, that is, with evidence supplied by a speaker or writer for the claim made by the main proposition. The verb *see* is in many ways an unremarkable English transitive verb which can, however, be used to add weight to an assertion that an event took place, by saying that someone actually saw it. *Hear* can be used in a similar way, but it adds less weight because the speaker claims only to have heard about the event, thus strongly suggesting that he did not actually see it. When used in this way, these linguistic devices are referred to as *evidentials*. Sometimes, they are verbs, as in the above examples, but their grammatical status can vary quite widely. Other possibilities include *reportedly, apparent(ly), alleged(ly), obvious(ly)*.

What is interesting about evidentials in the present context is that there are many languages in which evidentials constitute a grammatical category of which there must be an exponent in every sentence or, at least, in every past tense sentence. The details differ widely from one sentence to another. There are even some in which the pattern exemplified in example (7) above is standard for all past tense sentences. Specifically, this is a pattern in which there are two tenses, one for the event itself, and one for the evidential.

According to McLendon (2003), the grammar of Eastern Pomo, a Pomoan language of Clear Lake County, California, has an evidential category with four values. The distinctions are morphological. She gives the following examples:

Type	Example	Gloss
nonvisual sensory	p a · bék -ink'e	burned
inferential	p a · bék-ine	must have burned
hearsay	p a · bék - · le	burned, they say
direct knowledge	p a · bék-a	burned

The first form is used when the speaker actually felt the burning sensation. The second is used when the speaker saw circumstantial evidence. The third is for hearsay; the speaker is reporting what he was told, and in the last example, the speaker has direct, probably visual, evidence. The importance of these examples from our present perspective is that all sentences in Eastern Pomo that report past events must use one of these four evidentials. This happens to be a highly endangered language and the demand for translations into it is therefore small and diminishing. The problems it would pose for a translator, however, are quite severe because the information required to get them right is rarely explicit in English and other European languages.

Matters are worse in Matses (also known as Mayoruna), a language spoken by some two thousand people in the Amazon basin of Peru and Brazil and described in very great detail in David Fleck's Ph.D. dissertation (2003). This is a language where sentences referring to past events are required to have two tenses. One situates the time of the event described relative to the reference time, and the other refers to the time at which the speaker acquired the evidence that the event had occurred. Reports of events must always state just how and when the speaker came upon the information. A sentence with the wrong evidentiality counts as a lie.

The claim is that, if you ask a Matses man how many wives he has when his wives are not actually in sight, he would have to answer in the past tense saying something like *daëd ikosh*, which means something like "There were two last time I checked." Since he cannot actually see his wives at the moment, he cannot be sure that they are all still living and that none of them has run off with another man.

A considerable proportion of Guy Deutscher's highly entertaining book *Through the Language Glass* (2010) is devoted to languages with grammatical evidential categories that must have exponents, and to Matses in particular. To complicate matter further, Matses has three degrees of pastness, with different morphological correlates. The recent past covers approximately the past month. The distant past extends from there to approximately a lifetime—fifty years or so. The remote past covers everything before that.

The interplay between tense and evidentiality is more complex in Matses than in any other known language. The language is, of course, a curiosity. But it serves to reinforce very powerfully the point that the grammar of a language can force its speakers, and consequently anyone who translates into it, to express certain kinds of information which may be difficult, or impossible, to infer reliably from the information that the speaker or translator has access to.

5.1.5 Case

Case is a large and pervasive category which, in many situations, seems to have virtually no semantic content. These are situations where, like the subjunctive mood in French, a particular case is required in a certain syntactic environment. It cannot be said to carry any semantic load because no other case could replace it in that environment. In Latin, for example, all but a handful of prepositions can be followed only by a noun phrase in the ablative case. In English, morphological case distinctions occur only in pronouns but, following a preposition, only the accusative case is possible as in *He ran right past her*. In German, some prepositions require the following noun phrase to be in the accusative, and some in the dative, case. A very small number require the genitive. Some prepositions in the Indo-European languages that still retain a non-trivial system of morphological cases, allow the following noun phrase to be in one of two cases, and the choice has semantic consequences. The preposition *in* in both Latin and German, require the accusative when it refers to a situation involving motion— essentially, where it could be translated as *into*. So, *The dog is going into the house* would be *Canis in villam intrat* in Latin, and *Der Hund geht in das Haus* in German. When a static situation is involved, Latin requires the ablative and German the dative case. So *the dog is in the house* would be *canis est in villa* in Latin and *Der Hund ist in dem Haus* in German.

The canonical role of case is to mark particular noun phrases as standing in particular relationships to the verb of the sentences in which they occur. The sentence *Mary sent the reporter the captain*, is about a *sending* event which involved three participants. *Mary* is the *subject*, *the reporter* is the *indirect object*, and *the captain* is the *direct object*. We can attempt definitions of these three notions either in semantic or formal grammatical terms. Let us start with the semantic approach.

If one of the participants in the action described by a sentence is the instigator of the action, then that participant generally fills the role of the subject. This is the case with the sentence *Mary sent the reporter the captain*. It apparently describes something that Mary undertook, and in which the reporter and the captain had very little say. But not all sentences describe actions, or they describe actions that do not obviously involve an instigator. The sentence *John saw the reporter* describes a circumstance involving two individuals neither of whom played a causal role. John, however, was the participant that was most affected by the event and thus, in the absence of an instigator, *John* becomes the subject of the sentence.

The nominative case usually marks the subject of a sentence and sometimes this is all that makes it clear what is the subject. In the German sentence *Das Buch las der Mann* (The man read the book), the phrase *der Mann* (*the man*) is unambiguously nominative, whereas *das Buch*, taken out of context, could be nominative or accusative. It is only because the subject role is taken by *der Mann*, and because of what makes sense semantically, that we know that *das Buch* must be the object. The sentence *Das Buch ließ die Frau* would surely be taken as meaning *The woman read the book* even though the phrase *die Frau* taken by itself could be nominative or accusative. We disambiguate it mainly on the basis of the meaning, but also partly because the nominative precedes the accusative most of time, though not in this case, and especially when the morphology is ambiguous.

The association between nominative case and the subject of a sentence, and between accusative case and the object, is very strong, but there are divergences. A small class of German verbs, for example, take objects in the dative case. One such verb is *helfen* (HELP) so that in *Er hat mir geholfen* (HE HELPED ME), the pronoun *mir* (ME) is in the dative case. Other verbs that exhibit this behavior include *antworten* (ANSWER), *drohen* (THREATEN), *folgen* (FOLLOW), *trotzen* (DEFY), *gefallen* (PLEASE), *entfliehen* (ESCAPE) and *mißtrauen* (MISTRUST). In Icelandic, some verbs also have dative subjects as in *Mér erkalt* (I AM COLD), which is similar to the German *Mir ist kalt* which, in its turn, is similar to *Mir ist es kalt* (IT IS COLD TO ME). Much has been written by linguists about these so-called *quirky* cases.

The older Indo-European languages such as Sanskrit, Ancient Greek and Latin, had six to eight cases. The trend in their more modern descendants has been towards simpler case systems, led by English and the Romance languages where there are arguably two, or possibly three. The third case would be the genitive as in *his dog and her cat*, and French *sa fille et son fils* (HIS/HER DAUGHTER AND HIS/HER SON). Finnish, however is traditionally regarded as having fifteen and Hungarian eighteen.

We note in passing that the apparent similarity in possessive pronouns between English and French is misleading and a possible source of problems when translating into one of these languages from the other. The difference is simply that, in English, the pronoun takes its gender from that of the possessor whereas, in French, it takes it from the thing possessed. Thus, in English, Mary's brother is *her brother*, but in French, it is *son frère*, where *son* is the masculine form. Consequently, the translator into English must infer the gender of the possessor, which may not be explicit.

We observed that the semantic argument for assigning John the subject role in the sentence *John saw the reporter* was not especially convincing. While there is clearly something to this attempt to characterize the role of cases in purely semantic terms, it may turn out to be more a rationalization than an explanation. Consider the following examples:

1. My sister sold the teacher her car.
2. My sister sold her car to the teacher.
3. My sister sold the teacher his car.
4. ?My sister sold his car to the teacher.
5. The teacher bought my sister's car.
6. The teacher bought his car from my sister.
7. The car was sold to the teacher by my sister.
8. The teacher was sold the car by my sister

The message, or at least the main thrust of it, is substantially the same in all of these sentences. There are three or four participants: my sister, a teacher, and a car. The sentences all report an event in which the car originally owned by my sister becomes the property of the teacher. We are not given any idea whether the transaction was instigated by my sister, or the teacher, or someone else. The circumstances under which we would expect one or another of these sentences to be used are, of course, not the same.

The car referred to in these sentences belongs to my sister at the beginning of period during which the events took place, and to the teacher at the end. At the beginning of the period, it is her car and, at the end, it is his car. So it seems that we can refer to it in either way. However, we have prefixed example (4) with a question mark, following the linguist's convention for marking doubtful acceptability judgments. Perhaps the problem is that the sentence *My sister sold his car* is clearly aberrant, and adding *to the teacher* to the end is not enough to redeem it. Equally unacceptable would be *The teacher bought her car from my sister* unless, of course, the teacher was female.

There are, of course, no cases in the above examples, except for the possessive pronouns. The roles that would be filled by cases in a language like Latin or German are taken here by word order and prepositions. So, what are these roles if they are not semantic notions like *instigator* and *patient*? The best answer seems to be that they are roles in the little drama that is played out when we use particular verbs, in this case *buy* and *sell*.

The verbs *buy* and *sell* both evoke the same standard little drama, involving two people, some object or material that we can refer to as the *merchandise*, and some money. This particular drama is often referred to as the *commercial transaction*. Let us call the two people the *buyer* and the *seller*. Before the action begins, the seller owns the merchandise and the buyer owns the money. The action consists in reversing this situation so that the seller owns the money and the buyer the merchandise. There is a general understanding that the money and the merchandise are, by some standard, of roughly equivalent value, though the standard can vary widely from one situation to another and may be contested. The point is that, if you take my car by force, and throw me a $10 bill through the window as you drive away, I will be disinclined to say that I sold you my car.

The verbs *buy* and *sell* differ principally in the way the roles in the drama are mapped onto roles in the grammar of the language. The subject is the instigator of the action and generally the buyer, that is, the recipient of the merchandise. However, if there is an indirect object, as in *John bought Mary the car*, then this is the recipient. The subject precedes the verb in a declarative sentence and agrees with it in person and number. The direct and indirect objects are generally distinguished in one of two ways. Either they both follow the verb, with the indirect object preceding the direct object. The other possibility is to put the direct object after the verb and to follow that with a prepositional phrase containing, in the case of *buy*, the preposition *from* and the indirect object.

In the case of *sell*, the subject is the seller and the instigator, and the merchandise is the direct object. If there is an indirect object, it is either a noun phrase preceding the direct object, or a prepositional phrase with the preposition *to*.

The grammar categorizes verbs according to whether they can be used with direct and indirect objects. If a verb allows indirect objects, then it also allows direct objects. Verbs that allow direct objects are called *transitive* and those that do not are called *intransitive*. Transitive verbs can generally also be used in a different kind of construction known as the *passive* voice. Sentences (7) and (8) above are examples of this. The verb appears as a past participle together with some form of the auxiliary verb *to be*. Importantly for our present concerns, the noun that would have been the subject in the active voice appears with the preposition *by* and the direct object from the active sentence becomes the new subject. The *by*-phrase is optional, so that this can be a useful construction when one wants to leave one of the participants implicit.

As we have said, the functions that word order and prepositions fill in English are routinely filled by cases in many other languages. Here are some examples from German:

1. Meine Schwester hat dem Lehrer seinen Wagen verkauft. (My sister has the teacher his/her car sold)

2. Seinen Wagen hat meine Schwester dem Lehrer verkauft. (HIS/HER CAR HAS MY SISTER (TO) THE TEACHER SOLD)

3. Dem Lehrer hat meiner Schwester seinen Wagen verkauft. (THE TEACHER HAS MY SISTER (TO) HIS/HER CAR SOLD)

4. Meine Schwester hat seinen Wagen dem Lehrer verkauft. (MY SISTER HAS HIS/HER CAR (TO) THE TEACHER SOLD)

5. Der Lehrer hat von meiner Schwester seinen Wagen gekauft. (THE TEACHER HAS FROM MY SISTER HIS/HER CAR BOUGHT)

6. Der Lehrer hat seinen Wagen von meiner Schwester gekauft. (THE TEACHER HAS HIS/HER CAR FROM MY SISTER BOUGHT)

7. Der Lehrer hat den Wagen meiner Schwester gekauft. (THE TEACHER HAS THE CAR OF MY SISTER BOUGHT)

Many other variants are possible. For instance, German makes frequent use of a device known technically as *topicalization* which distinguishes, or emphasizes, one constituent of a sentence by moving it to the beginning. The topicalized constituent can even be the verb, as in *Verkauft hat meine Schwester dem Lehrer seinem Wagen* SELL MY SISTER DID HER CAR TO THE TEACHER.

The words *Schwester*, *Lehrer* and *Wagen* mean *sister*, *teacher* and *car* respectively. The word *verkauft* is the past participle of the verb *verkaufen*, meaning *sold*, and *gekauft* is the past participle of the verb *kaufen*, meaning *bought*. The word *hat* is an auxiliary very roughly corresponding to English *have* and it appears here because the German sentences that correspond best to the English examples quoted earlier use constructions like *has sold* rather than the simple past, *sold*.

The syntax of German main clauses is generally similar to that of their English counterparts. They begin with a noun phrase referring to one of the three participants in the commercial transaction. Following this is the auxiliary verb *hat* and the other two participants. The main verb comes at the end. The principal constraint on the relative order of the noun phrases that identify the three participants is that the subject of the sentence must be adjacent to—preceding or following—the auxiliary verb. Examples (1)–(4) show the variants.

Given the weak constraints on the relative order of the noun phrases, the burden of distinguishing subjects and direct and indirect objects must be assumed by other mechanisms, notably cases and prepositions. In (1)–(4), it is assumed by cases.

Like much of inflectional morphology, case systems are typically subject to a great deal of syncretism, that is, ambiguity as to what case a given affix represents. The phrase *meine Schwester*, for example, can be nominative or accusative, singular or plural. We will take it that the number ambiguity is resolved by context outside this sentence, or by the assumption that a single car is the property of a single person. The subjects of sentences come before the verb more often than not, but we have stronger evidence that the phrase is the subject of this sentence because the phrase *dem Lehrer* can only be dative, and the subject must be adjacent to the verb. This leaves *den Wagen* as the only candidate for the role of direct object. Similar reasoning resolves the ambiguities in examples (2)–(4).

The remaining three examples use the verb *kaufen* (BUY) which, like its English counterpart, does not admit indirect objects. Instead, it uses a prepositional phrase with *von* (FROM) to identify the seller. The preposition *von* requires its object to be in the dative case, hence the form *meiner Schwester* which is either genitive or dative. We see the same phrase as a genitive in example (7).

In German, as in French, possessive pronouns agree with the noun denoting the thing possessed, and not with the possessor. The first word of the noun phrase *seinen Wagen* could therefore be translated into English as either *his car* or *her car*.

5.1.6 Number

The category of tense is similar to that of number in that they both have strong semantic as well as grammatical components. A speaker generally chooses one tense rather than another in order to situate states or events in time relative to the present or to some other situations that are under discussion. In like manner, he chooses between singular and plural depending on whether one or more than one entities of the given kind are in question. In many languages, number has a stronger grammatical component because it is frequently manifested in more than one of the words in an utterance as a result of a common grammatical phenomenon called *agreement*. Thus, we say *The dog chases the cat*, but *The dogs chase that cat*. In English, this agreement is found only in the third person singular, but in other languages it occurs much more widely. In French, the most obvious rendering of *The little bird arrived tired* would be *Le petit oiseau est arrivé fatigué* whereas, for more than one bird, we would have to say *Les petits oiseaux sont arrivés fatigués*. All six words are affected.

Tense and number, in many languages, including all those in the Indo-European family, generally require every noun to be marked with a number and every verb with a tense. In other words, when using a noun, there is no way to leave unspecified whether one or more than one entity is being referred to. Similarly, there is no way of using a finite verb without specifying a tense. There are apparent exceptions to this general rule. There are, for example, nouns like *fish* and *sheep* that do not have distinct singular and plural forms.[28] The word *fishes* exists as a plural form in English, but with a special interpretation, which we ignore here. Likewise for verbs. However, we should probably regard these as examples of ambiguity rather than vagueness. In other words, a hearer of the sentence like *He ate the fish*, probably assigns the word *fish* to the singular or the plural category rather than simply leaving the matter vague. Notice that, if one of these words is used in a situation that involves agreement, the choice still has to be made. Consider the pair *The fish tastes good* as opposed to *The fish taste good*.

Even though there are English words that show no formal distinction between singular and plural, in most contexts they clearly function as either one or the other and not as something intermediate between the two. In the sentence *The sheep is asleep*, the word *sheep* is clearly singular. In *The sheep are asleep*, it is plural. The sequence *The sheep that was asleep have woken up* is ungrammatical because it requires the word *sheep* to be construed as both singular and plural. But what shall we say about the sentence *The sheep might be asleep*? There is a widely shared feeling that the sentence is ambiguous, and not simply indeterminate in the number of its subject. It is difficult to raise this feeling to anything higher than the level of an intuition. One might try to force the issue by providing a context like the following:

> There are two dogs and two sheep but we are not sure if they all came back to the yard. We know the dogs are there because we can hear them but the sheep might be asleep.

This presumably means that any sheep that returned to the yard—either one or two of them—might be asleep. However, the intuition that it is ambiguous persists. One can alternate between perceiving the word *sheep* as singular or plural but it is close to impossible to interpret it as both at the same time. Notice that a word or phrase that fixes the number as singular or plural does not have to precede the word being disambiguated, as in these examples:

> The Sheep could be asleep, couldn't it/they?

So this is just another instance of the kind of ambiguity found in Joseph Jastrow's Duck Rabbit (fig. 5.2) and, below, many geometrical line drawings. The point about the duck-rabbit is simply that one can see it either as a duck or as a rabbit, but not as both at the same time.

---

28. Many of the English nouns with this property name animals (*grouse, plaice, salmon*) or nationalities(*Portuguese, Lebanese*).

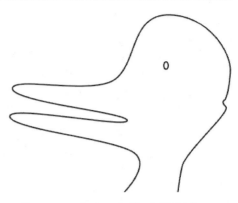

FIGURE 5.2 Jastrow's Duck Rabbit

The inventory of morphemes in a language is clearly very much larger than that of phonemes. Like phonemes, however, they constitute a set of distinct digits among the members of which similarities and differences rarely play any role. The morphemes *ample* and *amble* differ in only one phoneme, and even phonemes that differentiate them are phonetically very similar, but this give us no right to expect them to have similar meanings. The morphemes *time* and *thyme* are identical in their phonetic makeup, but they are entirely unrelated in meaning.

Like tense and case, number is a property that plays a role in determining the forms of words in many languages. It always shows a distinction between singular and plural, but some languages, like Arabic, have a separate dual category. Dual was a distinct category also in Indo-European and vestiges of it can be seen in English in words like *both, either,* and *between*. Observe that in translating from French into English, one must decide whether to translate the French word *entre* as *among* or *between*. Observe also that indefinitely many French phrases of the form *tous les trois, tous les quatre* can be translated into English as *all three of them, all four of them* etc., *tous les deux* must be rendered as *both of them* and not *all two of them*.

We have already observed that, like tense, a speaker associates a number with a noun for semantic reasons, but it is manifested in other words as a result of agreement. The semantic connection is generally quite transparent but, as with tense, it is sometimes largely conventional. In English, for example, we speak of *a pair of shorts, pants, pliers, scissors* etc. Many other languages use singular nouns to refer to these things. We talk about a person's *hair* as one thing whereas the French speak of *cheveux* (HAIRS). The English form *hairs* is much more likely to refer to body hair or when some subset of a person's hair is in question.

English—especially British English—allows the connection between semantic and grammatical number to be broken on occasion. It is possible, for example, to say either *The committee has decided the matter*, or *the committee have decided the matter*, presumably because the decision is thought of as having been made by the members of the committee, and it takes more than one person to constitute a committee. Notice, however, that we cannot say *a committee have been established to study the matter*, where the emphasis is on the committee as a single entity. Several words allow this double interpretation, such as *family*, *platoon*, *couple*, and *school*.

5.1.7 Apostrophe -*s*

In a serious discussion like the present one, that little tick mark that we refer to as the *apostrophe* probably deserves no more attention than its diminutive size suggests. It receives more than its fair share of attention from prescriptive grammarians who lie in wait for unwary writers who break the rules governing its use. But it is, in one way at least, quite remarkable and deserving of some brief examination.

The apostrophe plays some role in many languages, and at least three in English. We will concentrate on just one of them. We will not be concerned with its use to stand in for omitted letters, as in *isn't* and *I'm*, though this may have played some role in the modern possessive apostrophe. Neither will we be concerned with idiosyncratic plurals like *P's and Q's*. We will be interested in its use to mark possession, as in *John's books*, and fairly obvious extensions of this as in *a dollar's worth*, *a month's time* and *Beethoven's quartets*.

Those with some knowledge of a Germanic language will immediately observe the parallel between English apostrophe-*s*, and the genitive -*s* in most of these languages. This is the standard masculine and neuter singular form in modern German as it was in Old English. The parallel is not not accidental and, while there is some disagreement on the details of how it came about, the Old English form is behind the modern one. What is remarkable about the modern form is that, while it is still used as a marker of possession, it has acquired grammatical properties quite unlike those of any other inflectional affix. In particular it has become a suffix that can be applied to nouns, as expected, but also to noun *phrases*. Thus we can say, not only *John's books*, but also *the one you were talking about's title*. Observe the ambiguity in a phrase like *The scene at the movie's end*.

Syntactically, a noun phrase followed by an apostrophe-*s* functions substantially as a definite noun phrase and semantically, the -*s* fills substantially the same role as the word *of*. We can generally recast *the man who came to dinner's umbrella* as *the umbrella of the man who came to dinner*. The word *the* goes with *man who came to dinner* and not with his umbrella. To see this, observe that *a man who came to dinner's umbrella* would have to be paraphrased as *the umbrella of a man who came to dinner* and not *an umbrella of the man who came to dinner*.

5.1.8 Paradigms

Many languages, like Latin and Finnish, have rich inflectional systems, while others, like Chinese have virtually none at all. In those that have them, the members of certain major word classes, such as verbs, nouns, and adjectives, occur in a variety of *forms*. The forms correspond to different sets of grammatical *attributes* such as tense, number, case, and gender. To each attribute, there corresponds a set of values: singular and plural for the number attribute, masculine and feminine for the gender attribute, and so on. The collection of all the forms of a word, for all the relevant attributes and values constitutes a *paradigm*. The paradigms of nouns and adjectives are generally called *declensions*, and those of verbs, *conjugations*.

The following table shows one of the first paradigms traditionally encountered by learners of Latin, that for the word *mensa* (TABLE). The two attributes that are relevant for Latin nouns are *Case* and *Number*. The possible values of the *Case* attribute are given in the left-hand column. The values of the *Number* attribute, *Singular* and *Plural*, are given in the two columns on the right.

Case	Number	
	Singular	Plural
Nominative	mensa	mensae
Vocative	mensa	mensae
Accusative	mensam	mensas
Genitive	mensae	mensarum
Dative	mensae	mensis
Ablative	mensa	mensis

Generally speaking, different sets of attributes are associated with different word classes, or subclasses. Thus, in many Indo-European languages, gender, number and case are associated with nouns and adjectives. All forms of almost all nouns have the same value for the gender attribute. Values for the case and number attributes are determined by grammatical and semantic considerations. However, there are a few French nouns the are generally masculine in the singular an feminine in the plural. They include *amour* LOVE, *délice* DELIGHT, *orgue* ORGAN.

In many languages, the word that generally corresponds to *people* in English, has some interesting properties. One is that either it has no corresponding singular form, or it has no plural form despite its plural sense. The French word *gens* is always plural, whereas the cognate words in Italian, Spanish, and Portuguese are singular. The French word also has extraordinary gender properties. Adjectives in the same phrase that follow it are masculine. Those that precede it, however, are feminine. There is actually a good deal more to this particular story, but we will not pursue it further here.

Adjective forms have the same attributes as nouns but, in most cases, their values are derived, by agreement, from the nouns they modify. Therefore, while each noun generally has just one gender, adjectives have different cases depending on the nouns they modify. In some languages, they have additional attributes. In German, for example, each inflected adjective is either *strong* or *weak* depending on the grammatical construction in which it participates. The forms of a German inflected adjective therefore varies on four dimensions: Gender, Number, Case, and Strength. Displaying their paradigms on a two-dimensional page is therefore something of a challenge. Here is one way of doing it for the German adjective:

Strength →	Strong			
Number→	Singular			Plural
Gender→	Masculine	Feminine	Neuter	
Case ↓				
Nominative	guter	gute	gutes	gute
Accusative	guten	gute	gutes	gute
Genitive	gutes	guter	gutes	guter
Dative	gutem	guter	gutem	guten

Strength →	Weak			
Number→	Singular			Plural
Gender→	Masculine	Feminine	Neuter	
Case ↓				
Nominative	gute	gute	gute	guten
Accusative	guten	gute	gute	guten
Genitive	guten	guten	guten	guten
Dative	guten	guten	guten	guten

We show the strong forms in one table and the weak forms in another. Each table can be seen as two smaller tables, for singular and plural respectively, displayed side by side. These two tables have a row for each of the cases. The one on the left has a column for each gender, but the plural table has only one column because no gender distinctions are made in the plural.

Until well into the twentieth century, languages were widely considered respectable to the extent that their grammars were similar to those of Latin and Greek. In an effort to give English the respectability that its speakers thought it deserved, they would sometimes present paradigms for English words with grammatical categories taken directly from Latin. The result looked something like this:

Case	Number	
	Singular	Plural
Nominative	table	tables
Vocative	table	tables
Accusative	table	tables
Genitive	table's	tables'
Dative	table	tables
Ablative	table	tables

or even

Case	Number	
	Singular	Plural
Nominative	the table	the tables
Vocative	oh table	oh tables
Accusative	the table	the tables
Genitive	the table's	the tables'
Dative	to the table	to the tables
Ablative	by the table	by the tables

Language has an uncanny ability to bring out prejudice and silliness in people. Fortunately, this particular sort of silliness has been abandoned. Nowadays, paradigms of English words are rarely presented at all. One might, perhaps, not be surprised to see something like the following, say, in a book for teaching English to foreigners:

Case	Number	
	Singular	Plural
Simple	table	tables
Genitive	table's	tables'

There are, however, two good reasons why one does not. One is that the extremely small amount of information that the table contains does not merit such a weighty typographical device. The main piece of information is that regular English nouns are marked for is plurality with an -*s* suffix. The other piece of information in the display, namely that English nouns form genitives with an apostrophe and an *s*, in some order, is simply wrong, as we have seen.

It is a general characteristic of inflectional systems that paradigms are complete. In other words, every slot in the table corresponding to a word is occupied by some form. Clearly, this is not always the case. Many languages, for example, like English, have a noun meaning *people* that has no singular form (French *gens*, Italian *gente*, German *Leute*).

The learner of a second language, or even a first language, presumably has reason to be grateful for a system in which every slot in most paradigms is occupied, and by a form that is related in a transparent way to the other forms in the paradigm. If I see an unfamiliar animal and ask you what it is, you may answer *That is an aardvark*. When I get home, I may excitedly report *I saw three aardvarks today* with reasonable confidence that I got the right plural form. It does not always work, of course. If the animal had been an elk, the people at home might laugh discretely behind their hands.

Words that do not have a full complement for forms are said to be *defective*. It is perhaps not surprising that defective words tend to be fairly common so that everyone has the chance to learn their peculiarity. Examples include modal verbs like *may, must, can, should* and *might*. These have no infinitive forms; they do not take the -*s* suffix in the third person singular. The question of whether they really have tenses is moot. *Should, would* and *might* are sometimes thought of as past tense forms of *shall, will* and *may*, and indeed we can say *He thought I would do it* to refer to his expectation at some earlier time that my doing it would happen some time later. In other words, there was a time at which he might have been expected to say *I think he will do it*. Speaking of a time when he had no objections to my doing something, I could say *He said I could do it*. But these past tense forms also have a life of their own as present-tense verbs. Consider *I am not sure, but I think it might happen, I do not know if he will do it, but he certainly could* and *I do not know if he will do it, but he certainly should*.

Another set of defective words are verbs that describe the weather. They include the verbs in *It is raining, it was freezing* and so on. These verbs occur only in the third person singular. Notice, however, that their influence can spread through the adjacent text as in *It looks like rain* and *It is trying to rain*. Other western European languages also tend to use such so-called *impersonal* verbs to describe the weather but it is, of course, not universal. For *It is raining*, Russians say идёт дождь (*id'ot dozht*). Translated word for word, this yields something like *rain goes*.

We have remarked that some nouns occur only in the plural in standard English. Among these are articles of clothing like *pants*, *trousers*, and *pajamas*, and tools like *tongs*, *scissors*, *shears* and *glasses*. The members of these classes tend to be used in a phrase with the word *pair* as in *a pair of trousers* and *a pair of scissors*. However, some of them—especially those referring to clothing—can be used in the singular in special circumstances. We can, for example, speak of *pant legs* and *pajama tops*. Also, there is a dialect of English spoken by employees of pretentious clothing emporia who say things like *This is a very durable pant*. Nouns that are almost always plural are *arms* and *troops* (in the military sense). There is, however, the phrase *side arm*. There is also a minority dialect in which *scissors* is singular.

Other nouns that are found exclusively in the plural, at least in one of their senses, include *cattle*, *quarters*, *police*, *customs*, and *goods*. Words that occur only in the singular are harder to find. One example is *information*.

The difficulties posed by paradigms with missing parts for language learners are obvious, especially when the corresponding parts are not missing in the learner's native language. They are also puzzling for some theoretical linguists who have difficulties understanding how a prohibition against producing a word according to standard rules could be learnt. For the translator, they can hardly be regarded as a serious problem.

Somewhat more problematic than defective paradigms are those that display what is known as *suppletion*. A suppletive form is one that is not related to the other members of the paradigm according to the standard rules. In English, the standard rule for obtaining the third-person singular form of a verb from its infinitive is to add -*s*. Thus, from *walk*, we obtain *walks*. To get the past tense form or the past participle, we add -*ed* and get the form *walked*. But there are many verbs for which these rules do not work. The third-person singular of *have* is not *haves*, but *has*. The past tense of *swim* is *swam* and the past participle is different from this, namely *swum*. These forms are suppletive.

Translators, as opposed to interpreters, are, as we have noted, concerned with language in its written form. If we concentrate narrowly on this form, we may be inclined to see the paradigms of a great many English words as suppletive. The rule for forming third-person singular forms, as we have just stated it, would give us *wishs* from *wish*, *buzzs* from *buzz* and *watchs* from *watch*. The past tense and past participle rule would give us *loveed* from *love*, *tryed* from *try* and *freed* from *free*. Observe, however, that people learning English, either as natives or foreigners, do not have to learn the forms of these words individually as they do for *have* and *swim*. They learn to produce the forms by applying rules that are somewhat more complicated than we have suggested. Since it is peripheral to our main concern, we will not dwell long on the details of morphological rules, spelling rules, and the like.

The most satisfactory way of conceptualizing the system is in two parts. One is the truly morphological and the other has to do with spelling. We take it that, adding *-s* to the word *walk* yields something like *walk-s*. A spelling rule then removes the hyphen to give *walks*. Adding *-s* to *wish* gives *wish-s*. This time, there is a spelling rule that replaces *sh-s*, not by *shs*, but by *shes*. Thanks to this rule, we get something that is pronounceable. Adding *-ed* to *love* gives *love-ed*. Simply removing the hyphen from this would give something pronounceable, but the pronunciation would be wrong. The spelling rule that applies here replaces *e-e* by *e*. This is still a somewhat simplified account of the way the system operates but the remaining complexities are technical and beyond our present scope. The bottom line is that, if native speakers, or writers, can produce the correct forms of newly learned words, we do not have to treat them as suppletive.

The verb *to be* is famously suppletive, as are its counterparts in many other languages. There are no rules for deriving English *am*, *is*, *are*, *was* and *were* from *be*, or *be* from any of them. Likewise, there is no way of deriving French *suis*, *est* and *sont* from *être*, or German *bin*, *ist* and *war* from *sein*. Curiously, the present participle is formed in a very regular way in all of these and, indeed, in many Indo-European languages. Present participles are formed in English by adding *-ing*, in French by adding *-ant* and so on. Minor variations in the spelling implement simple standard devices for preserving the correspondence between the written and the spoken forms. Thus, in English, we have *running* rather than *runing* and *loving* rather than *loveing* and, in French, we have *mangeant* rather than *mangant*. Past participles, vary wildly.

Even literate native speakers are occasionally unsure about the forms, particularly of rare words. At one time or another, most of us have felt the need of a past tense for the verb *forgo* and have managed only in the nick of time to suppress *forgoed*. It has, in any case, nothing to do with *forthcome* and *forthcoming*. I have occasionally found myself on the brink of saying *he succame (succamb?) to the temptation*. In British English, the past tense of *dive* remains what it has been traditionally, namely *dived*. For many Americans, this has been replaced by *dove* which is, in fact, a neologism. Verbs that rhyme with *ride* sometimes cause hesitation in English speakers. Examples include *stride* and *thrive*. *I never thought I could have thriven so well*(?).

English verbs ending in a short vowel and a *-t*, especially if they are monosyllabic, often have past tense, and past participles that are the same as the present tense forms as in *bet, cut, let, set, shut*, and *wet*, and derivatives of these such as *upset, undercut, beset, offset, inset, put*, and *reset*. But there are no general rules here, for we also have *forget* (*forgot, forgotten*), *get* (*got*, British *got* and US *gotten*), *sweat* (*sweated*), *regret* (*regretted*), *fret* (*fretted*), *strut* (*strutted*), *vet* (*vetted*), *pet* (*petted*), *beget* (*begot, begotten*), *abet* (*abetted*), and *whet* (*whetted*).

As we have already remarked, there is a single, almost degenerate paradigm for English regular nouns and another for regular verbs. The verbal paradigm is almost as degenerate as the one for nouns. We can display it somewhat as follows:

3rd sing. present	walks
Other present	walk
Present participle	walking
Past	walked

Morphologically richer languages usually have several paradigms for each of the major parts of speech. Latin, for example has four regular conjugations for verbs and five declensions for nouns. French grammar books usually arrange verbs in three conjugations. The first contains verbs with infinitives ending in *-er*, the second contains only verbs with infinitives in *-ir*, and the third is a grab bag of the leftovers, including many with infinitives in *-ir*. Not surprisingly, the last of these manifests a great deal of irregularity and suppletion.

It is worth noting that the table for the paradigm for the Latin word *mensa* (TABLE) has twelve slots, though there are only six different forms (*mensa, mensae, mensam, mensarum, mensas*, and *mensis*).The table for the German strong adjectival forms has sixteen slots, but only five different forms (*gute, gutem, guten, guter, gutes*). The table for the weak forms also has sixteen slots, but only two different forms (*gute* and *guten*). This massive ambiguity of the forms, known as *syncretism*, is pervasive in inflectional morphology. The German *-er* adjectival suffix, for example, is nominative singular when the gender is masculine, but genitive or dative singular when the gender is feminine. The *-en* suffix accounts for almost all the weak forms. Among the strong forms, it accounts only for the masculine, accusative singular and the dative, plural in all genders. It is hardly surprising that morphological paradigms are such a persistent source of frustration for language learners.

Consider the following example: In the sentence *Der große Hund jagt die kleine Katze* (THE BIG DOG CHASES THE LITTLE CAT), the forms *große* (BIG) and *kleine* (SMALL) must be inflected because they each appear between an article and the noun they modify. Because they appear in this configuration, they are both weak forms, so that it is impossible to tell by looking at the forms in isolation, that the first is nominative singular, and the second accusative singular.

Now consider the following somewhat contrived sentence: *Schöne Gesänge junger Kinder gefallen alten Leuten* (BEAUTIFUL SONGS OF YOUNG CHILDREN PLEASE OLD PEOPLE). There are no articles in the sentence and the forms of all three adjectives are therefore all strong. The subject of the sentence is *Schöne Gesänge* (BEAUTIFUL SONGS) must be plural because *Gesänge* appears only in the plural part of the paradigm of *Gesang* (SONG). The adjective *schöne* (BEAUTIFUL) must therefore also be plural, and consequently genitive, because this is the only plural form in the adjectival paradigm that ends in *-er*. The phrase *junger Kinder* (YOUNG CHILDREN) must be genitive plural because *Kinder* can only be plural and *jünger*, if plural, can only be genitive. The phrase *alten Leuten* (OLD PEOPLE) must be plural because *Leuten* can only be plural and it must be dative because no object has yet been found for *gefallen* (PLEASE), a verb that requires its objects to be in the dative.

We have made a tortuous puzzle of this disambiguation process which native German speakers solve without thinking about it. Our point is only to highlight a pervasive feature of inflectional systems, namely that they display such massive syncretism as to make it almost seem that they were designed to keep foreigners at bay. German is by no means an extreme case.

5.2   The Tyranny of Grammar

A speaker is not free to choose whether or not to inflect an inflectable word. This is a matter that is prescribed by the grammar. It is sometimes said that inflectable words must always be inflected, but this is too strong. The German adjectival paradigms given above, for example, prescribe the forms that must be used when the adjective in question is used attributively, that is, when it is part of a noun phrase in which it modifies the principal noun. Accordingly, there is a contrast between *Das ist ein großes Haus* (THAT IS A BIG HOUSE), and *Das Haus ist groß* (THE HOUSE IS BIG). In the second example, the adjective is not part of a noun phrase whose head noun it modifies, but is predicated of the subject of a sentence with the verb *ist* (IS). Accordingly, it is not inflected.

It remains true, however, that most inflectable words must always be inflected and that, if inflection is not required sometimes, then the relevant contexts are prescribed as part of the grammar. Without question, a German adjective must be inflected if it fills an attributive role.

The semantic categories that are associated with inflections are generally few in number and abstract in nature. For the Indo-European languages, the attributes are aspect, tense, mood, case, number, and gender and none of them has more than six values. The numbers are larger in some other language families, but still quite small. Bantu languages like Swahili and Zulu do not place nouns in three genders, but into seventeen or eighteen classes with other semantic correlates. For example, there are classes for persons, animals, long thin objects, and abstract concepts. One class contains the names of plants, rivers, and some body parts. Other body parts belong in another class together with fruits and words borrowed from other languages. Importantly, all classes also contain many other words which have none of the canonical semantic properties just as Indo-European gender classes contain many words that have no natural gender. According to the standard analysis, the singular forms in a given class begin with a characteristic prefix. The corresponding plurals belong to a different class, with a different prefix. A different analysis would also be possible, with a smaller number of classes, each with a pair of corresponding prefixes. As with Indo-European genders, what is of primary importance are agreement requirements between nouns and other words.

5.3 Derivation

The system of inflectional morphology in English is very simple, though not nearly so simple as that of languages like Chinese, where it is virtually nonexistent. English derivational morphology, however, is quite complex, and mostly beyond our present scope. The distinction between these two kinds of morphology is by no means as sharp as linguists would wish it to be. The following, however, are among the criteria most frequently cited:

1. Inflection of the words in a given category (nouns, verbs, adjectives,...) is obligatory whereas derivation is optional.
2. Derivation applies to words to yield other words whereas inflection applies to stems to yield words.
3. Derivation can apply to a word with one part of speech to yield a word of a different one. This does not happen with inflection.

English has the derivational suffix *-ness*, which can be applied to many adjectives to give a noun with a systematically related sense. If a noun refers to something that is *slow*, then it has a property that can be referred to with the noun *slowness*. This suffix works in the same way with a great many, mostly Germanic, adjectives. The words *brightness*, *darkness*, *fairness*, *thickness*, *thinness* and a host of other examples are derived in the same way. If the adjective is not of Germanic origin, other means of deriving the corresponding noun are generally preferred. Nevertheless, we sometimes find it being used with adjectives of French origin to give words like *tenderness* and *rudeness*.

Many speakers cannot distinguish Germanic from other words but simply know what suffixes are appropriate for what specific adjectives. Another suffix that fills that same roles as *-ness*, but almost exclusively with adjectives of French origin is *-ity*, as in *luminosity* from *luminous* and *curiosity* from *curious*.

Sometimes, what would normally be a derived form has been displaced by a suppletive one a in the pairs *strong/strength*, *long/length*, *fast/speed*. These are clearly lexical items in their own right.

There are, of course, also standard derivational devices that work in the opposite direction, yielding adjectives from nouns. Thus, from *truth*, we have *true* with one sense, and *truthful* with another. Adding *-ize* to many adjectives that ascribe a property to the referent of the noun they modify, gives a verb which refers to the act of ascribing that property, as in *modernize*, *centralize*, *popularize* and *moralize*. The suffix *-ize* is obviously borrowed from French and there are many cases where the whole derived form has been borrowed from French because the adjective from which they appear to be formed does not actually exist in English. Examples are *baptize*, *canonize*, and *exorcize*.

Generally speaking, this French suffix can be used only with adjectives that are also of French origin. Another suffix that has the same meaning is *-en*, as in *strengthen*, *weaken*, *lengthen*, and *shorten*. It is used with many colors, as in *blacken*, *whiten*, and *redden*, but not all. We do not say *pinken* and, indeed, there is no derivational device that we can use in this case. This suffix also appears in the word *deaden* whose meaning one might expect to be essentially the same as that of *kill*. However, the meaning of *dead* that is involved here is clearly a very particular one that is used relatively rarely.

We use the term *derivational device* because it is not only suffixes that can fill this role, in English or other languages. The prefix *de-* is added to some nouns and verbs to give a verb with the underlying meaning of *remove* as in *delouse*, *devein* and *demilitarize*. The prefix *dis-* is sometimes also used in this way, as in *disarm*, *dishonor* and *disinherit*. Sometimes the meaning is less specific, introducing a general negative quality to the derived form, as in *disapprove* and *disobey*.

There are many instances in English of words that belong to more than one grammatical category with systematically related meanings. This happens frequently with nouns that are the names of tools, such as *hammer*, *saw*, and *chisel*, or components used in the construction of larger objects, such as *nail*, *pin*, *screw*, and *staple*. Perhaps these should be thought of as belonging to a larger class, meaning something like *apply*, and embracing words like *water*, *oil*, *fuel*, *paint*, *varnish*, *panel*, and *brick*. We can view these pairs simply as words that have more than one meaning, but this misses the fact that their meanings are related in a systematic way. One way to capture this would be to appeal to the already established notion notion of *zero derivation*. Just as a singular noun is English is marked with an empty suffix, so the verb in each of these pairs is derived from the corresponding noun with an empty suffix.

As we have said, a speaker must generally know what derivational form is appropriate for particular words so that the derived word is effectively a lexical item that speakers must learn. But this should not be taken as meaning that the system is entirely unproductive and, indeed, it is most clearly productive in cases where forms are derived from words that are themselves already derived. Thus, almost any verb that is derived using the suffix *-ize* can take the suffix *-able* to yield a new derived form as in *centralizable*, *popularizable*. Any derivation formed with *-able* can give rise to a new form in *-ity* as in *characterizable*, and *generalizable*. From these, we get *characterizability*, and *generalizability*, and from these *uncharacterizability*, and *ungeneralizability*. English speakers have no difficulty understanding the word *unredecontaminatablity* the first time they encounter it, or of constructing it if they have a use for it.

A multiply derived form is not just a sequence of prefixes, a stem, and a sequence of suffixes. Morphology of the language assigns it a structure just as syntax assigns a structure to phrases or sentences. Furthermore, a given sequence of morphemes can sometimes have more than one structure, and thus have ambiguous interpretations just as phrases and sentences can. Such ambiguities are far less common in morphology. One reason for this is that every phrase in the structure must have one constituent that contains the stem of the word so that, if the word has the form $p_1 \ldots p_m S s_1 \ldots s_n$, where S is the stem, there can be no sequence $p_i \ldots p_j$ of prefixes, or $s_i \ldots s_j$ of suffixes, that constitute a phrase.

There are, however, English words like *unlockable* which has the structures *(un((lock)able))* and *((un(lock))able)*. An unlockable door is either a door that cannot be locked, or a door that can be unlocked. Some parallel forms are *undoable, unintieable, unbuttonable, unfastenable*. With the first structure, *unlockable* could be translated into French as *inverrouillable* and into German as *unverschließbar*. With the second structure, it should rather be translatable as *déverrouillable* or *aufschließbar*. Once one sees that words with ambiguous derivational structures are possible, one might expect that there would be many of them, involving many combinations of derivational suffixes, but this turns out not to be the case. Observe that *un-* can attach to both adjectives and verbs, and that *-able* attaches to verbs to form adjectives. In order to get the kind of ambiguity exemplified in *unlockable*, we need just such a combination of a prefix and a suffix, and the kind of ambiguity found in *un-* is quite unusual. In addition, there appear to be few combinations of prefixes and suffixes have semantically coherent interpretations. The combination of *un-* and *-able* is by far the most productive.

A different, and less interesting ambiguity arises when a word can be split into morphemes in more than one place as in *unionize*, which is analyzable either as *un-ion-ize* or as *union-ize*.

5.3.1 Compounds

When two or more words are put together to form a new word, the result is known as a *compound* and the process of combining them in this way is called *compounding*. The question that this naturally raises is what distinguishes compounds from phrases formed through ordinary syntactic processes. There are a number of answers to this question and they are different for different languages.

The adjective *black* and the noun *bird* combine naturally to form the noun phrase *black bird* which can be used to refer to a bird that is black. The noun *blackbird*, on the other hand, refers to a particular species of bird, though not the same one throughout the English-speaking world. It is easy to tell that *blackbird* is a compound, because its components are not separated by a space. We can tell the compound from the phrase also in the spoken language because the stress falls on the first component of the compound, but the second component of the phrase. This is a common pattern in English.

Consider the sentences *He is a realestate salesman* and *He is a real estate salesman*. The stress falls on the first syllable in *realestate* but the last syllable in *real estate* and the meanings are quite different. The compound refers to a person who sells real property whereas the phrase refers to a real, as opposed to an unreal, estate salesman, whatever that may be. A secondhand clock may or may not have a second hand. A *red head* is a head that is red, but a *redhead* is a person that has a red head. A piano has a *keyboard* and a hotel has a *key board*.

It is by no means the case that the parts of a compound are always written separately. If the first word in *French teacher* is stressed, then we have a compound that refers to a teacher of French but, if the second word is stressed, then we have a phrase referring to a teacher who is French.

German and Finnish employ compounds a great deal more than English, and English employs them a great deal more than the Romance languages so that a translator must not expect that compounds will routinely translate as compounds. In German, the parts of a compound are not separated by spaces so the orthographic form of the resulting words can be very long, as in *Lebensversicherungsgesellschaftsangestellter* (EMPLOYEE OF A LIFE INSURANCE COMPANY. Chemistry is an especially prolific source of long compounds. As in English, the first member of a pair of words that form a compound generally receives stress, though this cannot always be maintained with long words.

The largest class of German compounds consists of nouns made up of other nouns. It is generally a lexical property of German nouns that, when they precede another noun in a compound, they must (i) be singular, (ii) be plural, or (iii) be separated by *-s-*, which is a historical genitive. We say that this is *generally* the case because there are exceptions and complexities that are beyond our present scope. To group (i) belong *Erdbeben* (EARTH QUAKE), *Schuhmacher* (SHOE MAKER), and *Gasthaus* (GUEST HOUSE). These constitute about 75% of German nominal compounds. To group (ii) belong *Kindergarten* (KINDERGARTEN), *Bilderrahmen* (PICTURE FRAME) and *Schweinefleisch* (PORK). The last group contains *Lebensversicherung* (LIFE INSURANCE), *Staatspolizei* (STATE POLICE) and *Gottesdienst* (CHURCH SERVICE).

Although *-s-* is indeed a historical genitive, it is the binding element that follows many nouns that are feminine and could therefore never have a genitive form in *-s*. Nouns that end in a derivational suffix, like *Bildung* (EDUCATION), *Fähigkeit* (CAPABILITY) and *Dummheit* (STUPIDITY) are all feminine, yet they form compounds with *-s-*.

An English compound can often be rendered into German as a compound, and conversely. However, this is by no means the case for other target languages, particularly those that belong to other families. The most felicitous translations of English compounds onto French, for example, often involves prepositional phrases or relative clauses. Lexicalized French compounds routinely consist of a noun modified by a prepositional phrase, as in *moulin à vent* (WIND MILL), *aide de camp* (AIDE-DE-CAMP) and *arc-en-ciel* (RAIN BOW). This also occurs in English, as in *daughter-in-law, master at arms* and *mother-of-pearl.* In another important class, the first word is the third person singular of a verb and the second is a noun. Examples are *porte-monnaie* (CHANGE PURSE), *gratte-ciel* (SKY-SCRAPER), and *couvre-feu* (CURFEW).

A number of English compounds derive from French phrases consisting of an adjective and a noun where the adjective follows the noun, as is often the case in Romance languages. Examples are *attorney/secretary/surgeon general, notary public,* and *heir apparent.* Notice that the plural form is obtained by pluralizing the first word.

Other kinds of compound are not hard to find and, while noun compounds are the ones that come most readily to mind, perhaps because the are the commonest, they can also belong to many other parts of speech. Consider adjectives *blood red, time honored, hard and fast, six-foot,* adverbs *fair and square, little-by-little, by halves,* verbs *come and go, stop and frisk* (also an adjective), *on and off, hell for leather,* prepositions *on and off,* and so on.

6

Syntax

6.1 Prescriptive Grammar

In everyday terminology, when the term *grammar* is not being used to refer to the declensions and conjugations of Latin or Greek, it is often referring to a real or imagined set of rules for distinguishing good language from bad language. Its principal utility is in enabling one to avoid the latter. If you believe that a sentence should not end with a preposition, it is because you believe that this is a rule of English grammar. If you believe that it is correct to say *My father and I built this house* rather than *My father and me built this house*, it is because you believe that there is a valid rule of grammar to this effect. Of course, this does not mean that you know what the rules say in detail and this is a matter upon which different people have different theories. If you think that the rule provides grounds for preferring *This house was built by my father and I* to *This house was built by my father and me*, you will invite the scorn of the pundits who will gleefully explain that those who understand the rule properly know that it justifies exactly the opposite conclusion.

Grammar as what distinguishes bad from good linguistic usage—so called *prescriptive* grammar—is not a matter of professional concern for most linguists. Members of this profession generally see themselves as scientists who must, therefore, concentrate on language as it is, and not on language as somebody thinks it ought to be. Apparent exceptions might be some socio-linguists interested in, say, how language functions in distinguishing social groups from one another. But, inasmuch as prescriptive grammar plays the role of rules of etiquette, to be observed by well-behaved members of society, then it influences linguists just as surely as anyone else. Many linguists, on discovering that a colleague had written the word *schemas* in the draft of a coauthored paper, would quietly replace it with *schemata*.

Viewed as a prescription for linguistic etiquette, grammar is, of course, often a matter of concern to translators. If a translator judges the author of a source text not to have followed some rule, he will presumably rarely go in search of some parallel infraction in his target text. But, if the passage in question is in a piece of prose fiction containing a character whose departures from linguistic norms play a role in the story, then he has the unenviable job of doing just that. Similarly, if the source text is deploring the state of language instruction in public schools, with copious examples, then there may be no alternative to seeking parallels in the target language.

There is doubtless more insistence on proper linguistic usage in the language of literate peoples, but agreement on just what the rules are is far from complete. Books like Fowler's "Modern English Usage",[29] and William Strunk and E. B. White's "The Elements of Style"[30] have been around for a century and continue to sell well. They are, of course, updated from time to time because the rules of etiquette change over time. For many Britons, the highest authority is the British Broadcasting Corporation. During my lifetime, however, they have sunk to using *agree* as a transitive verb as in *The parties agreed a truce at their meeting on Monday.*

Paul Shoebottom at the Frankfurt International School writes a blog on English usage, mostly for the benefit of foreign learners of the language. It contains some good advice but also illustrates some of the dangers of quickly classifying some of the things people say as *correct* or *incorrect.* This blog confidently declares that—

> ...it is incorrect usage to say *My car often broke down on the way home* if you are referring to one journey - it has to be *My car kept breaking down,* or *My car broke down several times.* (Shoebottom 2017)

The claim is that it is wrong to use the word *often* to refer to a set of events that take place within a short period, such as the drive home would presumably take. I share some of the feeling, but a very minor modification makes me happier. For example *My car broke down often*

---

29. Jeremy Butterfield, ed. 2015. *Fowler's Dictionary of Modern English Usage.* 4th ed. First published in 1926 as *A Dictionary of Modern English Usage.* Oxford: Oxford University Press

30. William Shrunk Jr. and E.B. White. 2000. *The Elements of Style.* 4th ed. First published in 1918 by Strunk alone; White made revisions and added a chapter for a 1959 version. Boston: Allyn & Bacon

on the way home seems like a clear improvement. And what about *On the way home, the turn signals often did not work?*

Prescriptivism in matters of language presumably comes in part from a well intentioned desire to keep ones usage elegant and beautiful by avoiding what one has been taught is ugly and in part from a feeling of superiority that comes from being able to display ones knowledge of arcane things. If you are caught saying *irregardless*, or *disinterested* when you should have said *uninterested*, then you are no better than the advertizer that wrote *Winston tastes good like a cigarette should.*

In *U and Non-U: An Essay in Sociological Linguistics* (1956), Alan S. C. Ross presented a set of pairs of English vocabulary items, the U (upper class) member of each pair being generally more earthy and the non-U member, more pretentious. He argued that the more earthy items tended to be used by the working class, but also by rich, educated, and more pretentious people, and the more pretentious items by poorer, more ordinary people. Nancy Mitford popularized the distinction in her essay "The English Aristocracy" (1956). Here are some example pairs:

U	Non-U
Expensive	Costly
False Teeth	Dentures
Pregnant	Expecting
House (a lovely)	Home (a lovely)
What?	Pardon?
Napkin	Serviette
Awful smell	Unpleasant odor
Rich	Wealthy
Curtains	Drapes

Some of these seem to reflect regional rather than social distinctions. For example, *expecting* and *serviette* are not used in these senses in the United States where *drapes* and *a lovely home* are more common than in Britain. Nevertheless, the point is well taken, that language usage differs on a variety of dimensions and, if the successful rendering of a text in another language requires these varieties to be reflected, then they suddenly become a central part of the translators' art.

Prescriptive grammarians concentrate most of their attention on the lexicon, and on syntax. Probably the most celebrated injunctions of the prescriptivists are those against split infinitives and sentences that end in prepositions. An example of the first of these is *to boldly go where none have gone before.* The second kind of infraction is quite common, especially in sentences that end in a relative clause, as in *This is the account you should take it from.* It is said that someone who knew Churchill was a stickler for carefully crafted English, went to such pains to avoid a sentence ending with a preposition in a memorandum he wrote for the prime minister as to render the sentence as a whole quite contorted. Churchill is said to have written in the margin *This is the sort of thing up with which I will not put.* It is perhaps worth pointing out that the sentence *This is the sort of thing I will not put up with* should probably not be thought of a contravening the injunction against sentences that end in prepositions because the words *up* and *with* function in it, not as prepositions but as verbal particles. They are part of the verb *to put up with.*

6.2 Productivity

Syntax is the next level of abstraction above morphology within modern linguistics. Just as morphemes are concatenations of phonemes, so phrases and sentences are concatenations of words. Furthermore, just as the number of entities and their configurations are greater in morphology than in phonology, so in syntax the numbers increase dramatically. Syntax has attracted a great deal more attention from linguists over the last fifty years than either phonology or morphology. There are two important and closely related reasons for this. One is that it is mainly in terms of syntax that the greatest mystery of language, namely its *productivity*, must be accounted for. The second is that the complexity of the phenomena encountered on this level has given rise to a large number of different theories and approaches, each with its own army of adherents.

When we speak of the productivity of language, we are referring to the fact that people can construct and understand an essentially infinite number of sentences, most of which they have never encountered before. Furthermore, they can differentiate between strings of words that are sentences, and others that are not. Accounting for this productivity became the dominating theme of linguistics with the publication of Chomsky's *Syntactic Structures* in 1957. Unfortunately, the view that was taken of the problem was lopsided in that it concentrated on the ability to distinguish sentences from non-sentences while largely ignoring a related problem that is surely at least as important, namely how it is that people can encode an almost limitless range of messages in hitherto unused sentences. This question is now at the center of attention for many linguists.

Determinedly approaching the problem from only one side led linguists to formulate problems like the following: how is it that, on the basis of the small and certainly finite set of sentences encountered by the age of, say, six, a child is able to infer the rules necessary to recognize and construct any of an infinitely large set of sentences? More particularly, how is it that a child can pull off this feat with few or no counterexamples, that is, with virtually no feedback when attempts to construct a sentence fail? No such dilemmas would even suggest themselves to an observer who adopted a more balanced vantage point. The notion that a child would have even the remotest chance of learning a language on the basis of a set of totally unmotivated examples, large or small, completely devoid of any context, would never even present itself. When a person is asked whether this or that string is a sentence, they fairly clearly take it as a question as to whether they can imagine a circumstance in which it might usefully be said, and this is an altogether different question.

However lopsided the view of many linguists may have been, the productivity question is important, indeed central, and highly complex. The fact that humans learn to control this complexity in the first few years of their lives while it remains completely beyond the reach of all other species encourages the view that the human brain must be genetically endowed with special equipment for processing language. After all, evolution has apparently favored animals with opposable thumbs, the utility of which is far surpassed by language, so it would hardly be surprising that creatures with language would have been accorded some advantage. But debate about how syntax arose or how children attain mastery of it does not bear directly on its role in translation.

Consider the sentence *Bobo gave Didi the duck*. Some readers of this may have seen the sentence before, but it is scarcely probable. In any case, our ability to understand it does not turn on our having seen it before. Using familiar rules of English grammar, we are able to decompose it into a subject, (*Bobo*), a verb (*gave*), an indirect object (*Didi*), and a direct object (*the duck*). From these grammatical relations, we are able to deduce that the sentence is about a giving event in which someone called Bobo was the donor, someone called Didi, the recipient, and what changed hands was a duck. The duck is presumably known from earlier in the text, since it has the article *the* rather than *a*.

Some other permutations of these same words, such as those in 1(a)–(d) below, we immediately recognize as not being sentences at all.

(1) a. * Bobo the gave Didi duck

    b. * Bobo gave the duck the to Didi

    c. * Bobo gave duck to Didi the

    d. * The to Bobo gave duck Didi

Following a well-established convention among linguists, we signal the fact that they are not sentences with a leading asterisk. Still other permutations, like those in 2(a)–(d) are clearly sentences. Their meanings, however, though similar in many ways, are different in the roles they assign to the entities referred to by the noun phrases. In 2(a), for example, the duck is the gift, and Didi is its recipient.

(2)   a. Bobo gave Didi to the duck

        b. Didi gave the duck to Bobo

        c. Didi gave Bobo to the duck

        d. To Didi Bobo gave the duck

By changing the membership of the set of words very slightly, we can create new sentences in which the assignment of entities to roles remains the same as in the original. Some examples of this are given in 3(a)–(e).

(3)   a. Bobo gave the duck to Didi

        b. Didi was given the duck by Bobo

        c. The duck was given to Didi by Bobo

        d. The duck Bobo gave to Didi

        e. To Didi Bobo gave the duck

Linguists generally agree that all these distinctions should be accounted for by a *grammar*, or, more specifically, by a set of *syntactic rules*. They differ, however, in the form that these rules should take. Our concern here is only to give a feel for the way these mechanisms work, and not to explore any of the great range of subtleties involved. The following illustrates a very simple kind of rule.

1. S →   NP   VP
           subj   *head*

2. VP → V_d NP   NP
             head   *iobj*   *dobj*

3. NP → Det   N
            det   *head*

4. N → duck

5. NP → Bobo

6. NP → Didi

7. V_d → gave

8. Det → the

Some rules are written on two lines. To begin with, we ignore the second line. The first rule says that the sentence (S) can consist of a noun phrase (NP) followed by a verb phrase (VP). The second says that the verb phrase can consist of a ditransitive verb (V_d) followed by two noun phrases. A *ditransitive verb* is simply a verb that takes both the direct and indirect objects. The verb *give* is the canonical example of such a verb. The third rule says that a noun phrase can consist of an article or, in linguistic jargon, a *determiner* (Det), followed by a noun (N). The remaining rules simply associate parts of speech with individual words. *Duck* is a noun; *Bobo* is a noun phrase; and so forth.

Let us now go back to our original sentence, namely *Bobo gave Didi the duck*. Using the grammar, we can replace each of these words by its part of speech, as follows:

$$NP\ V_d\ Det\ N\ NP.$$

We continue using a slight generalization of this operation. We look for something in our string that matches the right-hand side of some rule and replace it by the corresponding left-hand side. For example, the sequence *Det N* can be replaced by *NP* to give the new string

$$NP\ V_d\ NP\ NP$$

using rule 3. This string contains the sequence V_d *NP NP* which matches the right-hand side of rule 2. After the corresponding replacement, we are left with *NP VP* which we can replace with *S* according to Rule 1. We have thus established that, according to this grammar, the original string of words is a sentence.

We can summarize this set operations with the following, so-called *phrase-structure* diagram like the one in Figure 6.1. The nodes at the

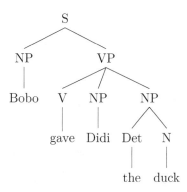

FIGURE 6.1

bottom of this inverted tree are simply the words of the original sentence. Labels occurring higher in the tree identify places where the process just described made a replacement in accordance with the rules. Notice that there are various different orders in which these replacements could have been made, all resulting in the same tree structure. A grammar that works this way is known as a *context-free phrase-structure* grammar, or simply a *context-free grammar*. The name comes from the fact that the possibility of applying a rule to construct a phrase depends only on material inside that phrase and not anything in the context to the left or right.

Only the first three rules in the above set allow for the construction of substantial phrases, that is, phrases that consist of more than one word, and, for these, we have written a second line of symbols under the ones we have been considering. This names the role that each particular member of a phrase plays in that phrase. The first rule, for example, constructs a phrase in which a noun phrase, filling the role of subject of the phrase (*subj*), is followed by a verb phrase, filling the role of *head* of the phrase. The second rule involves two noun phrases, but playing different roles. One way of incorporating these roles into the diagram would be as in Figure 6.2. The roles are printed in lower-case italics, and

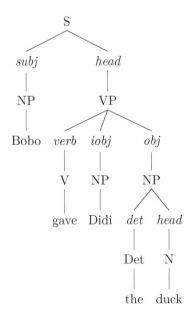

FIGURE 6.2

the grammatical categories, or parts of speech, in upper-case letters. In what follows, we will generally leave the roles implicit.

Introducing roles into the grammar in this way adds somewhat to the information the grammar can give us about a sentence, but it does not change the set of sentences we can analyze, or how many analyses we can get for each one. As we shall see shortly, linguists have found it necessary to introduce more sweeping changes that do affect these things.

Syntax is characterized by a great deal of ambiguity, that is, by numbers of sentences that have several different structures, generally corresponding to different meanings. Consider the following sentences:

1. He saw the boy with the telescope.
2. I had forgotten how good beer tastes.
3. Visiting relatives can be boring

In (1), the prepositional phrase can be taken as modifying either the noun phrase *boy* or the verb phrase *saw the boy*. In the first case, the boy that he saw was the one with the telescope. In the second case, he used a telescope to see the boy. In (2), what I had forgotten is either the taste of good beer or how good it is that beer—any beer—tastes. In the first case, the words *good* and *beer* constitute a phrase, whereas, in the second, *how* and *good* constitute a phrase. In (3), the trees have the same shapes for both interpretations, but in one case *relatives* is the object of *visiting* where, in the other case *visiting* modifies *relatives*.

Example (1) above, is a classic case of an ambiguity that arises when a noun is modified by a following prepositional phrase, and it can be compounded arbitrarily many times. Consider the sentence

4. He saw the boy with the telescope on the counter at the front of the store.

This contains five noun phrases with four prepositions between them and, assuming that there are no other ambiguities inside these phrases, the sentence as a whole has fourteen structures. Add another preposition and noun phrase and the number goes to forty-two, then 132^{31}.

Context-free grammar is a simple scheme, a version of which used to be widely taught to children and applied in an exercise known as "sentence diagramming". As a system for stating the grammatical properties of a language accurately and in detail, however, it is woefully inadequate. Even the eight rules we introduced above do not do a satisfactory job on the single example we designed them for. We should be able to add the nouns *child* and *children*, *ducks* and the verbs *give* and *gives* to

---

31. This sequence is called the *Catalan* numbers.

the grammar, and be in a position to analyze the sentences 4(a)–(d). The trouble is that it also provides analyses of 4(e)-(h).

(4) a. The child gives the duck to Didi

  b. The child gives the ducks to Didi

  c. The children give the duck to Didi

  d. The children give the ducks to Didi

  e. The child give the duck to Didi

  f. The child give the ducks to Didi

  g. The children gives the duck to Didi

  h. The children gives the ducks to Didi

At first, this does not look like a serious problem. All we have to do is to extend the grammar somewhat. We need two rules for forming noun phrases, one for singular phrases, and one for plural phrases. We must do the same thing for nouns and verbs. In fact almost the whole grammar is affected. It now looks like this:

1. S → NPsing   VPsing
        subj   *head*

2. S → NPplur   VPplur
        subj   *head*

3. VPsing → $Vsing_d$ NP   NP
              head   *iobj*   *dobj*

4. VPplur → $Vplur_d$ NP   NP
              head   *iobj*   *dobj*

5. NP → Det   Nsing
          det   *head*

6. NP → Det   Nplur
          det   *head*

7. N → duck

8. NP → Bobo

9. NP → Didi

10. V_d → gave

11. Det → the

Now suppose we were writing a grammar, not of English, but of German, where there are not only two numbers, but also three genders, but also four cases. We could therefore need $2 \times 3 \times 4 = 24$ different rules, just for constructing simple noun phrases. A similar explosion would occur in many places throughout the grammar. Furthermore,

German is by no means extreme in the demands it would place on a pure context-free grammar, and there are other reasons for unhappiness with this system.

The twenty-four rules that simple German noun phrases would require do nothing more than capture the idea that determiners and nouns agree in number gender and case. It turns out that, if the noun phrase contains an adjective, then they must also agree. The subject of a sentence must agree with the finite verb, and so on. We should be able to capture this pervasive notion in a manner that is simpler and more transparent. Here is a formulation of our toy English grammar that does that, and a little more.

1. $\begin{bmatrix} \text{cat} & S \\ \text{subj} & subj \\ \text{head} & head \end{bmatrix} \rightarrow \begin{bmatrix} \text{cat} & \text{NP} \\ \text{num} & num \end{bmatrix} = subj \begin{bmatrix} \text{cat} & \text{VP} \\ \text{num} & num \end{bmatrix} = head$

2. $\begin{bmatrix} \text{cat} & \text{VP} \\ \text{num} & num \\ \text{iobj} & iobj \\ \text{dobj} & dobj \end{bmatrix} \rightarrow \begin{bmatrix} \text{cat} & V \\ \text{num} & num \end{bmatrix} \begin{bmatrix} \text{cat NP} \end{bmatrix} = iobj \begin{bmatrix} \text{cat NP} \end{bmatrix} = dobj$

3. $\begin{bmatrix} \text{cat} & \text{NP} \\ \text{num} & num \\ \text{det} & det \\ \text{head} & head \end{bmatrix} \rightarrow \begin{bmatrix} \text{cat} & \text{Det} \\ \text{num} & num \end{bmatrix} = det \begin{bmatrix} \text{cat} & N \\ \text{num} & num \end{bmatrix} = head$

As before, each rule has two parts, with one item to the left of the → sign, and a string of one or more items on the right. Now, however, each of these items consists of two columns containing what we will refer to as *attributes* and *values*. Rule 1 says that a phrase of category S can be constructed out of a pair of items belonging to categories NP and VP provided they have the same values for the attribute *num*. A word in italics is to be understood as naming a variable which can take on any value but, if it occurs more than once in the rule, then it must have the same value in each place. In rule 1, the variable *num* must therefore have the same value in the verb as it does on the noun phrase.

Variable names also appear following the attribute-value pairs on the right-hand sides of the rules, separated from them by a "=". This causes the entire set of attributes and values associated with the word or phrase preceding the "=" sign to become the value of that variable. These variables also appear on the left-hand side of the rule so that they can be incorporated into the description of the phrase that is constructed. We apply this grammar to a string in the same way that we applied the earlier one but, by virtue of the attributes and variables that we have introduced, a remarkably richer set of events takes place. Now, when we analyze the sentence *Bobo gave Didi the duck*, we get a tree structure with the same shape as the one we got before, but the top node, instead of being labeled simply *S*, carries the following label:

$$
\begin{bmatrix}
\text{cat} & \text{VP} \\
\text{V} & \text{gave} \\
\text{Agt} & \begin{bmatrix} \text{cat} & \text{NP} \\ \text{num} & \text{sing} \\ \text{lex} & \text{Bobo} \end{bmatrix} \\
\text{iobj} & \begin{bmatrix} \text{cat} & \text{NP} \\ \text{num} & \text{sing} \\ \text{lex} & \text{Didi} \end{bmatrix} \\
\text{oobj} & \begin{bmatrix} \text{cat} & \text{NP} \\ \text{num} & \text{sing} \\ \text{det} & \begin{bmatrix} \text{cat} & \text{Det} \\ \text{num} & \text{sing} \\ \text{lex} & \text{the} \end{bmatrix} \\ \text{head} & \begin{bmatrix} \text{cat} & \text{N} \\ \text{lex} & \text{duck} \end{bmatrix} \end{bmatrix}
\end{bmatrix}
$$

All the information we need about the semantic structure of the sentence is in this single label. The information associated with the other nodes in the tree participated in the process of deriving this one, but can be discarded once this label has been constructed. Information that was encoded in a variety of different ways in different languages, notably word order and idiosyncratic morphology is now normalized in a quite radical way. So, once again, the effect is to reduce irregularity and the properties that distinguish one language from the other. Syntax is therefore placed closer to the apex of the Vauquois triangle than morphology.

Building a key notion like agreement into the notation used for linguistic rules and descriptions—the so-called *formalism*—enables the linguist to capture, and profit from, generalizations that he is able to make about language in general. If linguistics is the science of language then capturing generalizations must be one of its primary aims.

Another syntactic generalization concerns the relationship between sentences and several kinds of subordinate clause that are related to them in a systematic way. Consider the sentences in 5.

(5) a. That is the one that Bobo gave Didi

      b. Didi is the one Bobo gave the duck to.

      c. Bobo is the one that gave the duck to Didi.

      d. The duck is the one that Bobo gave to Didi.

      e. That is who Bobo gave the duck to.

      f. That is who gave the duck to Didi.

      g. That is what Bobo gave to Didi.

      h. Did Bobo give the duck to Didi?

      i. What did Bobo give to Didi?

      j. Who did Bobo give the duck to?

      k. Who gave Didi the duck?

      l. That is the duck that you said Bobo gave Didi.

      m. That is the duck that you said I thought Bobo gave Didi.

5(a)–(d) contain relative clauses based on the sentence we have been considering. In each case, the relative clause modifies the noun *the one*. The relative clause itself differs from the original sentence in that one of its noun phrase has been removed—*the duck* in (a), *Didi* in (b) and so forth. We can paraphrase these sentences by preceding each relative clause with the words *such that* and putting either *it* or *him*, as appropriate, in place of the noun phrase that has been removed. The result is as follows:

(6) a. That is the one **such that** Bobo gave **it** Didi

      b. Didi is the one **such that** Bobo gave the duck to **him**.

      c. Bobo is the one **such that he** gave the duck to Didi.

      d. The duck is the one **such that** Bobo gave **it** to Didi.

It seems, therefore, that our formalism for writing rules could profit from the ability to describe one kind of phrase as being the same as another but for the deletion of an item of a given kind, in this case, as noun phrase. We would be able to use such a mechanism in the other examples in 5 and also elsewhere.

Examples 5(e)–(g) contain what are sometimes referred to as *nominal* relative clauses. The roles played by the noun that the clause modifies in 5(a)–(d) and the relative pronoun are played by a single item, *who* or *what*.

Examples 5(h)–(j) are questions. The first of them questions the truth of the proposition—*Is it the case that Bobo gave Didi the duck?*.

In 5(i)–(j) The question needs a noun phrase from the original sentence as an answer. Accordingly, the question takes the form of the original sentence with that noun phrase removed and preceded by the word *who* or *what*.

Examples 5(l) and (m) illustrate the fact that the noun phrase that is omitted in forming these various kinds of sentence need not be one of the principal participants in the sentence, but may be embedded in anther sentence inside the main one at essentially any depth of embedding.

This is not the place to discuss the various more or less arcane conditions and restrictions governing this mechanism, such as the the missing noun phrase, while it can be the subject of a sentence, but cannot be extracted from inside the subject. So, while we get *This is the man you said wrote the book*, but not **This is the man the wife of wrote the book.* meaning *this is the man whose wife wrote the book.* Our point is that these are phenomena that are found in many languages so that it is appropriate to provide a mechanism to accommodate them.

The main thing that needs to be done to solve this problem is to introduce into the rule formalism something like the following: let X/Y be a phrase belonging to category X, but which is missing a component word or phrase of category Y. A sentence that is missing a noun phrase would thus be labeled as S/NP. The tree structure for a phrase of type X/Y must either have another phrase of type X/Y inside it, where there would normally be a phrase of type NP, or have nothing where there would normally be a phrase of type Y. With these conventions and the appropriate grammar rules in place the noun phrase *the guy you said gave Didi the duck* gets the structure in Figure 6.3. A relative clause is a phrase of category S/NP—a sentence that is missing a noun phrase somewhere. In this case, the gap where a noun phrase would normally be is inside another embedded sentence. We have shown its position with a bullet character. What is omitted, then, is the subject of this embedded sentence.

The human translator rarely has much difficulty in deciding among the various interpretations of a syntactically ambiguous sentence. Indeed, in most cases, it would be surprising if he even noticed the ambiguity. As with all ambiguities, however, the criteria that the reader or translator calls on to resolve them can be quite subtle. The example *I had forgotten how good beer tastes*, mentioned above, was first used by Ivan Sag in contexts that are generated by replacing X in the following pair of sentences in four different ways: *I just got back from X. I had forgotten how good beer tastes.* The four replacements are *Texas*,

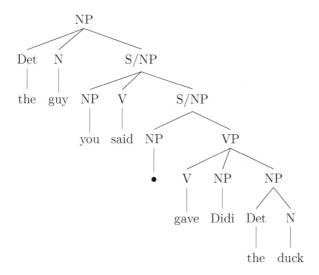

FIGURE 6.3

Utah, the Czech Republic and *Saudi Arabia*. Texas has a reputation for good beer, whereas beer is widely believed to be unobtainable in Utah. Similarly, the Czech Republic is famous for its beer, whereas Saudi Arabia is a dry country. So, for Texas and the Czech Republic, the the sentence is about good beer whereas for Utah and Saudi Arabia, it is about all beer. To add a little spice to the example, Sag points out that the common perception that Utah is a dry state is incorrect, and beer is indeed obtainable there.

Different translations are required of these sentences depending on which of the interpretations we take it to have. Sometimes, the extent of the semantic ambiguity corresponding to a particular syntactic ambiguity can vary depending on details of the situation being described. Suppose that we encounter the sentence *He took the letter to Mary* just after it has been established that someone wrote a letter to Mary. If the letter was intended go to Mary and it was to her that he took it, then it matters very little whether *to Mary* modifies *He took the letter* or just *the letter*. On the other hand, if he took the letter, thus preventing Mary from receiving it, then *to Mary* must be taken as modifying *the letter*. If the letter was not intended for Mary, but he took it to her anyway, then *to Mary* must modify *took the letter*. In some languages, these considerations do not matter because the ambiguity can be preserved naturally in the translation. In others, it could be crucial.

We have said that ambiguity is not a primary source of problems for translators. A moment's reflection reveals this to be a somewhat curious claim. What it seems to be saying is that sentences with more than one meaning generally have only one meaning for a translator and, presumably, the meaning they have for the translator is the right one. So, are we saying that translators have an insight into the meanings of sentences that is denied to the rest of us? They may indeed have to some very small extent, but this is not what is being claimed. When we say that a word, a phrase, or a sentence is ambiguous, we generally mean one of two things. Either the item could take on different meanings when placed in different contexts, or the item is assigned more than one analysis by the rules and conventions of some component of the grammar, such as the syntactic component. The upshot is that these ambiguities that are a minor concern for human translators, are a major concern for machine translation where sensitivity to context is primitive at best.

6.3 Signs

The Swiss linguist Ferdinand de Saussure analyzed language in terms of what he called *signs*, each of which is a pair consisting of a word or phrase and something which we will call the *sense* of the word or phrase. Just what should be understood by a sense is a complex matter to which we shall return. For the moment, we can limit our attention to common nouns, adjectives and verbs that are routinely used to refer to things, properties, events and states in the world. We will refer to all of these simply as *things*. We leave aside words whose function seems to be more grammatical, like conjunctions, prepositions, and auxiliary verbs, not to mention some less common kinds of noun, adjective and verb.

Following Frege (1892), we think of the sense of one of these words as a characterization of the kinds of thing it may be used to refer to. The word *fish* may be used to refer to a kind of animal that lives in water, that breathes through gills, is generally scaly and doubtless has various other properties that may be important even if we cannot call them to mind. People may be unsure where to draw the line between fish and other animals and may differ with other people on these matters. We will encounter striking examples of such doubt and disagreement later. Notice, however, that they do nothing to weaken our claim that words and other vocabulary items constitute a digital system. The existence of whales and porpoises, which share properties of fish and mammals, does not lead us to suppose that there should be a word with a sound that is somehow intermediate between those of *fish* and *mammal* that would naturally refer to these creatures. When we say that every instance of a word either absolutely is, or absolutely is not an instance of the word *fish*, we by no means intend to suggest that every thing in the world either absolutely is, or absolutely is not, a fish.

Someone might ask what we would say of a sound that is essentially the same as that of the English word *fish*, but occurring in an utterance in some other language or, for that matter, in an altogether nonlinguistic context. A steam engine, for example, might make a noise from time to time that sounded very like someone pronouncing the word *fish*. Our answer to such a person must surely be that it does not matter. We are interested in how languages work and not in the status of sounds that might momentarily be mistaken for language, or might be thought of as belonging to a different language than the one we are considering. De Saussure's point was that there is nothing about the phonetic or orthographic make-up of a word *fish* that makes it particularly appropriate for naming animals that live in water. And, indeed, the similar sounding French word *fiche* means nothing of the kind, but is used rather to refer to a piece of paper. If the German word *Fisch* means the same as the English word, it is because the words were both derived from a common ancestor at a time when English and German were closer to the one and the same language and not because of any natural association between the sound and the animal.

Digital systems make for robustness in transmitting information over transmission lines, which is one of the main reasons why compact disks are generally preferred to vinyl records. We have seen that language has that same robustness. But the digital nature of language also enables it to have a more crucial property, namely that of being a system of *signs*. A sign is a pair consisting of a linguistic unit, like a word or a morpheme, and something else which, for the moment, we can just refer to as its *meaning*.

In order to see why digital systems make much more versatile and effective systems of signs, let us consider the alternative system consisting of signs based on an underlying analog system.

Notice, first of all, that a language with these characteristics could not have a writing system that was in any way like the ones we are familiar with. Suppose someone made a number of sounds which, to our ears, sounded like the word *mate*. They would, in fact, all be different from one another to some degree, some sounding a little more like *met*, some somewhat more like *meet*, and some more like *net*. Since we are supposing that the system is analog, we must assume that every difference in pronunciation, however slight, has some significance; the greater the difference, the greater the significance.

Let us suppose that, when a speaker makes a sound, as nearly as we can tell, exactly like the word *mate* as we would say it when speaking with great care, that speaker is referring to the first officer on a ship, and that when he said something exactly like *met*, he was referring to a meeting that had taken place sometime in the past. We must now suppose that, if he uttered a sound that was intermediate between these two according to the appropriate metric, then he intended to refer to an entity that was somehow intermediate between the first officer of a ship and a meeting sometime in the past. It is extremely difficult to imagine such a system evolving naturally, and it would be outrageously difficult to construct artificially. It would enshrine a theory of phonetics that is isomorphic with a theory of the world, or of that part of the world that it could be used to talk about so that it would be hopelessly inflexible in the face of new information.

The corresponding digital system is incomparably simpler and incomparably more powerful. There is no notion of locality among symbols, and no reason to reflect the various kinds of locality in the meanings in the forms of the symbols. The relationship between the symbol and the corresponding meaning is entirely arbitrary. De Saussure insisted that linguistic signs consist of a *signifiant*, which we have been calling the *symbol* and a *signifié*, which we have called the meaning. The term *meaning* is indeed an unhappy choice. It is a grossly overworked term which has caused us no small amount of trouble in this book. In addition, it is clearly inappropriate for certain kinds of signs, especially those that occupy the lowest, or phonological level. Here, the *signifié* is in the realm of articulatory or acoustic phonetics and a long way from anything we normally call *meaning*.

De Saussure's notion of a sign extends naturally beyond that of a word-meaning pair to larger collections of properties. A third component might, for example, be the grammatical category of the word, and other properties might be words and grammatical categories in other languages. Viewed in this way, signs can be seen as the foundation of what we have referred to as the "standard model" of translation. Large translations are concatenations of smaller translations, and the smallest translations are signs which constitute a bilingual lexicon.

7

Machine Translation

7.1 History

The population of the world is increasing at a great rate and, as we pointed out at the beginning of this book, so is the world's need for translations. Ordinary people now routinely travel far beyond the boundaries of their village and even their country. Not only do they need to talk to the people they meet on these journeys, but they need to engage in commerce with them, to formalize agreements with them, to exchange news with them, and so forth. They also enter into competition with them and are therefore motivated to read what they write and listen to what they say.

On October 4, 1957, the Soviet Union launched into Earth's orbit a metal sphere, fifty-eight centimeters in diameter. It could be seen from all over the Earth and its pulsating radio transmissions could be picked up everywhere. This sphere, known as *Sputnik* (Спутник), Russian for satellite, occasioned a powerful shock in Western countries, most notably in the United States, where it gave rise to much disquiet on the question of who was winning the so-called *space race*. To control space was seen as the key to controlling the world.

It immediately became a matter of great urgency in America to discover in much greater detail just how far Russian space technology had advanced, what specific methods and techniques they were applying, and to put in place as soon as possible an American program that would overtake them. Naturally, most of what the Russians were doing was classified and it was clearly necessary to penetrate the vale of secrecy to the maximum extent possible. But it was clearly also important to get up to date on whatever could be found in the Russian open literature.

This brought the Americans to a major stumbling block. It turned out that almost all of the Russian literature was actually in Russian. To require Americans to learn Russian could very well be judged unconstitutional on the grounds that it amounted to cruel and unusual punishment.

By great good fortune, the launch of Sputnik took place just three years after what has come to be known as the *Georgetown-IBM experiment*. On January 7, 1954, researchers from Georgetown University Institute of Languages and Linguistics and the IBM corporation came together at IBM World Headquarters, 57th Street and Madison Avenue, to demonstrate a program running on an IBM 701 computer translating some fifty sentences from Russian into English.

Based on the results, Professor Léon Dostert, the leader of the Georgetown group, was moved to say "Five, perhaps three years hence, interlingual meaning conversion by electronic process in important functional areas of several languages may well be an accomplished fact" (IBM 1954).

The program demonstrated in the Georgetown-IBM experiment had access to a bilingual dictionary with just 250 entries, which leaves little doubt as to how well it was adapted to the particular text of forty-nine Russian sentences it would be given to translate. It had just six rules of grammar.

The following are three of the sentences used in the experiment together with the translation delivered by the computer. The original Russian text was transliterated into the Roman alphabet so that it could be transferred to punched cards and read by the computer

Mi pyeryedayem mislyi posryedstvom ryechyi.	We transmit thoughts by means of speech.
Vyelyichyina ugla opryedyelyayetsya otnoshyenyiyem dlyini dugi k radyiusu.	Magnitude of angle is determined by the relation of length of arc to radius.
Myezhdunarodnoye ponyimanyiye yavlyayetsya vazhnim faktorom v ryeshyenyiyi polyityichyeskix voprosov.	International understanding constitutes an important factor in decision of political questions.

The first of the six rules in the program, spelled out in English, was as follows:

```
Rule 1. Rearrangement. If first code is '110', is third
code associated with preceding complete word equal to '21'?
If so, reverse order of appearance of words in output
(i.e., word carrying '21' should follow that carrying
'110') - otherwise, retain order. In both cases English
equivalent I associated with '110' is adopted.
```

By the time Sputnik was launched, machine translation had still not become an accomplished fact. But the launch lent a sense of urgency to the enterprise of machine translation and attracted considerable funding to it. During the ensuing decade, research projects aimed at producing translating systems using a great variety of approaches sprang up all over the United States as well as in other countries. Needless to say, the Soviet Union initiated a similar program. But machine translation doggedly resisted becoming an accomplished fact.

In 1966, The American National Academy of Sciences constituted the Automatic Language Processing Advisory Committee (ALPAC) under the chairmanship of John R. Pierce and charged it with assessing the value that the government had received in return for what it had spent on language processing in general and machine translation in particular. They judged that value to have been very little and, as a result, funding for machine translation in the United States came to an almost complete stop. The committee took the view that machine translation needed to be treated as a much more complex undertaking than had originally been thought and recommended that resources be redirected towards providing a more secure foundation on which such an enterprise might be placed at some later stage. Eager to profit from this change in direction, the community of machine translation researchers relabeled themselves as *computational linguists* and thus a new field of science was born.

The history of machine translation is sometimes reckoned to have started a little earlier than Sputnik. Some even take it back to Leibniz and Descartes. Leibniz imagined what he called a *characteristica universalis*, or universal character. In French, he referred to it as *spécieuse générale*. It was inspired by Chinese characters and was supposed to be a universal language, free from the ambiguities and vaguenesses of natural languages that would make it possible to set mathematical and scientific discourse on a more secure footing. Some early approaches to machine translation relied on the notion of a so-called *interlingua* that was also intended to be a distillation of the semantic essentials of all natural languages.

To credit Leibniz and Descartes with foreseeing, or in any way foreshadowing, machine translation requires a considerable stretch of the imagination. The history is more often taken to have started with a letter written by Warren Weaver, director of the Division of Natural Sciences at the Rockefeller Foundation (1932–55) in March 1947 to the cyberneticist Norbert Wiener. Wiener was not greatly impressed, but in July 1949, Weaver elaborated on these ideas in a memorandum to his colleagues at the Rockefeller Foundation. His proposal was based on four main ideas, namely:

1. Resolution of ambiguities based on properties of the immediate context. He had convinced himself that most ambiguities could be resolved rather simply on the basis of very few words in the immediate vicinity of the word in question.

2. The problem of translation was a variant of the problem of code breaking, an enterprise in which Wiener had been engaged during World War II.

3. The problems of translation were essentially logical in nature. Although Gödel's incompleteness theorem had shown in the 1980s that logical problems were not always computable, it was thought that most of the problems that this would not prove an impediment in most practical cases.

4. It seemed likely to him that, for all their diversity, the languages of the world were united by more properties than separated them.

These four ideas, and especially the first two of them, are the foundation of what we have referred to as *syntactic* translation, or the *standard model* of translation. Perhaps the most celebrated sentence from the letter is on the second of these points. It reads

> When I look at an article in Russian, I say "This is really written in English, but it has been coded in some strange symbols. I will now proceed to decode." (1947)

We have seen nothing that should convince us that a machine translation system based on these ideas could not be immensely useful in a world with a desperate need for translation. But we have seen a great deal that strongly suggests that no such system could be the prototype of a system that would, in however distant a future, do what translators do. As Weaver himself said "Even if it would translate only scientific material (where the semantic difficulties are very notably less), and even if it did produce an inelegant (but intelligible) result, it would seem to me worth while." Certainly, it could be immensely useful in tracking Russian progress in the space race, and in the mere ten years that intervened between the Georgetown-IBM experiment and the launch of Sputnik, little of the early euphoria had dissipated.

Based on his experience in code breaking, Wiener had foreseen an approach to Machine Translation based on so-called *neural networks*. We do not need to go into these in great detail, though it is worth noting that neural networks are again attracting attention in the field.

A neural network consists of a large number of artificial *neurons*. These are devices, modeled by pieces of data in a computer program, each of which has a number of input channels, or *dendrites*, and an output channel, or *axon*. If the amount of input it receives at a given moment exceeds a given threshold, it produces an output. Inputs may come directly from the outside world or from the outputs of other neurons. Likewise, outputs can go to the outside, or to other neurons. Neurons are connected together in a random fashion, generally subject to the restriction that paths from one neuron to another be of a certain, very limited, length—usually two or three. If this number is n, we say that the network has n *layers* and that a neuron that receives an input after i steps is on level i.

Given that the connections in the network are random, it can only be expected to produce a random pattern of outputs for any given input. However, this situation can change after the network has been *trained*. Here is a simplified view of how training happens. A set of pairs in which inputs are paired with the outputs we want the network to produce for each of them. This is the *training data*. Many inputs are fed to the network. When an input belongs to the training data, then changes are made to the neurons that are effected. If the output is the one paired with the input in the training data, then the amount of input required to actuate these neurons is decreased. Otherwise, it is increased. The expectation is that this will cause the network to *learn* the desired associations between inputs and outputs.

Weaver did not specify how neural networks might be applied to the translation problem. The intuition is that the inputs to the network would be words together with other words from the surrounding context. The outputs would be translations of the words in the various different contexts. The details of the process need not concern us. What is important is that this very early proposal, sketchy and imprecise as it was, was in line with approaches to machine translation that became dominant much later. In particular, the rules that a computer uses in translating should not be formulated by humans and then embodied in programs. They should be formulated by computers as a result of processing large quantities of translations made by professional translators. There are now large numbers of researchers working an machine translation and the overwhelming majority of them never question the correctness of this view. We, however, will do so shortly.

The alternative view is, as we have said, that translating computers should learn their trade from people, presumably people who already know it. This what is generally referred to as the *rule-based* approach, though the human contribution may look more or less like rules. This was the approach that was adopted by the people who conducted that Georgetown-IBM experiment and most of the work that was done on the problem during the next forty or forty-five years.

7.2 Rule-based Machine Translation

As we pointed out at the beginning of Chapter 5, the field of linguistics can be seen as a number of layers with those having to do with sound or writing at the bottom, and those having to do with meaning at the top. Translation presumably interacts with linguistics on all of these layers to some degree. This is especially true of machine translation where processes that are automatic and unconscious in people must be provided for explicitly in computers.

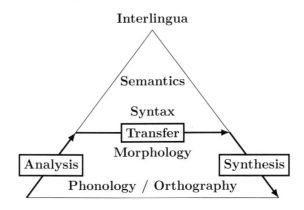

FIGURE 7.1 The Vauquois Triangle

The late, great French researcher on Machine Translation, Bernard Vauquois, often used a diagram like the one in Figure 7.1 to illustrate the relationship between linguistic theory and machine translation. It has come to be known as the *Vauquois Triangle*. The various sub-disciplines of the field are arranged in layers in their usual order, with phonology, or writing systems, at the bottom.

We imagine that the input that a hearer or reader receives has some natural representation on the lowest level. In the case of writing, this is presumably the actual letters, punctuation marks, and spaces of the text. In the case of speech, it is phonemes, intonation, pauses, and the like. The receiver of the message must derive higher level representations of the message from these, discarding distinctions that are interesting only on the lower level in the process. We will consider an example, simplifying the details greatly in order to bring out the aspects of it that we take to be most important.

Suppose I read the sentence *A helper fries fish for starving children*. Spelling rules reside at the lowest level of the hierarchy, and the relationship between the original written sentence, and the result of applying these rules might be depicted somewhat as follows:

A	helper		fries		fish	for	starving		children
A	help	er	fry	s	fish	for	starv	ing	children
			frie				starve		

The word *fries* can be analyzed as the single potential morpheme *fries*, or as either *fry* or *frie* followed by *s*. At this level of analysis, there is no basis on which to distinguish sequences of letters that represent actual morphemes of English. This information becomes available only on the morphological level.

For the word *starving*, there could three possibilities. It may be a single morpheme, or it may be a pair, the second of which is *ing*. The first member of the pair could be either *starve* or *starv*. But if we take it that the spelling rules are more finely crafted, recognizing the fact that English words do not end in *v*, then *starve* would be the only possibility for the first morpheme of the pair.

The most important effect of applying spelling rules is to make it more *regular*. More or less idiosyncratic variations in the spelling of a morpheme when it is combined with another morpheme are normalized. Notice that we do not take *children* to be a spelling variant of *child*, but rather a suppletive plural form which will be normalized on the next level. One of the results of normalization, or removal of gratuitous variation, is to make a text and its translation more similar than they would otherwise be. This will become more apparent as we look at higher levels. Doing this, however, will require more severe simplification in order to avoid committing ourselves to a particular theoretical stance or linguistic theory.

A morphological analysis of this sentence might be somewhat as in Table 7.1. The main thing that has happened here is that potential morphemes have been looked up in a lexicon to discover which ones might indeed be morphemes, and to associate grammatical information with them. In other words, what we have is a sequence of signs in de Saussure's sense. We take it, for example, that the word *a* at the beginning of the string represents either that letter itself, or the singular form of the indefinite article. If the second word of the sentence had begun with a vowel, then the first word would have been *an*, but

TABLE 7.1 Morphological Analysis

1	2	3	4	5
Alpha: a Det: indef, sg	As: help Ns: help Vs: help	As/A: comp Ns/N: agt	N: fries Ns: fry Vs: fry	N/N: pl V/V: prsg
		Nsg: helper		Npl: fries Vsg: fries

6	7	8	9	10
N:fish	P: for	V : starve	prpart:ing starving	Npl: child

the underlying morpheme would be the same as in this example, the distinction having been removed as a result of normalization.

Let us assume that the morphological lexicon does not have an entry for the word *helper*, but that the system expects to compose it from its constituent morphemes if required. In reality, this would probably not be done because automatic morphological-analysis systems rarely make any serious accommodation for derivational morphology, preferring to put all forms in the lexicon. We see in column 2 that the morpheme *help* can be classified as an adjective stem (As), a noun stem (Ns), and a verb stem (Vs). Column 3 shows the suffix *er* as a comparative suffix (comp) to be added to appropriate adjectives, as in the word *stronger*, or as an agentive suffix (agt) for use with nouns, as in the present case. Combining the noun stem *help* with the agentive suffix gives a singular noun, *helper* spanning columns 2 and 3.

Why do we not also analyze *helper* as a comparative adjective? The answer is that we are assuming that this is allowed only with adjectives whose entries in the morphological lexicon carry some special mark, which *help* lacks. The word *fries*, on the other hand, does have two analyses, one as a noun and one as a verb. The analyses of the remaining words in the sentence is essentially vacuous.

Suppose now that we have a translation of this sentence in another language. There may not be words in that language that correspond closely to *a* or *for* as they are used here but, if the language is not too exotic, the chances are that there will be words of *help*, *fry*, *starve*, and *child*, and that, from these, it will be able to get words more or less corresponding to *helper*, *fries*, *starving* and *children*. But we may be unlucky. German, for example does not have an clear equivalent for *fry*. *Braten* covers considerably more territory, and *frittieren* suggests deep frying. Be that as it may, we do not have to find lexical entries that correspond directly with the English words *helper*, *fries*, *starving* and *children* so long as we know how to construct these from the corresponding stem forms, that is, so long as we know how to conduct the reverse of the morphological analysis process in that language. If we understand the inflectional morphology of the two languages, we can get away with a smaller lexicon and, to this extent the two languages appear more similar to one another. This is why the morphological layer is narrower than the word level in Vauquois's triangle.

On the syntactic level, many of the morphemes that serve as morphological affixes are replaced by relations among other lexical items. There at least as many notational systems for representing the syntactic structure of sentences. A hybrid of some of the more popular ones is shown in Figure 7.2.

Large square brackets enclose the descriptions of phrases. To the left of each such description, or value, except the outermost one, is the name of an *attribute* which declares the role that the corresponding phrase plays in the larger phrase of which it is a member. Some attributes have simple alphabetic strings as their values. Values of the *cat* attribute are parts of speech, and values of the *pred* attribute are semantic predicates—essentially lexical items. This sentence is a phrase with four members. Its head is a verb, its agent and patient are noun phrases and it also has a modifier which is a prepositional phrase. A more realistic example would doubtless have many more attributes and values. One that we have shown on all the nouns in the structure is called *mass*. It has the value "-" for all nouns except *fish*, where it has the value "+". This is the attribute that permits this word to function as a "mass" noun, that is, without an article. This is important for this sentence.

Moving from the morphological to the syntactic representation involves a great deal of normalization. The grammatical number of nouns and noun phrases is represented separately from the predicate, and this is in a canonical form. Idiosyncratic morphological forms and paradigms, and suppletion have gone, and the components of the sentence do not constitute a string, so that there is nothing corresponding to word order any more. As a result, this representation of the sentence is almost certainly much closer to the representation of its translation in another language, whatever that language is. Accordingly, it occupies a shorter row in the triangle.

In addition to four progressively abstract levels of representation for sentences, Figure 7.1 shows three arrows labeled "Analysis", "Transfer", and "Synthesis" corresponding to the three main components that

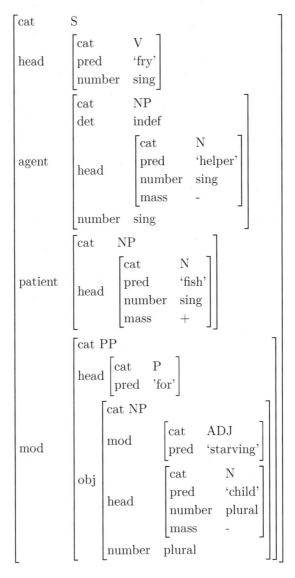

FIGURE 7.2 Syntactic Analysis

possible machine translation system would have if it conformed strictly to the Vauquois model. One of the first decisions that the designer of any such system would make is how far up in the diagram the transfer component should be placed. This is what determines what will be the most abstract level of representation that will be used.

The Analysis component of the system operates exclusively on the source text and, at least in principle, it could remain the same even if the target language were to change. Likewise, only one Synthesis component would be required for each target language. The only component of the system that contains information and about both the source and target languages is the one we have labeled "Transfer".

Needless to say, the Vauquois model is something of an idealization. Very few translation system have actually been built in which the transfer component was the only one that reflected properties of both languages. The advantages of the model, even if it is not adhered to strictly are, of course, enormous. Without the particular division of labor that it enshrines, it would require $n(n-1)$ complete systems to translate between pairs of languages chosen arbitrarily from a total of n. For the twenty-four languages of the European Union, this comes to 552. Without Vauquois, this is the number of Transfer components that would be required. With Vauquois, only n Analysis and Synthesis components would be required in the ideal case and, even if variants were some times required, there is reason to hope that the differences among them need only be minor.

The advantages offered by Vauquois's scheme are greater the higher the Transfer component can be placed in the hierarchy. Placing it right at the top, on the level we have labeled "Interlingua", would make it disappear altogether. Translation systems for arbitrary pairs chosen from a total of n would require a total of $2n$ components: one Analysis and one Synthesis component for each language. In the early days of machine translation research this was not regarded as a totally fanciful goal.

The Vauquois scheme, like all other approaches to machine translation, is based on what we have been referring to as the *standard model* of translation, according to which large translations are simply concatenations of shorter ones. Otherwise, they are simply pairs of lexical items, one from each of the languages involved. The only difference in the Vauquois model is that a lexical item in the source language must first be paired with one in the interlingua, then this must be paired with a lexical item in the target language. We can just about imagine ensuring that an interlingua could contain at least one item corresponding to every one in each of the languages to be covered, but we cannot easily imagine the inverse, namely that, for every lexical item in the interlingua, there will be a corresponding item in each of the natural languages. Some languages just have no vocabulary for *alimony, touch down, absolution, crescent wrench, quiche, strike out, braise* to name just a few examples.

The designers of machine translation systems who made a serious attempt to adhere to the Vauquois model have generally been academics whose immediate interests were theoretical rather than practical. One of the oldest and most successful commercial machine translation companies is SYSTRAN, founded by Dr. Peter Toma in 1968, mainly to translate Russian scientific and technical materials into English. Still today, it may well provide the best automatic translations in this field, and for these languages.

However, Systran is a hodgepodge of *as hoc* devices based on no easily discernible theory. Generally speaking, a system with a clear theoretical structure, such as the Vauquois model requires, will specify the rules to be applied on each of the levels in a special language, called a *formalism*, designed for just that purpose. Until recently, and possibly still today, everything in Systran was written in a general-purpose programming language. Systran provides the technology for Yahoo Babel Fish among others. It was used by Google's language tools until 2007. Systran is used by the Dashboard Translation widget in OS X.

Such formal structure as was to be found in systems intended for practical application, it was usually concentrated in the analysis component. This was partly because it clearly comes first in the sequence of processes, but partly also because of the intuition that this is where the severest problems would occur. Analysis is about exposing the intentions that the writer had in composing this text. Once this was known, it would surely be easier to find one among doubtless many possible ways of framing the same ideas in the other language. This line of argument has turned out to be somewhat misleading for various reasons. The supposed intent of the source text clearly consists of several layers. In simple cases, there is a primary message, but there are also subtexts of various kinds, suggestions, allusions, connotations of various kinds. Generally, only some of these can be carried over into the translation, and with often quite limited degrees of success. Once a few credible and robust analysis components had actually been constructed and attention came to be focused on transfer and synthesis, it became clear that they presented equally sever challenges.

For some forty years, starting in the 1950s, workers on machine translation saw themselves as scientists who approached their subject in a way that might give them the added satisfaction of practical translation systems. The analysis, transfer, and synthesis components would each contain massive numbers of rules which they would have to write and whose correctness and consistency would be proved by the working systems.

7.3 Statistical Machine Translation

In the 1970s, a group of researchers at the IBM Thomas J. Watson Research Center started work on a new approach to automatic speech recognition and, soon thereafter, to machine translation. Though new as an articulated program of research, these researchers can be seen as picking up the key ideas of Weaver's 1947 memorandum to the Rockefeller Foundation. Recall that Weaver had been motivated by the parallels that he saw between language translation and the breaking of secret codes. A text in Russian was essentially an English text that had been *encoded in some strange symbols*. This approach has a very natural appeal to a group of researchers who had been focusing on speech recognition.

There are a few obvious properties that speech recognition has that make it difficult. Different people say things in more or less different ways; a given person says one thing in slightly different ways on different occasions; different microphones and nearby reflective surfaces alter the quality of the sound; speed of articulation affects other properties of the sound; and so forth. To simplify somewhat, let us assume that there is a single, ideal way of pronouncing each word, or each phoneme, but that readers rarely receive them in this ideal form because of these various factors which corrupt them on the way from the speaker to the hearer. Seen this way, speech recognition is a lot like spelling correction. Jelinek and his colleagues at IBM referred to it as the *noisy channel* model of speech recognition.

From time to time, when reading an English text, I encounter a sequence of letters that I can interpret only on the assumption that it has been misspelled. I see the sequence *langauge* and assume, perhaps even without realizing it, that it should be *language*. How could a machine, that started out with no knowledge of English spelling, develop the ability to make this guess? There are surely three key facts that are crucially involved, namely (1) *language* occurs quite frequently; (2) *langauge* occurs quite infrequently; and (3) *langauge* is quite similar to *language* and can, indeed, be derived from it by simply interchanging a pair of adjacent letters. If I see the sequence *langauge* masquerading as an English word, I can estimate the probability that it should have been *language* based on the relative frequencies of the two strings and on the probability of *ua* being mistakenly written as *au*. I can also take into consideration the frequencies of *gu*, *ga*, *ag*, and *ug*.

The model that underlies this line of reasoning is that of a writer that knows the words he wants to send and a reader who knows how to recognize those words, separated by a channel that corrupts the words from time to time in minor ways. Some kinds of corruption are more common than others so that the reader can often guess where they have occurred and propose a more probable alternative.

Speech recognition is an altogether more challenging enterprise but it yields to essentially the same treatment. One important difference is that longer contexts have to be taken into consideration. Also, what the receiver thinks he hears may contain segments that he knows are not phonemes, but rather segments that could be one of a set of phonemes, each with its own probability. Suppose I hear an utterance containing a sequence of phonemes that sound a lot like *bury*, but which might also be *berry*, *bery*, *berrie*, *bury*, to mention only a subset. In trying to decide among the various possibilities, there are various kinds of knowledge that I can bring to bear. I know that very few of the possibilities are actual English words. However, if the sounds are embedded in a larger context, I may not be sure that they are intended as words rather than parts of larger words. If there is a larger context, then I may be able to make inferences based upon it to help me decide what words are more likely than others in that context. I can also use my knowledge of the likelihood that particular letters will be used to represent certain sounds. The letter *u* is very rarely used in English to represent the vowel in *bury*.

So, two types of information contribute to solving the speech recognition problem, one on the level of words, and the other on the level of phonetics and phonology. But the kind of information that we require on each level is the same, namely: how likely is a given hypothesis about the identity of a sound, given the hypotheses we could entertain about the identities of the surrounding sounds. If I did indeed hear the word *bury*, and come to the right conclusion about it, then information from the word level must play a major role because, as we have said, the letter *u* is very rarely used in English to represent the vowel in *bury*.

Speech recognition, as we have characterized it, can be seen as an application of the noisy channel model. We imagine a notation that can be used to capture the phonemes of English. It might be like the ones dictionary makers use to tell their readers how the words are pronounced. The sounds that speakers make map perfectly onto the symbols in this notation but, on the way to the hearer, the sequences of symbols get corrupted by the noise that surrounds them in the channel. The job of speech recognition is precisely to reverse the effect of this corruption and restore the original symbols.

When it is characterized in this way, it is easy to see the parallel between speech recognition and translation. It is just was Warren Weaver saw it when he wrote:

> When I look at an article in Russian, I say "This is really written in English, but it has been coded in some strange symbols. I will now proceed to decode." (1947)

In other words, what we have is another example of the noisy channel model. The writer has something in his head that he wants to put on paper. It is in English but the noise in the system is such that what actually gets onto the paper has been corrupted so much that it looks like Russian. As in the case of spelling correction, there is a statistical consistency to the corruptions that a particular channel introduces so that we can hope to reverse their effect probabilistically.

A statistical machine translation system usually has two principal components, referred to as the *translation model* and the *language model*. Given a word or short phrase in the source language the translation model provides a set of words or short phrases in the target language that might be used to translate it, together with the probability that it is the right one. These word pairs and probabilities are derived from a large corpus of translations by human, preferably professional, translators. Suppose that the French word *feuille* occurred in twenty sentences in a French/English corpus. Suppose that the word *sheet* occurred in eight of the English counterparts of these, *leaf* in six others and *paper* in three others. In the English versions of the three remaining sentences, no word occurs more than once. We might therefore judge that *feuille* should be translated as *sheet* with a probability $8/20 = .4$, as *leaf* with probability $6/20 = .3$, and as *paper* with probability $3/20 = .15$. In the remaining three sentences, as well as those already considered, it might be translated by some other word with a probability of $1/20 = .05$.

Needless to say, these are not the only ways in which the probabilities could be assessed. If the English counterpart one of the French sentences also contained another word with a high probability of translating *feuille*, then we might want to make allowances for this, or if *sheet*, though a good candidate for translating *feuille*, were an even better candidate for translating some other word in these sentences.

This can clearly only be a very simplified view of how statistical translation models work. For one thing, an English word that has a high probability of occurring in sentences that translates almost any French sentence is *the*. Very common words like this contain at least as much noise as signal. Provision must be made for what are generally called multi-word items. They include idioms, verbs like *take into account* and particle verbs like *put up*, *put up with*, *write down*, and *write up*. They include German compounds which writers invent on demand and which are far too varied to be captured in any lexicon.

There is another problem with this account of simple translation models that we cannot afford to finesse, namely that we cannot count on each sentence to be translated by just one sentence in the other language. It is true that single sentences translate single sentences most of the time but, if we were to count on this and there were a single exception early in a text, it could throw off the alignment of all the subsequent sentences. The first step in constructing a statistical machine translation system from a bilingual corpus is therefore to align the sentences. A simple and quite reliable way of doing this is based on the lengths of the sentences. Roughly, it consists in aligning a single sentence with a sequence of sentences if the number of words in the sequence is about the same as the number in the single sentence.

The component of the translation system that is referred to as the language model assesses the probability that a sequence of words is a sentence of the target language. Combined with the probabilities provided by the translation model that the words are translations of the words in the aligned sentence or sentences, this provides an overall assessment of a possible translation of a sentence.

The standard method of assessing the sentencehood of a string of words is by way of a so-called *n-gram* model. To characterize a particular model, we replace the n in this term with a morpheme denoting a particular small integer. Thus we have *unigram*, *bigrams*, *trigrams* and so forth. Language models are often based on trigrams, but the greater the number of words considered, the more effective the model and large commercial systems go up to 7-grams. The higher the number, the greater the computing power required to make and exploit the model.

The idea behind n-gram based language models is the following: a sentence that consists of, say, 20 words contains 17 sequences of 3 words, that is, 17 trigrams. Each word in the sentence begins a new trigram except for the last two. A typical English sentence generally contains more n-grams that occur in many other English sentences than one that does not.

To build a language model based on trigrams, we collect the n-grams in a large corpus of English, taking note of how many times each one of them occurs in the corpus. The frequency of an n-gram divided by the total number of n-grams in the corpus gives an estimate of the probability of each of them. We will assess the probability that a new sentence is English on the basis of the number of its frequently occurring n-grams also occurred frequently in the corpus. If the sequence *this is the* occurs frequently in many kinds of English text, its occurrence in a new text argues that that text is in English. The sequence *for by in* makes a less convincing case. The output of the translation model will presumably consist of English words, but it has no basis on which to order them as required in the target language. The strategy is therefore to consider many different orders and to accept only the ones to which the language models assigns a high score.

What we have said about statistical machine translation so far characterizes only the first of the five systems built by Jelinek and his team at IBM in the 1990s. The second of them, generally referred to as *IBM2* gave additional attention the problems of word order. The placement of words in the target text was, in part, a function of the absolute position of the corresponding word in the source. Ideally, the translation of the i-th word in a target text should translate the i-th word in the source. Placing it in position $i \pm j$ would incur a penalty proportional to j.

IBM3 introduced the notion of *fertility*, that is, of a probability distribution over the number of target words that a single source word might give rise to. French *du* probably often gives rise to two English words, namely *of the* whereas *de* often gives rise to an empty string of words.

This model also introduced *distortions*. A distortion is a function of a pair of integers $D(i, j)$ to the probability that the translation of a word at position i in the source sentence occupies position j in the target sentence. A person with any linguistic background is likely to find this especially strange idea betraying, as it does, a failure to appreciate the most fundamental fact about sentence structure, namely that locality does not correspond to adjacency in the string. Locality has to do with syntactic structure which is recursive and tree shaped. The German sentence *Den schwarzen Hund mit der langen Nase kaufte Hans* means *Hans bought the black dog with the long nose*, but if the English words are placed in the German order, they read *The black dog with the long nose bought Hans*. The reordering that has taken place in making the translation involves moving a single item to the end, namely *the black dog with the long nose*.

A very large number of more or less radical changes and additions have been made in the relatively short time since these models were proposed. The most important concern grammatical structure and phrases. In this field, the term *phrase* is taken to refer to a sequence if words, without regard to its grammatical status. The one thing that remains constant is human intervention in the construction of a operational system is limited to translating the corpus of sentences on which it is based into the target language. Such corpora do not have to be created specially for use in machine translation systems. They are created naturally by human translators for other purposes. Any other kind of intervention would count as the worst kind of apostasy. Machine translation is an exercise in Natural Language Processing (NLP), that is, big data and machine learning.

Speech recognition is a problem that yielded extremely well to approaches based on big data and machine learning. It is an apparently a very complex process that human beings learn with remarkable ease. But, like riding a bicycle, humans can perform the feat, but they cannot tell you how they do it. To get this information, copious records are kept of many instances of human performance and then these are reduced to a set of statistics that can be used to cause a machine make the same moves in comparable circumstances.

For this strategy to succeed, it must clearly be the case that the data that can be gathered by watching the process is all that is required to determine how it is done, and this requirement is met almost completely in speech recognition. But there are clearly cases of ambiguity which would confuse any system. Consider the alternatives, *After the flood, they decided they would have to raze the building on the south side of the square and build a lower one in its place.* and *After the flood, they decided they would have to raise the building on the south side of the square by about six inches.* Deciding among these alternatives rests on knowledge about what has to be done to a building before one can put another one in its place and that *razing* is not something that can be done *by six inches.* Compare *They understood that the proclamation had been read aloud* with *They understood what the proclamation had been read allowed.* The verb *allow* requires an object but, in the first examples there is nothing to fill that role. The only alternative therefore is to take the last words to be *aloud* and not *allowed.* The inverse of this argument applies in the second sentence where a role must be found for *what* to fill and this is conveniently supplied by *allowed.*

In speech recognition, decisions typically concern segments that are very few phonemes long. The relevant segments are immediately adjacent to one another, and call upon purely acoustic information from the input string. But, as we have seen, problems can arise that can be solved only by appealing to knowledge that the hearer can have acquired only from a much earlier part of the text, by engaging in a much deeper level of linguistic analysis, or by appealing to general knowledge that is nowhere to be found in this text. Not surprisingly, problems of these kinds are more frequent and more severe in translation than in speech recognition. Consequently, while we can expect the quality of machine translation to improve as more ingenuity, data, and computer power is brought to bear on it, the asymptote that it approaches will remain far below what human translators produce, and many consumers expect. The inescapable fact is that the information cannot be extracted from existing translations, because it simply is not in there. This is an important claim that needs the further support that we will now give.

Suppose that the sentence *We gave the monkey the banana when it was ripe* is to be translated into a language like French in which the adjective *ripe* and the pronoun *it* must agree with the noun they modify. The result in French might be *Nous avons donné la banane au singe quant elle était mûre*. A different pattern of agreements comes into play if one word is changed so that the sentence becomes *We gave the monkey the banana when it was hungry*. Now, it is not that feminine banana that is hungry, but the masculine monkey and the translation becomes *Nous avons donné la banane au singe quant il avait faim*.

The change in the verb from *était* to *avait* in this example is not a problem because the information needed to make the distinction is easily to be found in the lexicon. The question is, how do we know that it was the ripeness of the banana, but the hunger of the monkey that are in question? The answer is easy: bananas get ripe, but not monkeys. On the other hand, monkeys get hungry, but not bananas. This is part of our general knowledge of the world. Furthermore, the associations among these adjectives and nouns do not have to come from an adjacent piece of the text. For example, the first example might have been *We wanted the children to see what the monkey would do with the banana, but we waited to give it to him until it was really ripe*. In fact, the monkey and the banana could be arbitrarily far apart in the text. Furthermore, the inference required to derive the necessary conclusion, though natural, could be very subtle and complex.

In his magnificent paper *On Our Best Behavior* (2013) Hector Levesque invites his readers to consider the question *Could a crocodile run a steeplechase?*. He takes it, surely noncontroversially, that, even a reader that knew about crocodiles and steeplechases, would be very unlikely to have considered this question before. It is not one for which one could easily look up the answer and it might require considerable effort to find a relevant expert to whom one could appeal.

What is interesting about Levesque's question, and innumerable others that we encounter every day, is that we do not need to look up the answer or appeal to an expert. We come to the right conclusion about this and innumerably many other questions immediately, without special training or instruction. Furthermore, no computer or algorithm can come close to matching this ability. There is no knowing when the answer to a question of this sort might be crucial in a translation.

Levesque's paper introduces another prominent figure in artificial intelligence, namely Terry Winograd of Stanford University. In particular, he introduces what has come to be known as the "Winograd Schema" which is a pair of sentences of the form S_1 *because* S_2 where S_1 and S_2 are a pair of sentences. S_2 contains a pronoun that refers back to something mentioned in S_1 and which is different in the two sentences. A version of the first, and most well known of these is:

1. The town Council refused to give the angry women a permit because they feared violence.

2. The town Council refused to give the angry women a permit because they advocated violence.

The crucial observation is that *they* refers to the town council, or to the women according to whether *they* it is the subject of *feared* or *advocated*. We can be very sure of this, despite the fact that it turns on a quite complex set of semantic relations and specialized knowledge about the world. Notice that, if we are translating the first sentence into French, and we render town council as *conseil municipal*, then we must render *they* as *il*, whereas if we are translating the second sentence, then they can only be *elles*.

In accordance with standard practice, we have given a very specific form to the Winograd schema but, in fact, its two crucial parts can be in separate sentences with an arbitrary amount on intervening material. Consider, for example:

1. The women were really quite angry and decided to apply for permission to hold a demonstration. The town council considered the application last night. However, they refused them a permit because they feared violence.

2. The women were really quite angry and decided to apply for permission to hold a demonstration. The town council considered

the application last night. However, they refused them a permit because they advocated violence.

Examples of this phenomenon are extremely common. Here is another

1. It is best to get a seat in the front of the auditorium. You will find that much more comfortable. It will also be easier to see the screen.

2. It is best to place the computer facing the window. You will find that much more comfortable. It will also be easier to see the screen.

Presumably, the word *screen* in (1) refers to the kind of screen on which images are projected so that they can be seen by a number of people. In German, the word for this kind of screen is *Leinwand*. The second sentence refers to a small screen such as is routinely found as part of a personal computer. The German for this is *Bildschirm*. We have no difficulty knowing which to use because of our knowledge of lecture rooms and computers and not because of any statistical properties that adjacent words might have.

It is worth noting in passing that an example like this last one can present a different kind of problem if the translation is being made in the opposite direction. Consider the German sentence *Der Bildschirm zeigt genau das, was auf der Leinwand steht*. A more or less word-for-word translation would be *The computer screen shows exactly what is on the screen*. After a moment or two's reflection, it is clear what this probably means. But no reflection is required on the part of a German speaker who reads the original sentence, and none should be required in English. The trouble is that two things that are referred to by different words in German are referred to by the same word in English. This is a case where an inventive translator can bring pragmatic translation to the rescue, with something like *The computer screen shows exactly what the audience is seeing*. Other possibilities might be *The computer screen shows exactly what the audience would see*. The choice between *is seeing* and *would see* turns on whether we are talking about a situation in which we know there will be a particular audience, or a more generic one.

These examples illustrate a crucially important point concerning translation, namely that it calls upon a great deal more than purely linguistic knowledge on the part of the translator. One must know how a group of protesters, or a city council are likely react to the prospect of violence. One must have had at least minimal experience with computer screens and projectors to know which of them is being referred to in specific situations. Indeed, there is nothing a person might know that could not be crucial to carry out some translation task. High-quality machine translation would therefore require nothing less than a complete artificial intelligence. Just how frequently it would be called upon, and how difficult the questions would be that were put to it would, of course, differ with the type of text and the subject matter.

This is not to say that there might not be uses for fairly low-quality translations. When a web search brings up a page in a foreign language, the user is sometimes presented with a button saying "Translate this page". If the person conducting the search is familiar with the subject matter, he may be able to get all he needs even from a very poor translation. Alternatively, he may be prepared to employ a professional translator once he is satisfied that he has a page that contains the information he is looking for, and the machine translation may be good enough for this purpose.

Suppose that my sister, Alice, has inherited a safe which she believes contains some valuable items but for which she does not have the combination. I want to help and find out that there may be an enterprising French amateur engineer who has invented a fairly simple device that will rehearse the possible combinations and try them out very quickly until one is found that opens the lock. He has a web page where he appears to describe his device so that I may be able to make one myself. The trouble is that the page is in French.

The first paragraph of the web page looks like this:

> Dans une vidéo, Kamkar montre comment il a, au moyen d'un moteur 'pas à pas' permettant de contrôler très précisément les rotations, et d'un mini-ordinateur Arduino Nano, conçu un système qui fait tourner la serrure. Un module imprimé en 3D permet, lui, de brancher le moteur sur la serrure.

I copy this into the French input window of Google Translate and get the following in the English output window:

> In one video , he shows how Kamkar , using an engine ' step by step ' to control very precisely the rotations, and a mini - computer Arduino Nano, designed a system that turns the lock. A print module 3D allows him to connect the motor to the lock.[32]

I was not expecting anything large enough to be called an *engine*, but

32. This is actually taken from the web page at `http://datanews.levif.be/ict/actualite/un-mini-ordinateur-qui-decrypte-les-serrures-a-combinai sons-chiffrees-en-quelques-secondes/article-normal-395213.html`, accessed March 23, 2017

I notice the word *moteur* towards the beginning of the French text, so I am not too discouraged. Controlling rotations very precisely is just what I want. The words *A print module 3D* are confusing, but do nothing to suggest I am on the wrong track. I process some more paragraphs in the same way until I am convinced that it would be worth having a proper translation made of the page. The first paragraph of the translation looks like this:

> In a video, Kamkar shows how he developed a system using a motor and an Arduino Nano mini-computer to turn the lock, one step at a time, in a very precise manner. A device produced on a 3D printer allows him to connect this to the lock.

Some of the earliest machine translation systems built in the United States were used in essentially this manner to decide whether to send Russian documents to be translated in the traditional way.

High-quality translation routinely involves more than one person. One produces a draft which then goes to at least one reviser. The reviser must also be a translator. Indeed, translators generally become revisers only when they have acquired considerable experience as translators. If we broaden our view of the situation in which a machine translation system might be used to include a human reviser, we might be able to relax the requirement that the first version be of such high quality.

Needless to say, there is nothing new or surprising in this proposal. The so-called *extensive post-editing (EPE) application* of machine translation was a subject of experimentation since the earliest days of the field. The results, however, have been anything but clear. It seems to be possible to significantly reduce the total amount of human effort required to produce a satisfactory translation. But maintaining consistently high quality seems to be difficult because there is much more work for the revisers to do and the revisions are often of a trivial kind that would never arise in the work of a human translator.

Much remains to be learned about how how machine and human systems will be viewed by translators and consumers of their products. In Japan, the editing of machine translations has been taught as a specialty since the late 1980s. In 2013, Bruno Pouliquen *et al.* described a so-called *Language Translation Accelerator* (2013) called TAPTA4UN based on statistical machine translation systems based on United Nations corpora in six languages. The system was made available United Nations who could use it as and when they saw fit. The level of acceptability of the system by the translators varied greatly and seems to have differed considerably from one language pair to another.

It is easy to see translation as carried out by people in the usual way and fully automatic machine translation as the end points of a cline. This view is explored in Kay 1997. The position of a particular approach to the problem is a measure of the responsibility, or the initiative, taken by the man or the machine. The main approach advocated there takes the form of a specialized word processor referred to as the "translator's amanuensis". The particular protocol suggested there would seem quite cumbersome today. The idea that the source text would be presented in a source window, but also in a target window so that it would be the first draft of the translation. The final translation would be produced by editing this initial draft, replacing words and phrases by their translations in the target language. The reason for proceeding in this manner, rather than simply typing the translation, is that the program is provided with information on what source words and phrases correspond to what target words and phrases. Of course, this would not happen if the translator always deleted entire sentences before supplying the complete translation, but if he replaced relatively short sequences of source words one by one, information about their alignment could be amassed fairly quickly. After a while, the machine would be in a position to make suggestions for the translation of some words and phrases that the translator could accept or reject with a single key stroke.

The translator's amanuensis could clearly be augmented with a variety of tools, such as vocabulary lists, and previously translated documents from the same company or on the same topic. Such a collection of previously translated documents has come to be known as a *translation memory* which is the centerpiece of a widely used translator's aid called *Trados*. The original translator's amanuensis proposal focused on information that could be gleaned from the parts of a document that had already been translated and put to use as the work continued. It has been observed, for example, that different occurrences of an ambiguous word in the same vicinity are frequently used with the same sense. The corresponding translation in the target language could be available to the translator for insertion with a single key stroke.

Companies with a broad international presence typically make a lot of translations and it is generally the case that a document that is translated into one language has a high probability of also being translated into several others. This opens the opportunity of using early translations as a source of many kinds of information for use in later ones. To translate *The town Council refused to give the angry women a permit because they feared violence*, we need to know what *they* refers to in order to get the gender of the corresponding French and German pronouns right and we have argued that this will probably be beyond the capability of computer programs for a long time. But, if we have a translation into one of these languages, the problem is solved and the appropriate translation in the other language can be found easily. A wide variety of translation problems could doubtless be solved in this manner.

In his 2014 Ph.D. Stanford dissertation "Mixed-Initiative Natural Language Translation", Spence Green describes a so-called *mixed initiative* translation system. It incorporates a statistical machine translation system and capitalizes on the fact that, while such a system produces only one translation of a given sentence, it generally also considers many others that it assesses as less probable. The next sentence to be translated is presented in the source window and the most probable machine-generated translation in the target window. Every time the operator strikes that *Tab* key, the next word in the proposed translation is accepted and its color changed to reflect this. If the operator wants something other than the next word proposed, he types it and the system immediately looks for another, presumably less probable, translation among those that have been produced automatically and which begins with the sequence of words that has been accepted so far. There are various other moves that the operator can make, such as accepting parts of the proposed string, but in a different order.

Green describes a number of experiments that he performed to asses the quality of the results that professional translators could produce using his system and the effect of the system on the time it took them to produce them. On both counts, the results were very positive. Importantly, he was also able to report that the translators found the experience pleasant and satisfying.

7.4 Coda

Computers have a large and permanent place in the business of translation. They will continue to supplant the works of reference that had lined the walls where translators work. They will help ensure that company terminology is adhered to and will sometimes provide a first draft of the translation of a word, a sentence, or a document. They will improve the lives of translators in a variety of ways, many of which have yet to be imagined. In some circumstances, they will even replace human translators, and the translators will welcome this because these are the situations in which the work is the least rewarding. But growing need that the world has for translations will be filled by skilled professional translators until the day comes when computers can experience the same perceptions, curiosity, humor, pain, doubts, fantasies and fears as humans. When his day comes, there will no longer be any substantial difference between men and machines. Artificial intelligence will be artificial no more.

The idea that machines could learn to to do what translators do by applying machine learning and techniques for processing big data to the products of human experts is quite forlorn because the information simply is not there. What we have referred to as the *standard model* of translation, in which a large translation is a sequence of smaller translations right down to the level of lexical items, is totally inadequate as a model of what professional translators do. Textual adjacency is the wrong notion of locality in natural language. Above all, the intelligence and imagination that makes humans what they are, though crucial to the business of translation, is not encoded in the products.

Bibliography

Austin, J. L. 1962. *How to Do Things with Words*. Edited by J. O. Urmson and Marina Sbisà. William James lectures 1955. Cambridge, MA: Harvard University Press. (Cited on page 97).

Barker, Ray, and Christine Moorcroft. 2002. *Grammar First: Student Book 1*. New. Cheltenham: Nelson Thornes Ltd. (Cited on page 19).

Butterfield, Jeremy, ed. 2015. *Fowler's Dictionary of Modern English Usage*. 4th ed. First published in 1926 as *A Dictionary of Modern English Usage*. Oxford: Oxford University Press. (Cited on page 156).

Chomsky, Noam. 1957. *Syntactic Structures*. Mouton & Co. (Cited on page 158).

Cole, Peter, and Jerry L. Morgan, eds. 1975. *Syntax and Semantics, Volume 3: Speech Acts*. New York: Academic Press.

Cummings, D. W. 1988. *American English Spelling: An Informal Description*. John Hopkins University Press. (Cited on page 113).

Deutscher, Guy. 2010. *Through the Language Glass: Why the World Looks Different in Other Languages*. New York: Metropolitan Books/Henry Holt / Co. (Cited on page 130).

Diment, Dmitry. 2016. *Translation Services in the US*. Industry Report 54193. IBISWorld, April. http://clients1.ibisworld.com/reports/us/industry/default.aspx?entid=1446. (Cited on page 13).

Dryden, John. 1680. Preface to *Translation of Ovid's Epistles*. London: Jacob Tonson. (Cited on page 5).

Fleck, David William. 2003. "A Grammar of Matses." PhD diss., Rice University. Accessed March 21, 2017. https://scholarship.ric e.edu/handle/1911/18526. (Cited on page 130).

Freeman, John W. n.d. "Don Giovanni Synopsis." *Opera News* (). (Cited on page 62).

Frege, Gottlob. 1892. "Über Sinn und Bedeutung." *Zeitschrift für Philosophie und philosophische Kritik* 100:25–50. (Cited on page 170).

———. 1951. "On Concept and Object." Translated by P. T. Geach and Max Black. *Mind* 60 (238): 168–180. doi:10.1093/mind/LX. 238.168.

———. 1980. "On Sense and Reference." In *Translations from the Philosophical Writings of Gottlob Frege,* 3rd ed., edited by P.T. Geach and Max Black, translated by Max Black. Oxford: Blackwell. Originally published as "Über Sinn und Bedeutung." *Zeitschrift für Philosophie und philosophische Kritik* 100 (1892): 25–50.

Green, Spence. 2014. "Mixed-Initiative Natural Language Translation." PhD diss., Stanford University. https://purl.stanford.edu/jh270hf3782. (Cited on page 197).

Grice, H.P. 1961. "The Causal Theory of Perception." *Proceedings of the Aristotelian Society* 35 (supplementary): 121–152. (Cited on page 100).

———. 1975. "Logic and Conversation." In *Speech Acts,* edited by Peter Cole and Jerry L. Morgan, 41–58. Syntax and Semantics 3. New York: Academic Press. (Cited on page 99).

Hayot, Eric R.J. 2004. *Chinese Dreams: Pound, Brecht, Tel Quel.* Ann Arbor, MI: University of Michigan Press. doi:10.3998/mpub.3900 360. (Cited on page 6).

IBM. 1954. *701 Translator*. IBM Press release. New York, January 8. Accessed April 26, 2017. https://www-03.ibm.com/ibm/histor y/exhibits/701/701_translator.html. (Cited on page 174).

Jackendoff, Ray. 2012. *A User's Guide to Thought and Meaning*. 1st ed. New York: Oxford University Press. (Cited on page 55).

Jakobson, Roman. 1985. "Language and Culture." In *Selected Writings*, edited by Stephen Rudy, 101–112. Berlin: Walter de Gruyter.

Kay, Martin. 1997. "The Proper Place of Men and Machines in Language Translation." *Machine Translation* 12 (1-2): 3–23. doi:10. 1023/A:1007911416676. (Cited on page 196).

Labor Statistics, Bureau of. 2015. "Interpreters and Translators." In *Occupational Outlook Handbook*. December 17. https : / / www . bls.gov/ooh/media-and-communication/interpreters-and-translators.htm. (Cited on page 13).

Levesque, Hector J. 2013. "On Our Best Behavior." Presentated at IJCAI-13, August 3–9, 2013, Beijing, China, Unpublished manuscript, Dept. of Computer Science University of Toronto Toronto, Ontario Canada M5S 3A6. Accessed March 24, 2017. https://www.cs.toronto.edu/~hector/Papers/ijcai-13-paper.pdf. (Cited on page 191).

McLendon, Sally. 2003. "Evidentials in Eastern Pomo with a Comparative Survey of the Category in Other Pomoan Languages." In *Studies in Evidentiality*, edited by Alexandra Y. Aikhenvald and R.M.W. Dixon, 101–129. John Benjamins. doi:10.1075/tsl.54. 08mcl. (Cited on page 129).

Melčuk, Igor A. 1996. "Lexical Functions: A Tool for the Description of Lexical Relations in the Lexicon." In *Lexical Functions in Lexicography and Natural Language Processing*, edited by Leo Wanner, 37–102. Studies in language companion series 31. Amsterdam ; Philadelphia: John Benjamins. (Cited on page 93).

Mill, John Stuart. 1868. *A System of Logic, Ratiocinative and Inductive*. 7th ed. London: Longmans. (Cited on pages 52, 57).

Mitford, Nancy, ed. 1956a. *Noblesse Oblige: An Enquiry into the Identifiable Characteristics of the English Aristocracy*. Hamish Hamilton.

——. 1956b. "The English Aristocracy." In Mitford 1956a. (Cited on page 157).

Peirce, Charles Sanders. 1931–1958. *Collected Papers of Charles Sanders Peirce*. Edited by Charles Hartshorne and Paul Weiss. Cambridge, MA: Harvard University Press. (Cited on page 48).

Pouliquen, Bruno, Cecilia Elizalde, Marcin Junczys-Dowmunt, Christophe Mazenc, and Jose Garca-Verdugo. 2013. "Large-scale multiple language translation accelerator at the United Nations." In *Proceedings of the XIVth Machine Translation Summit*. Accessed March 21, 2017. http://www.mt-archive.info/10/MTS-2013-Pouliquen.pdf. (Cited on page 195).

Rosch, Eleanor H. 1973. "Natural categories." *Cognitive Psychology* 4 (3): 328–350. doi:10.1016/0010-0285(73)90017-0. (Cited on page 77).

Ross, Alan S.C. 1956. "U and Non-U: An Essay in Sociological Linguistics." In Mitford 1956a. (Cited on page 157).

Rozan, Jean François. 2004. *Note-taking in Consecutive Interpreting*. Edited by Andrew Gillies, Bartosz Waliczek, and Uta Hrehorowicz. 1956 Geneve, Georg. Cracow Tertium Society for the Promotion of Language Studies. (Cited on page 11).

Russell, Bertrand. 1905. "On Denoting." *Mind* 14 (3): 479–493. doi:10.1093/mind/XIV.3.398.

Schank, Roger C. 1991. *Tell Me a Story: A New Look at Real and Artificial Memory*. New York: Scribner. (Cited on page 89).

Schank, Roger C., and Robert P. Abelson. 1977. *Scripts, Plans, Goals, and Understanding: An Inquiry Into Human Knowledge Structures*. Hillsdale, NJ: L. Erlbaum. (Cited on page 89).

Shoebottom, Paul. 2017. "Usage." In *A Guide to Learning English*. Frankfurt International School. Accessed March 24, 2017. http://esl.fis.edu/grammar/easy/usage.htm. (Cited on page 156).

Shrunk, William, Jr., and E.B. White. 2000. *The Elements of Style*. 4th ed. First published in 1918 by Strunk alone; White made revisions and added a chapter for a 1959 version. Boston: Allyn & Bacon. (Cited on page 156).

Translation, Directorate-General. 2017. *Translation*. European Commission. https://ec.europa.eu/info/departments/translation.

Weaver, Warren. 1947. "Letter to Norbert Wiener." March 4. Accessed April 5, 2017. http://www.mt-archive.info/Weaver-1947-original.pdf. (Cited on pages 175, 176, 187).

————. 1949. "Memorandum on Translation." July 15. Accessed April 5, 2017. http://www.mt-archive.info/Weaver-1949.pdf. (Cited on page 175).

Wikipedia contributors. 2008. "example." In *Wikipedia, The Free Encyclopedia*. 13 May 2008 11:51 UTC. https://en.wikipedia.org/w/index.php?title=Translation&oldid=212089293. (Cited on page 1).

Wittgenstein, Ludwig. 1953. *Philosophical Investigations*. Translated by G.E.M. Anscombe. New York: MacMillan. (Cited on page 75).

Examples

Austen, Jane. 1813. *Pride and Prejudice.* Whitehall: T. Egerton. (Cited on page 121).

committee, trans. 1611. *King James Bible.* (Cited on page 12).

―――, trans. *Septuagint,* (cited on page 12).

Cup. 2017. In *Merriam-Webster Online,* s.v. "cup." Accessed March 28, 2017. https://www.merriam-webster.com/dictionary/cup. (Cited on page 72).

―――. 2017. In *Random House/dictionary.com,* s.v. "cup." Accessed April 6. http://www.dictionary.com/browse/cup. (Cited on page 73).

―――. 2017. In *Oxford Advanced Learner's Dictionary,* s.v. "cup." Accessed April 6. http://www.oxfordlearnersdictionaries.com/us/definition/english/cup_1. (Cited on page 74).

Fitzgerald, Edward. 1859. *Rubaiyat of Omar Khayyam.* (Cited on page 6).

Heine, Heinrich. 1827. "no title." In *Buch de Leider.* 33. (Cited on page 117).

―――. 1887. *Poems Selected from Heinrich Heine.* Edited by Kate Freiligrath Kroeker. Translated by James Thomson. London: Walter Scott. (Cited on page 117).

Jerome@Saint Jerome. 0400. *Vulgate.* (Cited on page 12).

Lazarus, Emma, trans. 1881. *Poems and Ballads of Heinrich Heine.* New York: R Worthington. (Cited on page 118).

LearnEnglish Kids. 2012. *Goldilocks and the three bears.* British Council. Accessed March 23, 2017. https : / / learnenglishkids . britishcouncil . org / sites / kids / files / attachment / stories – goldilocks – and – the – three – bears – transcript _ 2012_07_13_0.pdf. (Cited on page 35).

LinguisTech. 2017. *Translation Services.* Accessed April 6, 2017. http: //LinguisTech.ca/. (Cited on page 3).

Luther, Martin, trans. 1521. *Bible.* (Cited on page 12).

Mug. 2017. In *Merriam-Webster Online,* s.v. "cup." Accessed March 28, 2017. https : / / www . merriam – webster . com / dictionary / mug. (Cited on page 72).

———. 2017. In *Random House/dictionary.com,* s.v. "mug." Accessed April 6. http : / / www . dictionary . com / browse / mug. (Cited on page 73).

———. 2017. In *Oxford Advanced Learner's Dictionary,* s.v. "mug." Accessed April 6. http : / / www . oxfordlearnersdictionaries . com/us/definition/english/mug_1. (Cited on page 74).

Please. 2017. In *New Oxford AMerican Dictionary,* s.v. "please." Accessed April 6. http : / / www . oxfordreference . com / view / 10 . 1093/acref/9780195392883.001.0001/m_en_us1278753. (Cited on page 98).

Un mini-ordinateur qui décrypte les serrures à combinaisons chiffrées en quelques secondes. 2017. Accessed March 23. http : / / datan ews . levif . be / ict / actualite / un – mini – ordinateur – qui – decrypte – les – serrures – a – combinaisons – chiffrees – en – quelques – secondes / article – normal – 395213 . html. (Cited on page 194).

General Index

adaptation (of a work), 6
adjective, 4, 23, 81, 94, 112,
      114, 140–142, 180,
      191
adjectives, 170
agreement, 136–137
al-Mansur (caliph), 12
analog system, 46, 84, 111,
      171–172
antinomy, 92, 93
Arabic
    Baghdad as a translation
      center, 12
    translation to English, 125
Arabic, Classical
    grammar, 23
authentic translation, *see*
      translation, authentic
auxiliary verbs, 120

Baghdad, 12
Bible, translation, 12
bilingual dictionary, 3, 28–31,
      40
    Georgetown-IBM
      experiment, 174
bilingual speaker, 18, 30

Boeing Dreamliner, 13

case (grammar), 130–136
Caterpillar Corporation, 13
certificate of accuracy (of a
      translation), 16
Chinese
    morphology, lack of, 112
    tense, 120
    translation to English, 124
classifiers, 94–95
Clinton, Hillary (incident with
      peregruzka), 2
Coca-Cola (translating
      problem), 17–18
commands, 97
common names, 57
common nouns, 57, 170
Common Sense Advisory, 13
community interpretation, *see*
      interpretation,
      community
compositional (meaning), 49
compounds, 151–153
connotation (meaning), 49
consecutive interpretation, *see*
      interpretation,

Translation Index